JAY CONRAD LEVINSON

GUERRILLA MARKETING

HOW TO MAKE BIG PROFITS FROM A SMALL BUSINESS

PIATKUS

The sign of a good book

This fully revised and updated edition
first published in Great Britain in 1994 by
Judy Piatkus (Publishers) Ltd of
5 Windmill Street, London W1P 1HF

First paperback edition 1995

**The moral rights of the author
have been asserted**

*A catalogue record for this book is available
from the British Library*

ISBN 0-7499-1431-9 (hbk)
ISBN 0-7499-1316-9 (pbk)

Set by Professional Data Bureau, London SW17
Printed and bound in Great Britain by
Mackays of Chatham PLC, Chatham, Kent

GUERRILLA MARKETING

I dedicate this book to

Mike Lavin
Thane Croston
Alexis Makar
Lynn Peterson
Wally Bregman
Bill Shear
Leo Burnett
Steve Savage
Sidney Mobell
Norm Goldring

— guerrillas all.

Contents

Section I

The Guerrilla Approach to Marketing - Updated

ALTHOUGH MARKETING CHANGES so fast that there are daily and weekly publications solely devoted to chronicling the changes, the soul of guerrilla marketing remains unchanged. Updated, to be sure, but not changed at its core. Within a brand new world of marketing, the guerrilla thrives by warmly welcoming, then adapting to the myriad changes going on all over the place.

The world of marketing has evolved to a new age as computer technology asserts itself, as communications from satellites 23,500 miles away enable guerrilla marketers to advertise on television in prime time for under twenty dollars, **Guerrillas from** as an ugly recession has strengthened the bond between **outer space** people and their money, and as social causes such as domestic violence, saving rain forests, and curing AIDS have become part of the marketing scene. Although you'll be made aware of the most important changes, I hope this enlightenment is enhanced by the security you'll feel in the comforting fact that this updated guerrilla approach to marketing *works and is proven in action.* Ten years of success for thousands of guerrilla small businesses underscore this truth. Practitioners are now found around the world. The best will want to know

Who this book is for how guerrillas use the latest changes to their best advantage. I wrote this edition for them.

If your business is exceptionally well funded and you have stockpiles of money allocated to marketing whatever it is you are selling, you might take the standard approach and handle the marketing function with big bucks and textbook tactics. But if you have very little or a modest amount of money for marketing, I would advise you to take a radically different approach and handle the marketing function with big ideas and guerrilla tactics.

Guerrilla tactics do not put textbook tactics to shame, but they do provide you with an alternative to standard expensive marketing. They enable you to increase your sales with a minimum of expense and a maximum of smart moves.

You'll best understand the guerrilla approach to marketing once you study a standard marketing textbook. In the standard book, you'll learn of marketing goals and methods of attaining them. In this book, you'll learn of similar marketing goals and shortcuts to attaining them. You'll learn how to do what the big spenders do without having to spend big. Since very little comes to us for nothing, you'll have to do some extra work. But instead of relying on moneypower, you can rely on brainpower.

Goals and shortcuts

To keep up with the daily changes that occur in marketing is a Herculean task. I write a guerrilla marketing newsletter and a monthly guerrilla marketing column to accomplish all that Hercules would. The bare-bones essence of marketing has changed only in that we've become more enlightened by it. The weapons of marketing have undergone a revolution. This updated edition of *Guerrilla Marketing* is to keep you abreast of the current state of its art and its science. Although the true nature of guerrilla marketing remains the same, the breadth and technology of marketing has changed dramatically.

Saving the planet One major change is the use of environmental issues in marketing. Letting prospects know about your environmentally sound manufacturing practices gives them an additional reason to buy from you. Another factor small businesses must deal with is the recession, which has become a sort of unofficial perma-recession. And then there are the crucial advantages of cable and satellite television, not to mention fax machines and desktop publishing for the small-business owner. This updated edition shows you how to prosper from all of these changes.

Guerrillas know that the Intel 486 is the Colt 45 of the nineties and that it will be superseded by another name and number as time and human ingenuity advances. Do guerrillas welcome change? They thrive on it — because they know that their competitors have a tough time keeping up with change. This edition informs you about the marketing changes that will give you a leg up on your competition.

The Intel 486 is the Colt 45

Guerrillas already know that in the 1990s:

- 75 million baby boomers will enter middle age.
- The 18-to-34-year-old market will lose $100 billion worth of spending power.
- Dual-income households and the elderly will put a premium on time-saving products and services.
- Discretionary income will increase because of the trend toward smaller families and the fact that fewer households are being formed.
- The shrinking middle class will force retailers to aim more for the top and bottom. Some guerrilla companies will successfully manage to do both.
- Ulcers will increase for owners of companies that offer anything that has an unhealthy identity.
- Health care for those over 85 will expand 64 percent by the year 2000.
- Home remodeling will enjoy boom times because of the high cost of housing. Space-saving furniture sales will soar.
- Cosmetics and skin-care products will help the more

mature look like youngsters. Middle-aged models will become commonplace.

- Satellite transmission of local TV will grow rapidly, as will the galaxy of choices available, enabling guerrillas to aim directly at their market, geographically and demographically.

- VCRs will become so widespread that video brochures will be recognized as high-powered weapons, proving their effectiveness to all types of businesses.

Warmth in a cold world
- Tomorrow's marketplace will be populated by customers who are more demanding, less forgiving, in a hurry, and appreciative of warmth and attention to detail.

- The ultimate winners in the nineties and beyond will be companies that are right in front of the buyers at the time the buyers want to buy. Not easy, but possible.

- Your product or service will often be considered exactly the same as that of your competitors. This is because an enormous influx of marketing will create mass confusion and the perception that all offerings are created equal.

- Supermarkets will sell shelf space to companies just for the privilege of being displayed. Those same supermarkets will have computerized data their scanners compile on your purchases. This means you might buy Cornflakes and get a coupon offer from Weetabix.

- Ads will invite consumers to phone in or send for a free sample, enabling guerrillas to compile a list of people who have expressed interest in their product.

- New ways to influence consumer purchases, ranging from in-store TV to high-tech coupon machines, will be developed for use at the point-of-sale.

- There will be a growth spurt in frequent-buyer clubs, modeled after frequent-flier programs.

Brand-new markets This edition of *Guerrilla Marketing* for these times opens your mind to the brand-new markets of these times: working women, older people, ethnic groups. It brings into focus the **Brand-new** new marketing weapons of these times: video brochures, **weapons** newsletters, Freephone and 0898 numbers, infomercials, video monitors on shopping trolleys, postcard decks — as well as changes in the older ones: direct mail, tele-marketing, free publicity, trade shows, and catalogues.

Because of the inevitability of change in marketing, it will always be necessary to update the methods and tactics of guerrilla marketing while maintaining its soul and essence. Whereas the first edition of this book called to your attention the *three* most important marketing secrets, this updated **Three is now** edition gives you even more of a head start by imparting the **ten** *ten* most important marketing secrets.

One of the seven habits practised by effective people is called "sharpening the saw" — improving the things you do best. This edition sharpens the saw of guerrilla marketing. In doing so, it provides the guerrilla with a keener edge than ever. With thousands of new businesses launched each year, the guerrilla needs all the ammunition available to achieve victory. This edition was written to restock your guerrilla arsenal with ammunition, the kind that can make the difference between exceeding your projections or falling far short of them.

Even with the changes in marketing and markets, in media and methods, the guerrilla approach remains the sensible one for all marketers. For entrepreneurs, for new businesspeople, for small businesspeople, it seems almost mandatory. Ask the Successful small-business owners who have prospered in the ugly face of an ailing economy and they'll tell you it *is* mandatory that you make the attitude and smarts of the guerrilla part of your permanent mind-set.

If I ran a small or even a gigantic business, I'd take comfort in knowing that my marketing would work and had been proven on the front lines. I'd feel confident knowing that my marketing mind-set was state-of-the-moment. I'm delighted to let you in on the common sense that makes marketing work, but I'm even more gratified knowing the high level of success you will certainly attain as a guerrilla. As one guerrilla to another, I wish you well.

Please note: *Guerrilla Marketing* has been written using American examples, but the principles contained within the book are universal and apply equally to the UK and elsewhere.

1

What Is Guerrilla Marketing?

MARKETING IS EVERYTHING you do to promote your business, from the moment you conceive of it to the point at which customers buy your product or service and begin to patronize your business on a regular basis. The key words to remember are *everything* and *regular* basis.

The meaning is clear: marketing includes the name of your business, the determination of whether you will be selling a product or service, the method of manufacture or servicing, the colors, size, and shape of your product, the packaging, the location of your business, the advertising, the public relations, the sales training, the sales presentation, the telephone inquiries, the problem solving, the growth plan, and the follow-up. If you gather from this that marketing is a complex process, you're right.

See marketing as a circle that starts with your idea for generating revenue and completes itself when you have the blessed patronage of repeat and referral business. If your marketing is not a circle, it's a straight line that leads right to the bankruptcy courts.

This book can simplify the complexities, remove the mystique, show you exactly how any entrepreneur can use marketing to generate maximum profits from minimum investments. It can prevent you from making the many marketing mistakes businesspeople make every day.

What this book can do for you

Put another way, this book can help make a small business big. It can aid an individual entrepreneur in making a lot of money as painlessly as possible. Very often, the only factor that determines success or failure is the way in which a product or service is marketed. The information in these pages will arm you for success and alert you to the shortcomings that lead to failure.

Every type of entrepreneurial enterprise requires marketing. There are no exceptions. It's not possible to succeed without marketing.

Assume that you have a fine business background and are well versed in the fundamentals of marketing as practiced by the giant corporations. Admirable. Now forget as much as you can. Marketing for you as an entrepreneur is vastly different than it is for an esteemed member of the Fortune 500 (or the *Sunday Times* annual list of the UK's richest people). Oh, some of the principles may be the same, but the details are different. A good analogy is that of Adam and Eve. In principle, they were very much the same, but they varied in crucial details — and thank heaven for that. When they were lost, I'll bet Adam *never* asked for directions.

You're about to become a master of guerrilla marketing, the type of all-out marketing necessary for entrepreneurial success. Guerrilla marketing is virtually unknown to the large corporations. And be grateful that it is. After all, the large corporations have the benefit of big bucks. You don't.

So you've got to rely on something just as effective but less costly. You've got to rely on guerrilla marketing. I'm happy to report that your size is an ally when it **Your size** comes to marketing. If you're a small company, a new **is an ally** venture, or a single individual, you can utilize the tactics of guerrilla marketing to their fullest. You've got the ability to be fast on your feet, to employ a vast array of marketing tools, to gain access to the biggest marketing brains and get them at bargain-basement prices. Now you may not need to use every weapon in your potential marketing arsenal, but you're sure going to need some of them. So you'd best know how to use them all.

It may be that you will require no advertising at all. But you will require marketing. It may be that word of mouth is so favorable and spreads so rapidly that your venture can reap a fortune just because of it. If so, you can be sure that the word of mouth was motivated by effective marketing in the first place.

In fact, a strong word-of-mouth campaign is part of marketing. And so are business cards. And so is stationery. And the hours you're open. And the clothes you wear. And certainly your location is important in marketing.

Every component that helps you sell what you are selling is part of the marketing process. No detail is too insignificant to be included. The more you realize that, the better your marketing will be. And the better your marketing is, the more money you will make. I'm not talking about sales. I'm talking about profits — the dear old bottom line.

That's the good news. Here's the bad: one of these days, you're going to be an entrepreneur no longer. If you successfully put into practice the principles of guerrilla marketing, you will become fat and rich and famous and will no longer have the lean, hungry mentality of the entrepreneur.

Once you've reached that stage, you may resort to the textbook forms of marketing, for you might be too encumbered with employees, traditions, paperwork, management levels, and necessary bureaucracy to be flexible enough for guerrilla marketing. But somehow I have the feeling you won't mind that state of affairs too much. After all, Coca-Cola, Standard Oil, Procter & Gamble and General Motors were all started by entrepreneurs. You can be darn certain that they practised guerrilla marketing as much as possible in their day. You can also be sure that they do all their marketing by the numbers these days. And I doubt if they complain about it.

In time, some of those king-sized companies may be surpassed in size by companies that are now being founded and nurtured by entrepreneurs such as you. How will it happen? It will be the result of a combination of factors. And marketing genius will be one of them. Count on it.

At this point, I'm assuming you understand that you have to offer a quality product or service to be successful. Even the best marketing in the world won't motivate a customer to purchase a poor product or service more than once. In fact, **You must** guerrilla marketing can speed the demise of an inferior offer-**have quality** ing, since people will learn of the shoddiness that much quicker. So do everything in your power to ensure the quality of whatever it is you'll be selling. And once you've got that quality, you'll be ready for guerrilla marketing.

It is also mandatory for success that you have adequate capitalization — that is, money. Notice I didn't say that you need a lot of money. Sufficient capitalization to engage in guerrilla marketing will be enough. That means you'll need enough cash or cash reserves to promote your business aggressively for at least three months, and ideally for a full year. It might take $300; it might take $30,000. That depends on your goals.

Many small businesses offer superb products and highly desirable services. But fewer than one-tenth of one percent of those businesses will make it to the point of phenomenal **The elusive** financial success. The elusive variable that makes the differ-**variable** ence between merely being listed in the yellow pages and being listed on the Stock Exchange is the *marketing* of the product or service.

You now hold in your hand the key to becoming part of that tiny percentage of entrepreneurs who go all the way. By realizing that many facets of your business can fall into the category of marketing, you have a head start over competitors who do not see that there is a difference between *advertising* and *marketing*.

The more aware of marketing you are, the more attention you will pay to it. And the increased attention will result in better marketing of your offerings. A great deal of marketing isn't merely poorly executed these days; it's not executed at all! I'd venture a bold guess that fewer than 10 percent of new- and small-business owners have explored most of the market- ing methods available to them. These methods include canvassing, personal letters, telephone marketing, circulars and brochures, signs on bulletin boards, classified ads, out- door signs, advertisements in the yellow pages, newspapers, and magazines, and on radio, television, and billboards, direct mail, advertising specialties such as imprinted ballpoint pens, samples, seminars, and demonstrations, sponsoring of events, exhibiting at trade shows, T-shirt ads, and public relations. Guerrilla marketing *demands* that you scrutinize every single one of these marketing methods and more, many, many more — then use the combination that seems best for your business.

Few than 10 percent

Once you've launched your guerrilla marketing attack, you must keep track of which weapons are hitting your target and which are missing. Merely knowing can *double the effective- ness of your marketing budget.*

How to double your effectiveness

There are absolutely no advertising agencies that specialize in guerilla marketing. When I worked as a senior executive at some of the world's largest (and smallest) advertising agen- cies, I found that they didn't have a clue as to what it takes to help an entrepreneur succeed. They could help the big guys, all right. But they were helpless without the brute force of big bucks. So where can you turn to for help? The first place to turn is to this book. The next place is to your own ingenuity and energy. And finally, you will probably have to go to a marketing or advertising professional to get help with details in the areas where guerrilla marketing overlaps standard marketing. But don't expect the pros to be as tough in the trenches as you are. Most likely they operate better from high in a posh skyscraper.

Where to get help

Guerrilla marketing dictates that you comprehend every facet of marketing, then employ with excellence the necessary marketing tactics. To understand the nature of this idea, it may be useful to examine the real reason Japan was able to knock the United States off its perch as world leader in the TV, stereo, automobile and electronics industries.

Industry in the United States has been able to turn out excellent products with a low percentage of rejects — 5 percent. That means that of one million manufactured items, only 50,000 were rejects. Industry leaders recognized that the cost to lower that number would be greater than the profit would realize by achieving perfection. So it became an economic truism that you could run a successful manufacturing operation if you limited your rejects to 50,000 per million units. And the public became used to the concept: they complained about lemons, but weren't really all that surprised at them.

Japan, after a horrible defeat in the Second World War, suffered from an identity of poor quality. For years the phrase "Made in Japan" was enough to elicit a grin from a sophisticated purchaser. How did the Japanese overcome this problem? Japan decided to fly in the face of the economic truism that allowed for a 5 percent reject rate. Japan figured that if the public accepts products even though 50,000 per million are inferior, it might happily embrace products of which fewer than 50,000 were unacceptable. But according to the economists, this would cost a ton of money.

The Japanese, having nowhere to go but up, figured it was worth it. They improved the quality of what they made to the point that right now, they have only 200 rejects per million units. Two hundred rejects versus our 50,000 rejects! And Japan is still working on methods for lowering that 200 figure.

How did Japan do it? By reducing mistakes. Every error that could possibly be construed as a mistake was noticed by people actually hired by industry to count mistakes. In the category of mistakes were included shoddy workmanship, tardiness, breaks that lasted too long, minor flaws in detail work, low morale, and anything at all that impeded production. Weekly, departments within Japanese industrial firms would meet with their hired mistake counters. They were told the number of mistakes made that week, and they worked to reduce that number. By working at it assiduously, they dramatically cut the number of mistakes.

Through almost totally eliminating mistakes, Japan took over leadership in the TV, stereo, automobile and electronics industries. And as the number of mistakes went down, productivity went up. The country benefited in these two ways by this one action. In all businesses there are numerous opportunities and numerous problems. The Japanese exploited their opportunities and solved their problems. So it is with guerrilla marketing.

Guerrilla marketing involves recognizing the myriad opportunities out there and *exploiting every one of them.* Like the Japanese, don't overlook a thing. In the marketing of any product, problems are certain to arise. Solve these problems and continue to look for new problems to solve, problems of prospects and customers. Businesses that solve problems have a far greater chance of success than those that don't. Today and in the twenty-first century, businesses that save time for people will flourish. Why? Because lack of time is a problem and growing numbers of people in industrialized societies see it as such. The time-saving industry will become a major opportunity.

Going all out

You must spot these large opportunities, but you won't have the luxury of neglecting the smaller opportunities or overlooking minor problems. You've got to go all out.

Going all out is the foundation of successful guerrilla marketing. By going all out, the Japanese completely reversed the reaction to "Made in Japan" to the point where the phrase now means excellent craftsmanship, attention to detail, and nearly zero defects.

Energy alone is not enough, however. Energy has to be directed by intelligence. Intelligent marketing is marketing that is first and foremost focused on a core idea. All your marketing must be an extension of this idea: the advertising, the stationery, the direct mailings, the telephone marketing, the yellow pages advertising, the package, the whole thing. But it is not enough to have a better idea; you must also have a better argument and a focused strategy. Today many large and supposedly sophisticated companies go to one expert for a trademark, another expert for an advertising program, yet another expert for direct-mail planning, and possibly one more professional for location selection. This is not only costly, it is nonsense. Nine times out of ten each of these experts is pulling in a different direction.

Pulling in the same direction   What must be done is to have all the marketing pros pull in a common direction — a pre-agreed, long-term, carefully selected direction. When this is done, a synergistic effect is automatically created and five types of marketing tactics do the work of ten. The pre-agreed direction will always be clear if you encapsulate your thoughts in a core concept that can be expressed in a *maximum* of first, seven sentences, then seven words. That's right, a *maximum* of seven. Think it can't be done? Try it for your own business.

Here's an example. An entrepreneur wanted to offer courses in computer education, but knew that most people suffer from "technophobia" — fear of things technical. Advertisements for his proposed courses in word processing, accounting by computer, the electronic spreadsheet and more, produced little response. So he decided to restate the basic premise of his offering. At first, he stated it thus: "I wish to alleviate the fears that people have regarding computers, so that they will recognize the enormous value and competitive advantages of working with computers." Then, in an attempt to reduce this thought to a seven-word core concept, he reiterated his idea: "I will teach people to operate computers." This seven-word statement clarified his task. Clarified it for him, for his sales staff, for his prospective students.

Later he developed a name for his company, a name that reduced his core concept to three words: Computers for Beginners. This bypassed the problem of technophobia, stated his premise, and attracted hordes of beginners. Before he started this business, his concept ran six pages. By reducing and reducing his basic thoughts, he was finally able to achieve the succinctness necessary to assure clarity. And clarity led to success. It usually does.

It's a pretty simple idea to center all your marketing on a core concept. But you can be sure that when you begin to market your offering that way, you will be a member of an enlightened minority and well on your way to marketing success — a prerequisite for financial success.

The core concept

Here is what guerrilla marketing is *not*: expensive, easy, common, wasteful, taught in marketing classes, found in marketing textbooks, practiced by advertising agencies, or known to your competitors. Be grateful that it is not all those things. If it were, all business owners would be guerrillas, and your path to success would be a paved and marked one rather than a secret, unmarked route to the end of a rainbow with a bigger pot of gold than you ever imagined.

2

Entrepreneurial Marketing: The Guerrilla Difference

IN AN ARTICLE IN THE *Harvard Business Review*, John A. Welsh and Jerry F. White remind us that "a small business is not a little big business." An entrepreneur is not a multinational conglomerate but a profit-seeking individual. To survive, he must have a different outlook and must apply different principles to his endeavors than does the president of a large or even medium-sized corporation.

Not only does the scale of small and big businesses differ, but small businesses also suffer from what the *Harvard Business Review* article calls "resource poverty". This is a problem and opportunity that requires an entirely different approach to marketing. Where large ad budgets are not necessary or feasible, where expensive ad production squanders limited capital, where every marketing dollar must do the work of two dollars, if not five dollars or even ten, where a person's company, capital, and material well-being are all on the line — that is where guerrilla marketing can save the day and secure the bottom line.

A large company can invest in a full-scale advertising campaign run by an ad agency, and that company has the resources to switch to a different campaign if the first is not successful. And if the company ad manager is smart, he or she will hire a different agency the second time around. This luxury is not available to entrepreneurs, who must get it right the first time. Entrepreneurs who are guerrillas get it right because they know the secrets — and so will you. **Get it right the first time**

This is not to say that I hold the techniques employed by the big corporations in contempt; quite the contrary. While creating advertising for companies such as Quaker Oats, United Airlines, Citicorp, Visa, Sears, and Pillsbury, I frequently employed big-company marketing techniques. I was acting properly. But to suggest that the individual entrepreneurs I advise employ the same techniques would be irresponsible, not to mention financially wasteful. Instead, I resort to the techniques of guerrilla marketing, techniques that might get me laughed out of a Procter & Gamble or Chrysler Corporation conference room.

Many of the approaches and some of the techniques overlap. Entrepreneurs must govern tactical operations by marketing strategy. And all their marketing efforts have to be weighed against that strategy. They also need to examine all of the marketing avenues available to them. The critical difference is the bottom line. They must keep a far keener eye on the bottom line than do the giant firms. **The critical difference**

They must spend far less money testing their marketing tactics. And their marketing must produce results at a fraction of the price paid by the biggies. They may not necessarily handle their marketing efforts better than large companies, but they will be more personalized and realistic in their use of marketing.

Large companies think nothing of producing five television commercials for purposes of testing. Small companies dare not even think the same thought. Large companies employ many levels of management to analyze the effectiveness of their advertising. Small companies entrust the judging to one individual. Large companies look first to television — the most far-reaching of all the advertising media. Small companies generally look first to small newspaper ads in local papers. Both are interested in sales that generate profits. But each must achieve its goals in a dramatically different way.

Often, large companies aim for leadership of an industry, or to dominate a market or large market segment, and they use marketing ploys designed to attain those lofty ambitions. But **Flourish by** small companies, or individual entrepreneurs, can flourish **gaining a tiny** merely by gaining a tiny slice of an industry, a fraction of a **slice** market. Different wars require different tactics.

Whereas large companies must advertise from the outset and continue to advertise with virtually no interruption, smaller enterprises may be able to advertise only in the beginning and then rely solely upon guerrilla weapons and word-of-mouth advertising. Can you imagine what would happen if Budweiser beer depended on word-of-mouth advertising? Miller beer would sell a lot more six-packs.

An individual entrepreneur may be able to get enough business just by dealing with one gigantic company. An acquaintance of mine was able to survive financially (and in gracious style, I might add) merely by conducting small seminars for one large banking firm. No large company could exist off the income he was generating, but my friend was able to zero in on that one firm until he got his first assignment. After that there were others, and still others. This year, he is conducting his seminars for a large chemical company. Working with companies of that size, he needs very few customers. Needless to say, his marketing was tailored to this reality.

A descriptive brochure sent to a single large corporation may result in enough business to keep an energetic telephone marketing trainer in the chips for a long time. Try finding a Stock Exchange-listed company that could do the same. Impossible.

Many entrepreneurs get all the business they need by posting signs on bulletin boards. A large company would never consider such a possibility. If it did, it would be known as Shrinking, Inc., in short order. The point is obvious: sauce for the small goose is not necessarily sauce for the large goose. And vice-versa.

For example, business cards can be plain and straightforward for big-company executives. The executive's name, company name, address, and phone number are enough. Perhaps a title is also necessary. But for a smart practitioner of an individual enterprise, that business card ought to contain a lot more information. For example, I know a typist whose card has all of the above, along with the message "Legal, theses, statistical, manuscript, résumé, and business typing." Her card does double duty. It has to. That is what guerrilla marketing is all about.

A business card can double as a brochure, a circular, a wallet-sized advertisement. It can open up to become a mini-brochure. People appreciate such mini-brochures. These people know that their time and space are at a premium and that your card saves them time while taking up very little valuable space. The cost to produce such a card is not much more than one pays for a standard card, but the need is different. Lacking a large stockpile of cash, the small businessperson must make use of all the advertising media available. A business card can be more than a mere listing of one's name, address, and phone number; it can be an advertising medium.

The guerrilla business card

A huge corporation can run radio or television commercials and tell the audience, at the end of each message, to obtain the address of the nearest dealer by consulting the yellow pages. Now that's just fine when you dominate that section of the yellow pages with the largest ad and the most recognizable trademark and line. But the individual entrepreneur dare not direct listeners or viewers to the yellow pages. That would only alert his prospective customers to the competition, or to the dominance of certain competitors. Instead, the astute entrepreneur directs his prospects to the phone directory, where there will be no competitive ads and where his organization's small size will not appear as a detriment.

Perhaps the biggest difference between an individual businessperson and a large corporation is in the degree of flexibility each possesses. Here the balance tips in favor of the small business. Because it hasn't indoctrinated numerous

You have more flexibility

levels of management and a gigantic sales organization in the tactics and strategies of its marketing plan, it can make changes on the spot. It can be fast on its feet and can react to market changes, competitive ploys, undeveloped service niches, economic realities, new media, newsworthy events, and last-minute offers.

I recall how a major advertiser once was offered an unbelievably good media buy for a fraction of its normal price. Because the offer did not fit into the company's engraved-in-bronze plan, and because the person to whom the offer was made had to check with so many bosses, the company had to turn down the offer. A tiny business then accepted it: a thirty-second commercial just before the Super Bowl, for the incredible price of $500. The cost of this commercial slot normally sold for ten times that amount. But because of lack of flexibility, the giant corporation was unable to get in on the bargain. Speed and flexibility are part of the very essence of guerrilla marketing.

A success-bound entrepreneur must learn to think about marketing and advertising on a different wavelength than does a corporate advertising executive. While you must think about the primary marketing tools much as the executive does, you must also develop a sixth sense for the other opportunities available to entrepreneurs. It may be that a personal letter or visit is in order. A corporate manager might never consider such mundane tactics. Perhaps a telephone marketing campaign is in order. Can you picture Coca-Cola getting involved in telephone marketing to consumers?

The *Fortune 500* may have big bucks in the same way the brontosaurus had a weight problem. But like the furry, quick mammal, you've got the flexibility, the speed, the disregard of image, that enables you to use radio commercials and also hire high school students to hand out printed circulars on street corners. You don't have a body of rules to follow, a committee to answer to, a set structure to follow. You're a guerrilla. You are the organization. You answer to yourself. You make the rules and you break the rules. And that means you get to be amazing, outrageous, surprising, unpredictable, brilliant and quick.

You also just may be able to enjoy the rare luxury of sitting back and relying upon consistent word-of-mouth advertising. If you're really good at your work, and know how to generate word-of-mouth marketing, it might be enough to keep your coffers brimming. I know of no *Fortune 500* companies that can enjoy that amenity.

Incidentally, please understand that what appears to be word-of-mouth advertising is often a combination of newspaper, magazine, radio, direct-mail, and word-of-mouth advertising. But it's the mouth that gets the credit and not the media. Don't delude yourself into believing that you can succeed with no media advertising. Winning with that strategy would be like winning the lottery with your first ticket. It happens, but don't bet your boots or your business.

It's not really word of mouth

Still, it is possible to generate word-of-mouth advertising. There are several ways to accomplish this. The first, of course, is to *be so good at what you do*, or to offer products that are so obviously wonderful, that your customers will want to pass on the good word about you. Another way to get the ball rolling is to give brochures to your new customers. This reminds them why they patronized you in the first place and spurs word-of-mouth endorsements. A third way to obtain positive recommendations is literally to *ask for them*. Nobody is better equipped to talk up your company than you — or perhaps your best customer. Tell all your customers: "If you're really satisfied with my service or products, I'd appreciate it if you'd tell your friends." Finally, *you can bribe your customers*. Tell them, "If I get any customers who mention your name, I'll send you a free gift (or give you a 10 percent discount) next time you're in." Which of these methods should you employ? As a guerrilla, you should use all of them. Testing will tell.

The point to remember is that no large corporation can succeed by means of word-of-mouth advertising alone, and some entrepreneurs can. But do yourself a favor and don't leave everything up to the recommendations of your happy customers. They probably have more important things to talk about. Even for a guerrilla, consistent marketing is crucial to success,

An overall marketing plan for a person engaged in individual enterprise might consist of a listing in the yellow pages, a mailing of circulars and business cards, a posting of signs, and a follow-up telephoning to prospects to whom the promotional material was sent. That four-pronged effort (yellow pages, mailing, signposting, and telephoning) might be all it takes to get a business off and running. You can be certain that no big company has a marketing plan so short and simple — and inexpensive.

Imagine a staple gun and a handful of circulars as the only marketing tools necessary to conduct a business. IBM would boot me out of its corporate offices for suggesting such a thing. But many a successful home-typing service uses these devices and none other. A typist I know started out by typing her circulars, thereby lending credibility to her typing ability. Then she posted them with her staple gun on bulletin boards throughout local college campuses. These days, she posts no more circulars, and her staple gun gathers dust. Word of mouth has taken over, and she gets all the business she needs through referrals.

Entrepreneurs can enjoy month after month of profitable business merely by advertising in the classified pages. I'm sure you've seen rafts of ads by independent contractors while perusing the classified ads. You do look through them, don't you? The classified ads are recommended reading for entrepreneurs. They give you ideas. They alert you to the competition. They clue you in as to current prices. You'll read a lot more about them in chapter 13. The point I'm making here is **An important** that classified ads are an important tool for independent **tool** businesspeople. They are not a tool for large companies. I doubt if the most professional advertising agencies in the world are well versed in proper use of the classified pages. But the classified pages may be invaluable to free-lance earners.

In *How to Start and Run a Successful Home Typing Business* (Aames-Allen Publishing, Huntington Beach, California, 1980), Peggy Glenn, the author, who also writes of word processing at home, lists an eleven-point advertising program:

1. Hang fliers on campuses and near student gathering places.
2. Ask each school department to allow you to post your fliers.
3. Post a flier in the faculty lounge.
4. Post your flier at placement offices and counseling centers.
5. Leave fliers at the graduate study office.
6. Advertise in the campus newspaper.
7. Post a small sign on the community library bulletin board.
8. Post fliers for special groups such as engineers.
9. Visit a few college departments to see if they need your help.
10. Visit the principals of schools in your community with fliers.
11. Visit private and special schools in your area, leaving fliers.

She admits that this is a lot of advertising. To a typist, it is. To a large company, it isn't. That illustrates clearly how marketing is different for entrepreneurs — inexpensive, yet comprehensive.

Still, there are ten highly significant marketing secrets that must be known by all advertisers, large and small, if they are to succeed. Even the tiniest of entrepreneurs must be aware of them. And that awareness will begin the moment you start reading the next chapter.

3

The Ten Most Important Marketing Secrets

IT FLOORS ME that these secrets are secrets at all. Instead, they ought to be truisms, engraved on brass plaques in the offices of all who market or plan marketing. Yet these proven gems of marketing wisdom have somehow escaped the ken of large and small marketers alike. I sincerely believe that it is next to impossible to market a product or service successfully unless these secrets are known and put into practice. I also believe that merely by learning these secrets, then living by them, you're 80 percent of the way toward a successful marketing campaign.

If you have a small business and want it to become a large business, forget it — until you put these secrets into practice. And if you allow these concepts to become part of your mental marketing framework, you've got a giant head start on those who do not.

The big ten So as not to keep you in suspense any longer, I'll reveal the secrets right here and now. They can be summarized in ten words, each ending in the letters "ent": commitment, investment, consistent, confident, patient, assortment, subsequent, convenient, amazement and measurement.

1. You must have *commitment* to your marketing *program.*
2. You must think of that program as an *investment.*

3. You must see to it that your program is *consistent*.
4. You must make your prospects *confident* in your firm.
5. You must be *patient* in order to make a commitment.
6. You must see that marketing is an *assortment* of weapons.
7. You must know that profits come *subsequent* to the sale.
8. You must run your firm to be *convenient* for your customers.
9. You must put an element of *amazement* in your marketing.
10. You must use *measurement* to judge the effectiveness of your weapons.

Let's start with the first. If you're not committed to a marketing or advertising program, it's probably not going to work for you. I tell my clients that the single most important word for them to remember during the time they are engaged in marketing is *commitment*. It means that they are taking the marketing job seriously. They're not playing around, not expecting miracles. They have scant funds to test their marketing — they must act. Without commitment, marketing becomes practically impotent.

You evolve a marketing plan, revise and rerevise it until it is *a powerful plan for your purposes*. You put it to work, and then you stay with it, no matter what (in most cases). You watch it slowly take effect, rise and falter, take a bit more effect, slide back a bit, start taking hold even more, stumble, then finally grab on and soar, taking you with it. Your plan is working. Your cash register is ringing. Your bank balance is swelling. And it all happened because *you were committed to your marketing program*.

Let's examine that last paragraph. What if you weren't patient enough during the time your plan "slowly" took effect? You might have changed the plan. Many entrepreneurs do. What if you dropped the plan the moment it faltered? You would have lost out. Many marketers do. What if you lost your cool when your sales slid backward? You might have scrubbed the plan. Suppose you dropped it when it stumbled, as virtually all marketing plans do, at least temporarily. Disaster would have ensued. But because you stayed with the plan, because you were committed to it, it finally took hold and did what you wanted it to do. Your success was very much due to your understanding of the concept of commitment. If you had not been in touch with the essence of the concept, you probably would have taken one of the many tempting opportunities to kill the plan — and would have killed your chances **Understanding** along with it. But you understood what commitment means, **pays off** and it paid off for you.

A new sleep shop was opening in Boulder, Colorado. The owner of the business had heard about me, so we arranged to meet. We hit it off. We discussed the idea of commitment to a marketing program. He admitted that he knew zilch about marketing and turned the whole thing over to me. I developed a marketing plan, secured his approval, then reiterated the necessity for him to commit himself to the program. Mind you, I'm talking about a guy with one little store in a relatively small town.

The marketing started and nothing happened. Six weeks later, my new client called me to tell me he was still committed to the program, but that he hadn't seen much proof of it working for him. He also let me know that he was completely relaxed about the whole thing because he felt he understood about commitment. After twelve weeks, he called to tell me he was beginning to see hints that the program was taking effect. After six months, he opened his second store. After nine months, he opened his third, and at the end of the year, he had five stores. He remained committed to the marketing program and within six years had forty-two stores in Colorado, Iowa, Kansas, Wyoming, and Missouri.

I sincerely doubt that he would have progressed to a point where he could even have justified a second store if he had not stayed with the plan, if he had not understood what I meant about commitment. He had many chances to waver, many chances to become a disbeliever. He had a ton of reasons to veer from the plan. Naturally, it was a well-conceived plan, a plan perfect for his purposes. Commitment to an unwise plan is just plain stupid. And you won't have any way of knowing if your plan is good or bad at the outset — except for low-cost testing, your own intuition, and the counsel of others in whom you believe. But once you believe in your plan, you've got to back that belief with *patience*. Patience is another way of saying commitment.

My sleep shop client's plan called for weekly newspaper advertising, daily radio advertising, strong in-store signs, weekly sales training, consistent customer follow-up, and free gifts for customers during promotions. That was in the seventies. In the eighties, it was augmented by daily TV advertising three weeks out of every four. And for the nineties, though the business was sold for an obscene sum, it might be supported even more by a video brochure. But the framework would remain the same — because the mind-set of the owner would remain that of a guerrilla.

My advice to you is to create a sensible plan, then stick with it until it proves itself to you. How long might that take? Maybe three months, if you're lucky. Probably six months. And maybe even as long as a year. But you will never, never, never know whether the plan is working within the first sixty days. Commitment is directly related to time. The longer you live by a plan, the deeper your sense of commitment. If your boat sinks in the ocean and you start swimming to shore, you should not give up if you haven't hit the beach within one hour — even five hours. To survive, you've got to be committed to swimming to that beach. Think of that when you consider altering your marketing plans after a short time.

How long does it take to work?

In working with small clients, I consider the greatest stumbling block to be their inability to understand commitment. Lest you misunderstand, think about the following list

The greatest stumbling block

each time you run an ad and achieve less of a response than you expected:

1. The first time a man looks at an ad, he doesn't see it.
2. The second time, he doesn't notice it.
3. The third time, he is conscious of its existence.
4. The fourth time, he faintly remembers having seen it.
5. The fifth time, he reads the ad.
6. The sixth time, he turns up his nose at it.
7. The seventh time, he reads it through and says, "Oh brother!"
8. The eighth time, he says, "Here's that confounded thing again!"
9. The ninth time, he wonders if it amounts to anything,
10. The tenth time, he will ask his neighbor if he has tried it.
11. The eleventh time, he wonders how the advertiser makes it pay.
12. The twelfth time, he thinks it must be a good thing.
13. The thirteenth time, he thinks it might be worth something.
14. The fourteenth time, he remembers that he wanted such a thing for a long time.
15. The fifteenth time, he is tantalized because he cannot afford to buy it.
16. The sixteenth time, he thinks he will buy it someday.
17. The seventeenth time, he makes a memorandum of it.
18. The eighteenth time, he swears at his poverty.
19. The nineteenth time, he counts his money carefully.
20. The twentieth time he sees the ad, he buys the article.

The guerrilla from 1885

The above was written by one Thomas Smith in London back in 1885. So much for commitment. Now let's talk about another "ent" word, the second of the ten most important marketing secrets of all — *investment*.

Marketing and advertising should be considered *conservative investments*. They are not miracle workers. They

are not magic formulas. They are not instant gratifiers. If you
don't recognize that marketing is a conservative investment, **Marketing is**
you'll have difficulty committing yourself to a marketing **not instant**
program. **gratification**

Suppose you buy a blue-chip stock. If it drops after a few
weeks, you don't sell it. You hold on to it, hoping it will go up.
And in all likelihood it will. Such is the nature of a conservative investment. Think of marketing the same way. If it
doesn't produce instant results, that's because most marketing
doesn't. If it does produce instant results, good for you — but
don't figure it will always be that way.

Also, don't expect marketing to suddenly double your
sales. Although that has happened, it is unusual. Marketing
will contribute to slow but steady increases for you. At the end
of a year, you'll be able to say that you've invested X dollars
in marketing you and received X plus Y in sales. just the way
conservative investments are supposed to pay off. Recognizing this, you'll feel good about making a conservative investment in marketing the next year, and the year after that. If you
expect more from marketing, chances are you'll be disap-
pointed. If you expect only that, chances are you'll be gratified. And successful.

Stupid example time: I worked with a client who had never
engaged in newspaper advertising. We developed a marketing
plan for his four opticians' shops, a creative strategy, and a
media plan. We discussed commitment. Then we ran the ads.
After four weeks, my client called to tell me he was dropping
the entire advertising program. When I inquired why, he told
me he had expected his sales to at least double by this time.
Yes, he admitted, I had explained that advertising does not
work this way. But no, he decided, he didn't want to spend
money that didn't produce instant sales.

I wish I had informed him up front that his advertising
expenditure was a conservative investment. Perhaps he would
have better understood its powers. But instead, he dropped
the plan and lost his money. Obviously he didn't have an iota

of understanding of the investment concept. People don't invest money and then pull out when there is zero chance of recapturing the expense. But he did. And mind you, he was no dummy in real life. Only in marketing. He was expecting miracles, instant results, dramatic changes. Marketing just does not work that way. So don't expect it. Don't plan for it. Don't lose money because of it. In fact, whenever you spend one dime for any type of marketing, you should actually use the term *investing* to describe your expenditure. By *investing* your money in marketing, you'll earn a lot more money than by *spending* your money in marketing. See the difference?

The third major marketing secret is to make your marketing consistent. Don't change media. Don't change messages. Don't drop out of the public eye for long periods. When you are ready to market your product or service, be prepared to put the word out consistently. Consistently means regularly — and for a goodly period of time. It means that instead of running a couple of large newspaper ads once every few months, you'll run smaller newspaper ads, and run them frequently. Instead of airing fifty-five radio commercials in one week every few months, you'll run twelve radio commercials per week every week. You can even drop out of sight one week out of four. As long as you are a consistent marketer, you can pull out of the media for brief periods.

Familiarity breeds sales   Consistency equates with familiarity. Familiarity equates with confidence. And confidence equates with sales. Provided that your products or services are of sufficient quality, confidence in yourself and your offering will attract buyers more than any other attribute.

That's why the fourth secret is to make prospects *confident* in your offering. Confidence is ultra-important to you. More than quality. More than selection. More than price. More than service. Confidence will be your ally. And commitment, as proven by consistent marketing, will breed confidence.

I have a retail furniture client now who has been with me for about twenty years. When she first started marketing her product, she spent a fortune advertising on television. Could she afford it? Of course not. But she believed that television was her key to success. With the number of dollars she had to invest, television was her key to doom because she could only afford to run two commercials per week, even though they were on the highest-rated show at the time. But ratings are virtually meaningless with only two spots a week. It doesn't take a guerrilla to know that she'd be ill-advised to expect TV to produce profits with so few commercials. We'll discuss TV in greater detail later, but for now, suffice it to say that unless you can utilize a medium effectively, you should not utilize it at all.

My client was able to salvage her business from her disastrous TV experience, and she came to me. We talked about commitment, investment and consistency. We talked about the other seven secrets as well. Since that day, she has run a tiny ad every Sunday in the newspaper, and her sales have continued to rise. Without increasing her marketing expenses as a percent of her gross revenue, she has dramatically increased her sales. It happened over a period of several years. Her store has quadrupled in size, and her profits have followed suit. She's even back on television — this time running ten commercials per day, two weeks out of every four. The key to her glittering success was consistent advertising. She calls her tiny Sunday newspaper ad her "meal ticket". And she's right. She tells me that almost everyone who comes into her store says they've seen the ad. You'd find that hard to believe if you saw the size of the ad. But you'd find that easy to believe if you knew that she's been running that and similar ads in the same newspaper on the same day for years. People are familiar with her operation. They're confident in her offerings. And they buy from her.

Guerrillas have meal tickets

Along with her commitment, her treating marketing like an investment, her being consistent and patient, she has since added a multitude of weapons to her marketing arsenal. This assortment of weapons is generating all sorts of new, higher-than-projected profits for her. Guerrillas know that the wider the assortment of weapons you use, the wider the grin on your face when you review your financial statements.

Does she do follow-up mailings to all of her customers? Of course she does. She has learned that marketing doesn't end with the sale; instead, it's the marketing you do *subsequent* to the sale that leads to the juicy profits. It costs five times as much to sell to a new customer as it does to sell the same thing to an existing customer. So my client is always mailing to existing customers — and benefiting from the repeat sales that are the inevitable payoff.

The inevitable payoff

Her store is known as a very *convenient* place to buy. It's open seven days a week. Hours are extended for the convenience of her customers — not for her own convenience. She accepts every credit card under the sun. She takes checks, arranges partial payment plans, delivers, installs, is accessible twenty-four hours a day via voice mail and fax, and even the parking is convenient.

Although she takes much of her business for granted, she knows that her marketing must *amaze* people. So her marketing mentions that her custom-designed furniture is available at factory-direct-prices because she has her own factory. The prices are amazing and so is the homemade touch. It enables her to custom-design furniture and offer it at an off-the-floor price. This element of *amazement* attracts attention to her ads.

Most amazing of all, she has doubled the effectiveness of all her marketing! How did she do such a wondrous thing? The answer is *measurement*, as if you didn't know. She measured the effectiveness of all her marketing, asking people where they first heard of her.

In this way, she was able to eliminate the weapons and newspapers that weren't pulling their weight while doubling up on those that gave her the biggest bang for her bucks. The result: a doubling of her profits. The reason: measurement, also called "sourcing" by those in the know.

These ten secrets — as embodied by ten words — are the

most valuable secrets you'll learn in this book. They are also extremely difficult rules to follow.

Valuable but difficult

Your friends, employees, coworkers, partners, family and suppliers may advise you to change your marketing plan when they don't see instant results. These same well-meaning people will question a marketing program that does not produce a dramatic increase in sales over a short period of time. And they'll be the first to tire of your marketing, become bored with your ads or commercials, be ready for a major change in your message or media. But your customers won't feel that way at all. They'll go through the process of developing confidence in your offering, and you should do everything in your power not to undermine that process. Now that you know these secrets, you won't.

The guerrilla moral: when you do develop your marketing plan, don't give it your stamp of approval until you are ready to commit yourself to it. Don't okay it until you are ready to invest in it with a realistic expectation of return. And don't start implementing it until you are prepared to stay with it on a consistent basis. This is not to say that you can't make changes. Of course you can. And maybe you should. But you can make changes while remaining consistent.

In quick review:

- Your task: make prospects *confident* in you.
- Your secret weapon: *commitment* to your plan.
- Your personality: *patience* describes it.
- Your marketing: an *assortment* of at least twenty weapons.
- Your format: the spirit of *consistency*.
- Your finances: some wisely *invested* in marketing.
- Your energy: apparent prior to and *subsequent* to the sale.
- Your operation: the essence of *convenience*.
- Your creative message: it always *amazes* readers.
- Your unglamourous but ultra-profitable chore:

Your mission is clear

measurement of who came in to buy and where the heck they heard of you.

There. Now you can never say you weren't made fully aware of the ten most important marketing secrets. Merely by knowing them and making them a cornerstone of your business, you have a head start on your competition. Now, let's increase that head start. Let's examine what it takes to develop a successful plan in the first place.

4

The Blueprint: Developing a Guerrilla Marketing Plan

IN ORDER TO ENGAGE in successful marketing, you absolutely must start out with a marketing plan. But how do you develop one? You engage in research, attend to all details, and give the matter quite a bit of deep thought. Rest assured, the difference between many a success and failure is market planning and nothing else.

A word that you should now start to use and understand is positioning. Positioning means determining exactly what niche your offering is intended to fill. Once, I read of an airline that commenced operations during a time when most airline business was drastically down. By establishing a solid marketing plan, the new airline took off with astounding speed. It positioned itself as a high-frequency, no-frills airline that specialized in flights of less than two hours and in connecting passengers with long-distance routes of other airlines. That was a unique position. No other airline in the region offered such benefits. Success came rather easily.

To attract further attention, the airline held seat-clearance sales, gave away free fifths of Chivas Regal scotch and Jack Daniel's bourbon, and introduced other innovations into a rather staid industry. None of this happened by accident. All of it came as a result of intelligent market planning and brilliant positioning.

One of the best-known names in American advertising

circles is David Ogilvy. After placing several billion dollars' worth of advertising, Mr. O. listed thirty-two things his advertising agency had learned. Of the thirty-two, he said that the single most important decision had to do with positioning the product. He claimed that marketing results depended less on how advertising was written than on how the product or service was positioned.

The spring-board for marketing
The guerrilla marketing plan or strategy should serve as the springboard for marketing that sells. When doing your own market planning, review your offering with regard to your objectives, the strengths and weaknesses of your offering, your perceived competition, your target market, the needs of that market, and the trends apparent in the economy. This should be instrumental in your establishing a proper position. Ask yourself basic questions: What business are you in? What is your goal? What benefits do you offer? What competitive advantages? When you know the true nature of your business, your goal, your strengths and weaknesses, your competitors' strengths and weaknesses, and the needs of your target market, your positioning will be that much easier to determine, your strategy easier to plan.

Who are you marketing to ?
You must also ask and answer: who is my target market? The answers you may have had when you started in business may vary in the nineties. Many enormous new markets are being identified, and many guerrilla marketers are enjoying record-breaking profits by aiming at those markets. Guerrilla fact: the more markets you have, the more profits you have.

Three markets that have already emerged as viable target audiences and will be bombarded with marketing in the nineties and throughout the coming century are *older people, women*, and *ethnic groups*.

Marketing to older people
The University of Michigan informs us that older people rely on mass-media marketing even more than on friends and family when it comes to consumer information. Surveys from several sources show that older folks rank health first, financial security second, a closer relationship with God third, and

a closer relationship with family fourth. Younger people rank their free time above all else.

Guerrillas know that when communicating with older people, you should use the term "older" rather than "elderly" or "senior citizen". No games, please. When using graphics, show older people as actively old and living life to its fullest. Avoid anything trendy. Older people respond well to products and services that appeal to their autonomy and independence. Their eyesight is faltering, so use large type in your printed material. Do you know the magazine with the largest circulation in the United States? It used to be *Reader's Digest*; then it was *TV Guide*; now it's *Modern Maturity*.

The woman of today has more interests and can be reached through more marketing vehicles than ever before. And the power of women is staggering: although 79 percent of bed purchase decisions are made by women, 77 percent of the time a man writes the check for the bed. Similar percentages can be found in many other fields offering expensive items, beginning with houses and cars, usually the most expensive purchases people will make in their lifetimes.

The woman of the nineties

Guerrillas not only include women as a target audience in their general marketing, they also direct much of their marketing directly to women and only to women. Their purchasing power is growing with their stature in business.

Let's compare the mother of today, age thirty-seven, with her mother:

Task	% of Time spent by Her Mother	% of Time Spent by Today's Woman
Job	31	31
Kids	24	34
Husband	15	14
Personal	5	9
Chores	8	5
Cooking	16	8
Parents	3	5

Don't overlook ethnic groups

Now also recognized as a potential lode of purchasing power are ethnic groups, many of whom are affluent, educated, and, happily for the guerrilla, have no brand loyalties — yet.

To reach ethnic communities, consider placing ads in their newspapers, experimenting with direct mail, and sponsoring events aligned with the groups that are your target audiences. Remember that some ethnic groups rely on native language media for their consumer information.

Four criteria to meet

When you are focused clearly upon your market or markets, you can clarify your market position. Once you zero in on that position for your product or service, you should measure it against four criteria: (1) Does it offer a benefit my target audience really wants? (2) Is it a real honest-to-goodness benefit? (3) Does it truly separate me from my competition? (4) Is it unique and/or difficult to copy?

Unless you are completely satisfied with your answers, you should continue searching for a proper position. When you have finally answered the questions to your own satisfaction, you'll end up with a sensible position — and that should lead you to your goal. Accurate positioning doesn't just happen. It takes a lot of clear thinking, quite a bit of effort. But it's the key to marketing that works. And no guerrilla would think of doing one speck of marketing without a proper marketing plan that includes a positioning statement.

Just before starting on your marketing plan, you should practice thinking big. At this point, your imagination is not a limiting factor, so let it expand to open your mind to all the possibilities for your venture.

If you want, you can make your finished plan up to ten pages long. But at first, try stating it in one paragraph.

The guerrilla marketing plan

Guerrillas create strategies that are seven sentences long:

1. The first sentence tells the purpose of the strategy.
2. The second tells how you'll achieve this purpose, focusing upon your benefits.
3. The third tells your target market — or markets.

4. The fourth, the longest sentence, tells the marketing weapons you'll employ.
5. The fifth tells your niche.
6. The sixth tells your identity.
7. The seventh tells your budget, expressed as a percentage of your projected gross revenues.

Suppose you call your business Prosper Press and you intend to sell books about free-lancing. Let your strategy start with the words:

"The purpose of Prosper Press marketing is to sell the maximum number of books at the lowest possible selling cost per book. This will be accomplished by positioning the books as being so valuable to free-lancers that they are guaranteed to be worth more to the reader than their selling price." Let the paragraph continue: "The target market will be people who can or do engage in free-lance earning activities." Next, the paragraph might say, "Marketing tools to be utilized will be a combination of classified advertising in magazines and newspapers, direct mail, sales at seminars, publicity in newspapers and on radio and television, direct sales calls to bookstores, and mail-order display ads in magazines. The niche to be occupied is one that stands for valuable information that helps free-lancers succeed, the ultimate authority for free-lancers. Our identity will be one of expertise, readability, and quick response to customer requests. Thirty percent of sales will be allocated to marketing."

That's a long paragraph. And it's a simplistic paragraph. But it does the job. It's for a product rather than a service, for an earning venture that entails hardly any contact with the public. This mail-order venture requires very little in the way of marketing, considering all the options. It works beautifully in real life; has worked since 1974.

The plan starts with the purpose of the marketing — that is, it starts with the bottom line. From there, it connects with the benefits that will beautify that bottom line and with those who **Dissecting the plan** will contribute to that line — the target audience. The marketing tools are then listed. Next comes the positioning statement, which explains why the offering has value and should be purchased, what the product stands for. The identity (not the image, which is phony compared with the honesty of an identity) comes next. And the cost of the marketing wraps it up.

Take a moment to understand clearly the crucial difference between an *image* and an *identity*. Image implies something artificial, something that is not genuine. *Identity* defines what your business is really about.

A business owner gets together with his staff and they develop an image, which is defined by many dictionaries as "a façade". Their marketing reflects this image. People come in and see that the business isn't exactly what they expected. They feel ripped off. They feel distrustful of the company.

Another business owner gets together with his staff and they develop an identity, based on truth. Their marketing reflects this identity. People come in and see that the business is exactly what they expected. They feel relaxed. They know they can trust this company. After all, it said nothing about itself that wasn't true.

Which of these two business owners is the guerrilla? What's better for your company, a phony image or an honest identity? We both know the right answers.

Now let's examine a marketing strategy for a computer tutor:

The purpose of Computer Tutor marketing is to book 100 percent of the company's available time for computer education, at the lowest possible cost per hour. This will be accomplished by establishing the credentials of the educators, the location of the operation, and the equipment. The target market will be local small businesspeople who can benefit from learning how to operate a small computer. Marketing tools to be utilized will be a combination of personal letters, circulars, brochures, signs on bulletin boards, classified ads in local newspapers, yellow page advertising, direct mail, advertising specialties, free seminars, sampling, and publicity in local newspapers, on radio, and on television. The company will be positioned as the prime source of one-on-one, guaranteed instruction in the operation of small computers; positioning will be intensified by office decor, employee attire, telephone manners, and location selection. Our company's identity will be a blend of professionalism, personal attention, and warm, human regard for our students. Ten percent of sales will be allocated to marketing.

Most marketing plans, especially if they are reduced to one paragraph, seem deceptively simple. But *unless* they are simple, they are difficult to execute. A complete marketing plan, which can run as little as three paragraphs — the marketing plan, the creative plan, and the media plan — or as long as 10 or even 110 pages (not recommended), should serve as a *guide*. It need not spell out all the details.

The chairman and chief executive officer of the Coca-Cola Company recognized this need for simplicity when he said, "If I had to state our business plan in one sentence, it would be this: 'We are going to build on our marketing strength in order to achieve profitable growth in the decade ahead.' "

Naturally, the marketing plan does identify the market. It lays out the framework for creating the advertising — as will be seen in the next chapter. It specifies the media to be utilized, along with costs, as will be seen in chapter 6. And that's really all it has to do.

A business plan may require support documents such as **A business** results of research, the overall competitive situation, financial **plan** projections, and other details. But to include those details in the marketing plan itself is to muddy the waters. That's one reason guerrilla marketing plans are brief. A good road map lists the name or number of the highway wherever appropriate, not wherever possible. Like maps, marketing plans with too many details are difficult to follow.

The briefer your marketing plan, the easier it will be to follow. Bolster it with as many support documents as you wish. But don't include support information in the plan itself Leave the details for other times, other places, other documents. The marketing plan should be the essence of simplicity. If it is not, chances are you haven't thought it through enough. And your employees, once they've read it, should immediately grasp your goals and be on your wavelength because your strategy is clear and direct. Most marketing strategies befuddle instead of enlightening employees. Then again, most employees are never made privy to the marketing strategy of the companies for which they work.

Your prime purpose Once you have given your plan the proper thought, brevity, and focus, you can expand it in those areas pertinent to your business. While expanding it, never forget that your prime purpose is to obtain maximum profits. Profits are very different from sales. Anyone can achieve sales. It takes a guerrilla to consistently turn honest profits. These profits will be obtained if you clearly list your goals — all of them, including timing, budgets for everything, and projections. Without projections, you won't have a measuring stick. Your expanded plan should look first to the long range, then to the near future. By looking far enough into the future, you will realize what it takes to get you where you want to go in the style you desire.

You might want to consider what market share you are targeting, what key personnel may be necessary to command that share, what inside services you'll need, and what outside services can be utilized to negate the need for inside services. Whether you list all the potential pitfalls in writing or not, you should think about how to deal with them. If you know what to expect in the way of obstacles, you'll better be able to surmount them as they pop up. And pop up they will.

Expanded marketing plans Many expanded marketing plans include a situational analysis. This entalls learning about your key customers, your expected competition, the possibilities, the probabilities, and the reality of the marketplace at the moment. While you are analyzing your situation, always remember to keep your eye on your bottom line. Don't let business get in the way of the purpose of business. The means should not interfere with the end.

Computers now enable us to project results based upon hypothetical instances. An expanded marketing plan or business plan may examine those "what if" situations. It should have the framework for incorporating alternative courses of action based upon contingencies. If you wish, it can embrace lists of objectives, priorities, monitoring methods, problems, opportunities, and responsibilities. But an expanded marketing plan is more of a luxury than a necessity. And too many entrepreneurs get water-logged with details to the point that the flame of their initial thrust grows dim and turns to smoke. Huge corporations do the same when they get carried away with technology and distracted from their original dreams.

Yearly, you should re-examine your marketing plan — whether brief or expanded. Your goal should be to maintain it. The conservative philosophy should apply: if it is not necessary to change, it is necessary not to change.

But whatever bells and whistles you have attached to your basic plan, whatever M.B.A. documentation you have affixed to it, you must still know who you are, where you are going, and how you will get there. You must start with a bare-bones marketing plan, short and simple. And you should not confuse a marketing plan with a business plan. A longer plan can go into details of growth, exact expenditures, and details. But the plans I have included a few pages back are enough to enable you to start and succeed. The first example is for a real company. The second is for a fictional company. These plans can be implemented by entrepreneurs who have a bent toward either mail-order book marketing (you can write or buy the books) or computer education (you can do or delegate the teaching). Both follow a simple formula that can serve as the basis for virtually any venture.

Such plans allow for some flexibility, but not a great deal. For example, Computer Tutor may run only one magazine ad one time in one regional edition, and run radio commercials every single day of the year. The marketing plan would still be fulfilled.

A good marketing plan should not allow for too much flexibility. After all, the plan is created to be followed. If you **When to make** want changes, make them *before* you write the plan. And don't **changes** forget *to commit yourself to it.*

Once you have positioned your business with a marketing plan that tells what your advertising is going to say. And finally, you create a media plan that tells the exact media details: costs, names of newspapers or radio stations, dates and sizes of ads, frequency of advertising, advertising specialties to be employed, tacks for obtaining free publicity, and the identity of your business.

Okay, you've got a marketing plan that tells how you'll promote your earning endeavor. You've got a creative plan that dictates your message and your identity. You've got a media plan that tells exactly where you'll spend your money. Now, if you've got the rest of your earning act together — the financial side, the legal issues, the accounting, the ability to offer a lot of quality in either your products or your services, and the right mental attitude — you can start earning money.

Many people start at this point, get cold feet when they see the early results, and stop marketing while they think things over. Think but do not stop. Stopping is not a good idea. If after starting a business and embarking upon a marketing program — which is to say, investing serious cash in promoting the business (serious being anywhere from $100 per month to $1,000,000 per month) — you decide to stop marketing for a while, turn immediately to this page and read the following list of reasons why you *should* continue to market:

1. *The market is constantly changing.* New families, new prospects, new lifestyles change the marketplace. When

you stop advertising, you miss evolving opportunities and stop being part of the process. You are not on the bus. You are not in the game.

Why you must continue to market

2. *People forget fast.* Remember, they're bombarded with tons of marketing messages (an estimated 2700) daily. An experiment proved the need for constancy in marketing by running advertising once a week for thirteen weeks. After that period, 63 percent of the people surveyed remembered the advertising. One month later, 32 percent recalled it. Two weeks after that, 21 percent remembered it. That means 79 percent forgot it.

3. *Your competition isn't quitting.* People will spend money to make purchases, and if you don't make them aware that you are selling something, they'll spend their money elsewhere.

4. *Marketing strengthens your identity.* When you quit marketing, you shortchange your reputation, reliability, and the confidence people have in you. When economic conditions turn sour, smart companies continue to advertise. The bond of communication is too precious to break capriciously.

5. *Marketing is essential to survival and growth.* With very few exceptions, people won't know you're there if you don't get the word out. And when you cease marketing, you're on the path to nonexistence. Just as you can't start a business without marketing, you can't maintain one without it.

6. *Marketing enables you to hold on to your old customers.* Many enterprises survive on repeat and referral business. Old customers are the key to both. When old customers don't hear from you or about you, they tend to forget you.

7. *Marketing maintains morale.* Your own morale is improved when you see your marketing at work, and especially when you see that it does, indeed, work. Your employees' morale is similarly uplifted. And cutting out marketing seems a signal of failure to those who actively

follow your advertising. That won't be many people, but it will be some.

8. *Marketing gives you an advantage over competitors who have ceased marketing.* A troubled economy can be a superb advantage to a marketing-minded entrepreneur. It forces some competitors to stop marketing — giving you a chance to pull ahead of them and attract some of their customers. In all ugly economic situations, there are winners and losers.

9. *Marketing allows your business to continue operating.* You still have some overheads: telephone bills, yellow pages ads, rent and/or equipment cost, possibly a payroll, your time. Marketing creates the air overhead breathes.

10. *You have invested money that you stand to lose.* If you quit marketing, all of the money you spent for ads, commercials, and advertising time and space becomes lost as the consumer awareness it purchased slowly dwindles away. Sure, you can buy it again. But you'll have to start from scratch. Unless you are planning to go out of business, it is rarely a good idea to cease marketing completely.

Just look at it this way: does stopping marketing save you money? It does in the same way that stopping your wristwatch saves time. In other words, don't kid yourself

I hope I have talked you into living with your commitment to your marketing program. This in no way means that you are going to market your business successfully. A marketing plan is necessary — in fact, crucial — for a company or an entrepreneur. But a marketing plan is a bit like a fancy, comfortable, **The fuel that** powerful, great-looking car without gas. The fuel that powers **powers your** your vehicle is the marketing itself what it says, how it looks, **business** what it feels like. That's where the creative process comes into play in marketing. And that's when it's got to be used with style and power. There's a way of making sure those creative juices flow. I'll let you in on some of the secrets in the following pages.

5

Secrets of Developing a Creative Marketing Program

PROBABLY THE MOST ENJOYABLE part of the marketing process is the creative part. And if you want to succeed in making your small business big, you should realize that the creative part applies to every single aspect of the process. We'll start by going into ways you can make your advertising itself creative. Later, we'll explore how you can be creative in media selection, marketing planning, and public relations.

I'm not sure who first said it, but almost any marketing person worth his or her salt will tell you that *marketing is not creative unless it sells*. You can pretty much ensure that you'll end up with creative marketing if you start out by devising a *creative strategy*. Such a strategy is similar to a marketing plan, but limited to marketing materials only — and directed solely at their content.

The creative strategy

If you think there's a simple formula for establishing such a strategy, you're absolutely right. Here, in the simplest terms possible, is a typical three-sentence creative strategy:

The purpose of Mother Nature breakfast cereal advertising will be to convince our target audience, mothers of children twelve years of age and younger, that Mother Nature breakfast cereal is the most nutritious and healthy boxed cereal on the market. [This is the purpose of the creative message.] This will be accomplished by listing the vitamins and minerals in each serving of the cereal. [This explains how the purpose will be achieved.] The mood and tone of the advertising will be upbeat, natural, honest, and warm. [This tells the mood and tone, the personality of the product.]

In this one paragraph we have listed the purpose of the advertising, the method by which the purpose can be achieved, and the personality the ads or commercials will have.

The first step in developing a creative marketing program is writing a simple creative strategy. You can get a great deal of insight into writing one for yourself if you practice first by writing creative strategies for current advertisers. Pick a newspaper advertiser, a television advertiser, and a direct-mail advertiser and compose three-sentence creative strategies that apply to each of them. Do the same for your competitors. That will help you figure your own positioning and prevent you from becoming a me-too company.

After you've got your own strategy — one to which you have devoted much time and thought — you can embark upon a seven-step program to assure yourself of successful marketing. Let's check all seven steps.

Seven steps to creative marketing

1. *Find the inherent drama within your offering.* After all, you plan to make money by selling a product or a service or both. The reasons people will want to buy from you should give you a clue as to the inherent drama in your product or service. Something about your offering must be inherently interesting or you wouldn't be putting it up for sale. In Mother Nature breakfast cereal, it is the high concentration of vitamins and minerals.

2. *Translate that inherent drama into a meaningful benefit.* Always remember that people buy benefits, not features. People do not buy shampoo; people buy great-looking or clean or manageable hair. People do not buy cars; people buy speed, status, style, economy, per-

formance, and power. Mothers of young kids do not buy cereal; they buy nutrition. So find the major benefit of your offering and write it down. It should come directly from the inherently dramatic feature. And even though you have four or five benefits, stick with one or two — three at most.

3. *State your benefits as believably as possible.* There is a world of difference between honesty and believability. You can be 100 percent honest (as you should be) and people still may not believe you. You must go beyond honesty, beyond the barrier that advertising has erected by its tendency toward exaggeration, and state your benefit in such a way that it will be accepted beyond doubt. The company producing Mother Nature breakfast cereal might say, "A bowl of Mother Nature breakfast cereal provides your child with almost as many vitamins as a multivitamin pill." This statement begins with the inherent drama, turns it into a benefit, and is worded believably. The word almost lends believability.

4. *Get people's attention.* People do not pay attention to advertising. They pay attention only to things that interest them. And sometimes they find those things in advertising. So you've just got to interest them. And while you're at it, be sure you interest them in your product or service, not just your advertising. I'm sure you're familiar with advertising that you remember for a product you do not remember. Many advertisers are guilty of creating advertising that's more interesting than whatever it is they are advertising. But you can prevent yourself from failing into that trap by memorizing this line: *forget the ad, is the product or service interesting?* The Mother Nature company might put their point across by showing a picture of two hands breaking open a multivitamin capsule from which pour flakes that fall into an appetizing-looking bowl of cereal.

5. *Motivate your audience to do something.* Tell them to visit the store, as the Mother Nature company might do. Tell them to make a phone call, fill in a coupon, write for more information, ask for your product by name, take a test drive, or come in for a free demonstration. Don't stop short. To make guerrilla marketing work, you must tell people exactly what you want them to do.

6. *Be sure you are communicating clearly.* You may know what you're talking about, but do your readers or listeners? Recognize that people aren't really thinking about your business and that they'll only give about half their attention to your ad — even when they are paying attention. Knock yourself out to make sure you are putting your message across. The Mother Nature company might show its ad to ten people and ask them what the main point is. If one person misunderstands, that means 10 percent of the audience will misunderstand. And if the ad goes out to 500,000 people, 50,000 will miss the main point. That's unacceptable. One hundred percent of the audience should get the main point. The company might accomplish this by stating in a headline or subhead, "Giving your kids Mother Nature breakfast cereal is like giving your kids vitamins — only tastier." Zero ambiguity is your goal.

7. *Measure your finished advertisement,* commercial, letter, or brochure against your creative strategy. The strategy is your blueprint. If your ad fails to fulfill the strategy, it's a lousy ad, no matter how much you love it. Scrap it and start again. All along, you should be using your creative strategy to guide you, to give you hints as to the content of your ad. If you don't, you may end up being creative in a vacuum. And that's not being creative at all. If your ad is in line with your strategy, you may then judge its other elements.

The key to creative advertising is starting with a smart creative strategy. The test of creative advertising is sales and profits. If what you want to sell doesn't sell and generate profits for your business, you are not truly being creative. And creativity doesn't end with the creation of your advertising.

Once you have highly creative marketing weapons — in the form of ads, commercials, signs, circulars, store decor, whatever — you must be creative in the way you use them. I know of a deodorant company that did a lot of TV advertising to introduce its product during the winter. Why the winter, when people are not buying as much deodorant? Because this company lacked the funds to go head-to-head with the big guys. So instead of vying for public attention during the summer, when its competition would be shooting the big guns, it attracted attention during the winter, when no other deodorant companies were advertising and it had the stage to itself

How guerrillas use marketing weapons

There are other ways to be creative. You can be creative in the use of personal letters by having them hand delivered or by sending them via Express Mail, Federal Express, or some other out-of-the-ordinary delivery service. You can canvass creatively by wearing a unique outfit and handing a small gift to each prospect. You can be creative in your use of signs by putting them in unusual places, such as in the hands of paid picketers (one of the most unique advertising vehicles know). Show creativity in the Yellow Pages by the size of your ad, its message, color, and its graphic treatment. Be creative in the use of newspaper advertising by running six small ads in one issue, rather than one large one.

Going all out

As you can see, there are limitless ways to exercise creativity in all facets of marketing. In one of my earlier books, *Earning Money Without a Job*, I told of a couple who got married in their boutique, after informing the local newspapers and TV station about the wedding. Naturally, they received a lot of free coverage. (I hope they didn't get married simply to get free publicity.)

A former boss of mine used to remind his staff that you can

Your socks in your mouth

be creative by coming downstairs with your socks in your mouth — but what's the point? There should be a reason for your creativity. And it should never detract from your message. Well-directed creativity is hard to find, hard to develop, and hard to compete against. That's why guerrillas place such emphasis on *creativity with a point to it.*

When practicing guerrilla marketing, you must be more creative than your competition in every aspect of marketing. Merely doing it by the numbers isn't enough. You've got to do it properly, do it intelligently, do it clearly, do it creatively, and do it consistently to assure yourself of successfully marketing your product or service. You don't have to know how to write or draw to be creative. All you've got to do is supply the creative idea. You can always hire a person to write or draw

Who will be creative for you?

for you. But it's not easy to hire a person to be creative about your business for you. That task should fall to you. And you should revel in it. Now let's look at a few examples of creativity in action:

Example A: An accountant wanted to increase his business, so he wrote a tax newsletter and sent it, free of charge, every three months, to a large list of prospects. By doing this, he established himself as an authority and dramatically improved his business. Not an earthshaking act of creativity, but it worked like crazy for the accountant.

Example B: A waterbed retail store wanted to rid itself of the counterculture identity associated with waterbeds, so it relocated in an elegant shopping center, required its staff to dress to the teeth, and hired a man with a voice like God to serve as the announcer on its radio commercials. Great results all around.

Example C: A jeweler wanted to attract attention to himself every Christmas, so he invented outlandishly expensive Christmas gift ideas. One was a Frisbee with a diamond in the center. Price: $5000. One was a miniature hourglass with real diamonds instead of sand. Price: $10,000. One was a jewel-encrusted backgammon set with a price tag of $50, 000. The jeweler sold hardly any of these items. But he attracted national publicity and his December sales soared.

Notice that in none of these examples did I talk about the creativity one usually associates with ads themselves. That's the obvious place to be creative. But these examples show how you can be creative in your prospecting, store decor, employee attire, methods of gaining free publicity, and many other ways. If whenever you engage in marketing you train yourself to think that the opposite of creativity is mediocrity, you'll start forcing yourself to use marketing tools in the most creative manner possible.

In case you're wondering where creativity starts, I'll tell you. It starts with *knowledge*. You need knowledge of your own product or service, knowledge of your competition, knowledge of your target audience, knowledge of your marketing area, knowledge of the economy, knowledge of current events, and knowledge of the trends of the time. From this knowledge, you'll not only develop a creative marketing program, but you'll also be able to produce creative marketing materials. **Where creativity starts**

I find that I can glean a lot of knowledge by keeping abreast of world events in the usual manner. I read one weekly news magazine and ten monthly special-interest magazines. I watch the late TV news most nights. And I read one daily newspaper. Some people are far more attuned to world happenings than that. But that's enough for me. It lets me in on the world situation, the local situation, and up-to-the-minute trends. It also allows me to get a look at the marketing of others — especially competitors of my clients.

If you're not keeping up, you're falling behind. And guerrillas just can't afford to fall behind. **Keep up or fall behind**

Armed with all of this knowledge, you are able to do what

many people define as the essence of creativity: you can combine two or more elements that have never before been combined. For instance, when 7UP wanted to boost its sales up there with CocaCola and Pepsi-Cola, it referred to itself as "The Uncola". This put it in the category of the colas, yet proudly proclaimed that it was different. By combining the prefix *un*, which means "not", with the word *cola*, 7UP exercised great creativity. The advertising person who dreamed up the concept used his knowledge of the art scene at the time by employing psychedelic art in advertisements both in print and on television. His knowledge of his product, his competition, his target audience, and the trends of the day resulted in exceptionally creative advertising. And the proof of that creativity was in the increased sales enjoyed by 7UP. Where did it all start? It started with basic knowledge.

The Marlboro cigarette company exercised creativity when it combined the ideas of a cowboy and a cigarette. The AT&T telephone company used creativity when it combined the ideas of an emotionally charged situation and a telephone ("Reach out and touch someone"). Avis Rent-a-Car showed creativity when it capitalized on being the second largest, rather than the largest, car rental company, and flatly stated, "We try harder." In all of these cases, plus thousands more, creativity started with plain and simple knowledge.

As a guerrilla, you are obligated to become knowledgeable about a broad range of topics. Guerrillas are generalists, not specialists. Guerrillas know that to remove the mystique from **Thinking** the creative process, they must think backward. They must **backward** start by picturing the mind of their customer at the moment that customer makes a decision to purchase. What led to that decision? What were the thought processes? What made them take place? What were the customer's buttons and what did you do to push them? Thinking backward takes you to the needs and desires that are crucial to motivation.

Let's take a moment to examine marketing in the light of psychology. "Skinnerian marketing" would dictate that you modify behavior. This means saying, showing, or doing something that causes a customer to change his or her behavior so as to act in the way you want that customer to act. You gently nudge the customer to buy, to call, to visit, to compare, to clip a coupon, to follow your command.

"Freudian marketing" is addressed to the unconscious — the most powerful part of a person's mind. "Skinnerian marketing" is addressed to the conscious — less powerful, but more easily activated.

Guerrilla marketing is addressed to both the unconscious — and the conscious. It changes attitudes while modifying behavior. It comes at the customer from all directions. It persuades, coerces, tempts, compels, romances, and orders the customer to do your bidding. It leaves little to chance. It is the essence of precise planning.

What guerrilla marketing does

In the nineties, guerrilla marketers understand their role in the community. Their marketing might change attitudes while modifying behavior, yet have very little to do with the product or service itself. I quote from a very successful ice cream company's brochure: "At Ben and Jerry's, we're as concerned about our responsibility to the community, both local and global, as we are about making great ice cream." Then they prove their devotion to humanity by sponsoring altruistic causes such as the Children's Defense Fund, voter registration, peace on earth, saving rain forests, less military spending, and more recycling. Ben and Jerry say, "Business has the responsibility to give back to the community." And this is their creative platform. It sells sanity. It sells honesty. It sells nobility. It sells ice cream. Ben and Jerry sponsor concerts to help spread the word, not about their ice cream as much as about their desire to save the planet.

In the 1950s, this would have been considered crazy. In the 1990s, it's considered brilliant marketing as well as humanitarian. Ben and Jerry's is famous for its good deeds. But Sears? Sears is pushing for recycling these days. And so are Safeway, Bank of America, Coca-Cola, American Airlines,

3M, Du Pont, UPS, and guerrillas throughout the nation whose names are not yet famous. Backing a noble cause is an option when developing a creative strategy.

Apparel-maker Liz Claiborne buys ads aimed at helping victims of domestic violence. Patagonia, the outdoor clothing company, promotes environmental awareness. Esprit, the clothing maker, urges people to vote. In 1992, $262 million **Cause-related** was spent on "cause-related marketing". This includes causes **marketing** such as AIDS, healthy eating, and helping the homeless.

This corporate philanthropy started well before the nineties. American Express promoted restoration of the Statue of Liberty in the mid-1980s.

Do creative strategies based upon noble causes work? In 1992, 83 percent of shoppers said they had changed brands based solely upon environmental concerns. Eighty percent of shoppers said a company's environmental reputation is important. Consumers even said they'd spend a 5.5 percent premium for "green" products.

Be careful about centering your creative strategy around rapid societal changes that are more anecdotal than factual. The guerrilla is alert for changes, but knows the difference between a real change and a media-perceived change.

Because industrialized nations are experiencing a major decline in 20-to-29-year-olds, the group that starts new households, the slowdown in sales of big-ticket items is predicted to persist throughout the nineties.

Guerrillas adapt their marketing, their creative message, and their entire philosophy to the realities of the times. Instead **Go with the** of pushing against the river of change, they go with the flow. **flow** And their profitability attests to the wisdom of this attitude.

6
Secrets of Selecting Marketing Methods

IF YOU ARE CONSCIENTIOUS, you can create a dynamite marketing plan, a brilliant creative strategy, and promote a noble
cause. Still, there are many places you can go wrong. One way
is to run the right advertising in the wrong media. But how do
you tell the right from the wrong?

Every method of marketing has its own particular strength. **The strengths**
Radio is the most *intimate* of the media, allowing you to spend **of the media**
chunks of time in one-on-one situations with your audience.
Sometimes the listeners will be in crowded restaurants. But
other times they'll be in their cars or in their homes — alone.

The newspaper is a prime medium for disseminating the
news. And that strength can become your strength. Advertising in the newspaper, other than in the classified section,
should be newsy, interruptive, and to the point.

Magazines are media with which readers become more
involved. Whether they buy individual newsstand copies or
subscribe, they take a good, long time to read them. So you can
attempt to capture the editorial "mood" of the magazine in
your ads. You can put forth more information because readers
will be willing to take more time reading a magazine ad than
a newspaper ad.

Television is the most comprehensive of the media. It
enables you to convince your prospects by means of actual
demonstrations. Such powerful selling devices as

demonstrations are not possible by any other means — except seminars, fares, and live contacts with audiences. Television allows you to combine words with pictures and music, and to get into the minds of your potential customers in more ways than any other medium. Television advertising can also be very costly, so it must be done properly or not at all. This is not a medium with which to dabble.

Still, cable and satellite TV has put the medium within the reach of *all* advertisers, down to the tiniest. To a guerrilla, this **Prime time for** is glorious news. Many a small business is becoming a big **guerrillas** business as a result of it. Don't take this as permission to play around with TV. Instead, think of it as an invitation to give serious consideration to what some describe as "the undisputed heavyweight champion of marketing."

Direct mall allows you to take the most careful aim at your target audience. Created skillfully, direct-mail advertising enables you to go through the entire selling process — from securing your prospects' attention to actually obtaining sales by means of coupons the prospects can complete and freephone numbers they can call. Like TV, direct mail can be very costly when misused. And it's quite easy to misuse. This will continue to be true as postage rates continue to rise and the number of mailed pieces increases. To a guerrilla, postage rates don't mean nearly as much as response rates. If it costs twice as much postage to get three times the response, only a nitwit would save on postage rates. Guerrillas aren't fazed by the blizzard of direct mall assaulting their prospects each day. They know how to break through that barrier: with follow-up mailings, with telemarketing, with unique mailing packages.

Outdoor signs and billboards are superb at *reminding* people of your existence and your reason for being. They do not work well all by themselves, except in rare instances. But **The power of** they work well in combination with other marketing methods. **inside signs** Signs inside are a different matter altogether because they generate impulse reactions right where they ought to — at the place of purchase, where about 75 percent of purchase decisions are made, according to a 1991 study. Worded and designed right, they *capitalize upon the momentum generated by your other marketing*. The great Leo Burnett, founder of one of the three best ad agencies in the world, always reminded us to "plan the sale when you plan the ad." He loved the immense power of inside signs. They would be designed to take off from where the ads left off. These days, those signs might be a video message, a hologram, a moving sign. And you don't need your own inside premises to capitalize upon the power of inside signs. The inside of many other premises will work very well, thank you. As long as your prospects are there, you should try to be there. Consider airports, hotel lobbies, club bulletin boards, stores owned by people with whom you have established tie-in arrangements.

Canvassing takes more time than any other method of marketing, but it is highly effective. It has few limitations and gives you *personal contact*. In many cases, it is difficult to handle the canvassing yourself. But you can delegate the job to a professional salesperson or a college, even a high school, student, depending upon the complexity of your sales presentation. Canvassing is greatly strengthened by mass-marketing methods, which help remove you from the category of complete stranger.

Yellow Pages marketing and classified advertisements hit the *very hottest of prospects*. These people are taking the time to look up the kind of information you're offering, so you don't have to expend much energy getting their attention or selling the general benefits of your product or service. This advertising also places you in direct confrontation with your competition. Just knowing that should enable you to be more precise with your message.

Brochures offer the greatest opportunity to go into *great detail* about your product or service. People expect a lot of information from a brochure, so you should feel encouraged to give it to them. This is not an invitation to be boring, but it is a hint that you can be very informative.

Telephone marketing allows you to be even more intimate than you can be in radio advertising — as you know, the most intimate type of advertising among the mass media. This type of marketing provides you with *great flexibility*. It can be used as an adjunct to direct mail or any other marketing method. It can stand alone. It can take a person from total apathy about your product or service to complete readiness to purchase. And you can take orders if your prospects have credit cards. As a guerrilla, you take credit cards — all of them. Just in case folks are up to their limit on Visa and MasterCard, take American Express, Diners Club, plus any other cards available. This may seem mercenary, but to prospects, it's convenience, and they appreciate you for making it so easy to buy from you.

Tiny signs on bulletin boards serve to *make you part of the community*, increasing the amount of confidence people have in you. They are also extremely inexpensive, and if your product or service can fill unanswered needs, such signs frequently prove to be the most fruitful of marketing methods. Like Yellow Page and classified ads, signs on bulletin boards tend to attract serious browsers. Such is not the case with, say, television advertising.

Advertising specialties such as T-shirts and calendars work like billboards and signs to *remind people of your existence*, but they can't do the entire selling job. They can, however, pave the way to acceptance of your offering when used in conjunction with other marketing vehicles. The same goes for the sponsorship of teams and events.

A shot in the sales curve Many businesses get a terrific shot in the sales curve by marketing at trade shows and exhibits. They find the opportunity there to *make contacts with purchase-minded people* who are thinking about the primary topic of the show or exhibit. The ability to reach people who have this type of mind-set is a great advantage. There are fewer barriers preventing completed sales. Some companies and entrepreneurs obtain all the business they need by this one method of marketing. If you fall into that category, your life will be simpler.

Public relations, encompassing community relations, publicity, and even joining clubs and organizations, is another marketing method that should always be considered. It fits in well with virtually all other methods and often is the key to success. Involvement in community relations — meaning service to your community — helps you make powerful contacts, especially if you work your tail off for the community and not merely to serve your business needs.

Publicity adds a great deal to your *credibility*, and at worst puts your name in the public eye, though guerrillas do not buy into that old lie that "even bad publicity is good publicity as long as they spell your name right." Bad publicity is harmful for your company and your goals. Avoid it at all costs.

Joining clubs and organizations seems also to do what community service does — put you in contact with people who can help you. It seems a bit self-serving to join with that purpose in mind, but many do. And it serves their purposes well. I have a subtle point to make here: *guerrillas are aggressive in their marketing, but they are never crass.*

With all of these marketing methods available, and all are examined later in this book with chapters of their very own, which do you, as a guerrilla, choose? The answer should be obvious: *as many as you can do well.*

Choose the weapons you can use well

Once you have selected the marketing vehicles that can propel you to your goal, be sure you use them in an orderly, logical manner. This can best be accomplished by using a *marketing calendar.*

A marketing calendar will help make all the elements in your program mesh. It enables you to plan your budget and helps you avoid unforeseen expenditures. It prevents you from engaging in hit-or-miss marketing. It protects you from marketing lapses. It precludes surprises. It aids enormously in planning, buying, and staffing. Clients who operate from one say that after three years, a marketing calendar is their most precious business asset. They tell me it's akin to getting into heaven without the inconvenience of dying.

Most marketing calendars address themselves to the weeks of the year, to the marketing vehicles that will be employed during those weeks, to the specific promotions or events in which you will be engaged, to the length of each promotion, and, when applicable, to whether or not coop funds from manufacturers will be available to help pay the bill. In addition, some calendars include the cost of the marketing for each promotion.

Armed with such a calendar, as all guerrillas should be, you can see far into the future. The marketing process will come into clearer focus for you. And you will find it considerably simpler to be committed to your marketing program, to see it as the investment it is, and to recognize the consistency that is built into it.

A moment ago, I told you that a guerrilla makes use of as many marketing vehicles as he or she can implement effectively. A marketing calendar lets you know whether or not you can use these methods properly, because it forces you to come to terms with the costs and realities of utilizing the media you have selected.

Just as you shouldn't run just one week's worth of TV commercials or join a club with no intention of coming to meetings, you should not employ a marketing vehicle unless you are going to use it like a pro. And that means putting time, energy, money, and talent into it. It also means selecting marketing tools that are compatible with your business.

All of the compatible marketing methods that you can possibly employ with skill, and on a regular basis, should be put to work for you. In chapter 4, we saw that the entrepreneur billing himself as Computer Tutor became committed to using fourteen methods of marketing. And that didn't even include decor, attire, and location. Computer Tutor has the option of being a single individual or a multi-employee company, yet its marketing plan calls for the utilization of personal letters, circulars, brochures (we'll get into the difference between these in chapter 12), signs on bulletin boards, classified ads in local newspapers, display ads in local newspapers, magazine advertising, radio advertising, direct-mail advertising, advertising specialties, free seminars, sampling, and publicity in newspapers, on radio, and on television. Sounds like this is going to cost Computer Tutor a huge sum of money. But it won't. You don't have to spend a double bundle to market like a guerrilla. In fact, you may be doing it wrong if you do spend too much money. Mind you, you won't get all that marketing for free. You'll have to pay, or, rather, invest. But it is possible to engage in a large number of marketing methods and save money with each.

Naturally, you start the process of selecting marketing methods by first identifying your target audience. The more exactly you know who your prospects are, the easier it will be **Who are your** to attain accuracy with your marketing plans. Kids don't read **prospects?** newspapers. Teenage girls rarely read business magazines. Adult males hardly ever subscribe to *True Romance*. Those are the realties of the marketplace, and you have to tailor your selection of marketing methods to them.

Select as many methods as you can. Select only the ones you be able to do right. And select the ones that will be read, seen, or heard by your target audience.

Although marketing budgets are as unique as snowflakes, you might get a better bead on your target if you study the budgets of three fictitious companies. One is a small contracting company, Let George Do It, one year old, located in a town of 40,000, but within a marketing area of 150,000. The second is a two-person computer education organization, Computer Tutor, three years old, outside a city of 500,000, in a market area composed of 600,000 people. The third is a retail stereo store, Sounds Great, five years in business, smack-dab within a city of one million people.

Let's suppose that Let George Do It grosses $4000 monthly **How George** in sales. The owner is willing to spend 7.5 percent of his sales **does it** dollars for marketing — a total of $300 per month, or $3600 per year. Computer Tutor takes in $20,000 in monthly sales and invests 10 percent of that in marketing: $2000 monthly, or $24,000 per year. Sounds Great grosses an average of $50,000 in monthly sales. An aggressive 12.5 percent is put back into marketing, permitting $6250 for marketing each month, or $75,000 per year.

Because these companies are not brand-new, they do not have to invest extra heavily in advertising to get public attention. They already have a logotype; they have business cards, stationery, and invoice forms. They even invested from $500 (Let George Do It) to $5000 (Sounds Great) for professional marketing consultation before they got started in marketing. So they each have a marketing plan, a creative strategy, and a media strategy. Their investment with the consultants has also netted them advertising themes, clear identities, and a visual format. Incidentally, the only way Let George Do It obtained such a large amount of consultation for such a low price was by building a sun deck for the marketing consultant as part of a barter arrangement. Computer Tutor and Sounds Great worked a similar agreement, if I know my guerrillas. Look at the following table to see how these guerrillas would apportion their funds.

George has selected many marketing methods, as you can see. His primary marketing medium is newspapers, yet he obtains quite a bit of business through his signs posted on bulletin boards and his free seminars. Neither cost him any extra money, and both are successful, according to George, because of his newspaper advertising. George installed a skylight for a graphic artist, who in return gave him nearly $1000 in artwork: layouts, illustrations, even type and a finished mechanical, all ready for the printer. George set up his trade-show booth at the Home Improvement Show, where he distributed his circulars freely and established a mailing list. George's $300 monthly investment in marketing runs 7.5 percent of his sales this year. He projects that next year that same $300 will represent only 5 percent of his sales. That is

Let George Do It ($300 Monthly)

Marketing Method	Monthly Cost	Comments
Canvassing	$ 0	Main investment is time
Personal Letters	$ 0	Main investment is time
Circulars	$ 20	Cost of $240 yearly, amortized
Brochures	$ 50	Cost of $600 yearly, amortized
Signs on Bulletin Boards	$ 0	Posts his own circulars
Classified Ads	$ 40	Runs ads in two newspapers, once weekly
Yellow Pages	$ 20	Small listing, one directory
Newspaper Display Ads	$100	Runs ads in one newspaper, once weekly
Direct Mail	$ 10	Postage only, since he mails his circulars
Free Seminars	$ 0	Distributes his brochures at these
Trade Show Booth	$ 10	Built booth himself, one-time cost amortized
Public Relations	$ 20	Cost of materials only, handles his own publicity
Production	$ 30	Amortized over one year, traded for a painting by George

how much he expects his sales to increase as a result of his consistent marketing program. (By the way, the prices quoted here were from 1984; they are remarkably similar ten years later. I guess that's the upside of a recession.)

Time to take a look at Computer Tutor's marketing budget:

Computer Tutor ($2000 Monthly)

Marketing Method	Monthly Cost	Comments
Personal Letters	$0	Uses these to gain corporate jobs
Circulars	$30	Cost of $360 yearly, amortized
Brochures	$80	Cost of $960 yearly, amortized
Signs on Bulletin Boards	$30	Monthly fee to have company's flier posted
Classified Ads	$40	Uses one newspaper twice a week
Yellow Pages	$30	Medium listing, one directory
Newspaper Display Ads	$940	One ad weekly, two newspapers
Magazine Ad (One Time)	$100	One full-page ad in Time, amortized over one year
Radio Spots	$400	Spends $400 weekly; on one FM station
Direct Mail	$100	Postage only, since company mails circulars
Advertising Specialties	$30	Cost of computer-oriented calendars
Free Seminars	$0	Distributes brochures at these
Sampling	$0	Offered to corporations
Public Relations	$20	Amortized for one publicity push yearly
Production	$200	Amortized over one year — all production of circulars, brochures, ads, commercials

Computer Tutor gets a lot of referral business. The brochures spur word-of-mouth recommendations. The company's newspaper ads sell people completely, cause people to phone Computer Tutor, where they receive even more of a sales pitch, and motivate people to send for a free brochure. The radio spots direct people to make a phone call. Although Computer Tutor spends nil for telephone marketing per se, it engages in quite a bit of it as a result of responses to the newspaper and radio advertising.

Computer Tutor would love to demonstrate its proficiency on TV, but simply cannot afford it. Each year, a publicity stunt such as free computer lessons for city-hall employees results in free TV coverage. The 10 percent of sales invested in marketing will drop to 7.5 percent next year because of an increase in sales. Actual marketing outlays will remain the same.

The marketing expenditures for Sounds Great are even more ambitious:

An ambitious
guerrilla

Sounds Great ($6250 Monthly)

Marketing Method	Monthly Cost	Comments
Brochures	$200	General brochures with no prices
Point-of-Purchase Signs	$205	One-time cost, amortized over one year
Yellow Pages	$200	One large listing in two directories
Newspaper Display Ads	$2800	Two large ads weekly, two newspapers
Radio Spots	$1400	Consistently run on three FM stations
Television Spots	$500	Two one-week TV splashes, amortized
Direct Mail	$300	Three yearly mailings, amortized
Free Seminars	$0	Held at store, sales made afterward
Searchlight	$20	For one yearly promo- tion, amortized
Production	$625	Amortized over one year

It's interesting to note that Sounds Great, which has the largest of the three budgets examined here, utilizes the fewest marketing methods. However, two methods are used very seriously: radio and newspaper advertising. The radio rates are very low, since spots are purchased through the company's internal ad agency (more about that in chapter 7) at a very favorable one-year contractual rate. The newspaper ads are also available at one-year contract rates, at a substantial discount. Television advertising is used with force, but only two times a year. The cost for the TV time is $3000 for each week.

Like other guerrillas, Sounds Great is now spending a large

amount — 12.5 percent — on marketing. This tactic has eliminated several competitors who spent less boldly. Although they were larger than Sounds Great, their marketing did not reflect this. Sounds Great, like all smart guerrilla marketers, plans to spend the same amount on marketing next year, but figures this will represent only 10 percent of sales. The year after, that same amount should represent 7.5 percent of sales. The plan is to spend no less than 7.5 percent on marketing, because the stereo business is highly competitive.

Desktop publishing might cut some of these costs, especially if they include newsletters and a lot of direct mail. But marketing is not a do-it-yourself process (see chapter 27), and desktop publishing is best left to people who know how to do it with style. If that includes you, perhaps you can save money on production when it comes to brochures, circulars, signs, and the aforementioned direct mail.

When advertisers discuss media, they talk of *reach* and *frequency*. Reach refers to the number of people who will be exposed to the message. *Frequency* refers to the number of times each person will be exposed. Although in some endeavors you should strive for reach, in most, frequency will help you even more. Remember, familiarity breeds confidence, and confidence serves as the springboard to sales. **Reach and frequency**

Before you select any method of reaching the people you wish to reach, think these thoughts: It is not necessary to say everything to everybody, nor is it possible. If you try to say everything to everybody, you'll end up saying everything to nobody or nothing to everybody. Instead, you should strive to say something to somebody. Your marketing message is the "something". Your target audience is the "somebody". Just as you take care in selecting what you will say, you should take equal care in selecting to whom it will be said. Saying the right thing to the wrong people is not acceptable guerrilla marketing. I know that advertising on television does wonders for your ego, but if your prospective customers don't watch much television, it is folly. **Say something to somebody**

I suggest that you set out with the idea that you will employ absolutely every marketing method listed in this chapter, maybe even more. Then start cutting down the list on the basis of who your audience is, whether you can utilize the method properly yourself, and whether you can afford it. With the methods that are left on your list, go to glory. Plunge into each as if it is your one and only. When you combine two marketing methods with two other marketing methods, the total is more than two plus two. A synergistic effect is created whereby two plus two starts to equal five and six and seven. And when you combine five marketing methods with five others, your possibilities for success increase manyfold.

The more methods of marketing you employ, and the greater your skill at employing and selecting them, the larger the size of your bank balance. The idea is to combine the right marketing message with the right marketing media. That's the guerrilla truth.

7
Secrets of Saving Marketing Money

SAVING MONEY IS IMPORTANT to everyone. To consumers. To large companies. And to entrepreneurs — especially to entrepreneurs. Don't forget, entrepreneurs for the most part are suffering from resource poverty. So not a penny can be wasted. And all money should pull more than its own weight. But is this possible? Bright entrepreneurs make it possible. This chapter suggests several ways to stretch your marketing money without decreasing their effectiveness one iota.

Stretching your money

First of all, *don't feel that you must constantly change your marketing campaigns.* This costs unnecessary production money and dilutes the overall effect of your marketing. Stick with one campaign until it loses its pulling power. That's hard to do for most advertisers. In the beginning, most people will like your ad. Then you'll become bored with it. Next, your friends and family will get tired of it. Soon your fellow workers and associates will feel ho-hum about it. And you'll be tempted to change the ad.

Don't do it! Let your accountant tell you when to change ads. That's right, your accountant — the person who takes long looks at your profit picture. You can be sure your accountant won't get tired of an ad that is still pulling in business. The important thing is the public's reaction to an ad. It takes a long, long time for the public to get tired of advertising run on a scale that can be afforded by most small businesspeople. By remembering this, you will stretch your media money and save production costs.

Another way to save impressive sums is to *make use of the* **Bartering** *concept of barter*. Maybe your local radio station or newspaper doesn't want what you are selling. But they do want something. In all likelihood, you'll be able to trade with someone who has that something they want. When that happens, you'll get your media ads for a fraction of their usual cost, since you'll be paying with your own services or goods *at their full retail price*.

Here's an example of bartering: a stereo dealer wanted radio commercials but felt he couldn't afford the cost. He offered to trade recording equipment, but the station just wasn't interested. The station was interested, however, in constructing a new lobby. The stereo dealer found a contractor who wanted new stereo equipment. Result: the contractor received $5000 worth of stereo and television equipment; the radio station got its new lobby; the stereo dealer received $5000 worth of radio time. Yet the dealer's cost was only $2500 in equipment. In fact, his cost was even less than that, because he traded discontinued merchandise that would have had to be discounted.

When I first learned of the world of barter, it was very much like my first time scuba diving. An entire world existed every day within my own world — and I wasn't at all aware of it. To give you an inkling of the magnitude of barter in today's economy, consider that in 1991, 55 percent of media was not purchased, but obtained by barter.

Getting co-op You can also *save money by getting access to cooperative* **funds** *advertising funds*. Many large advertisers pay cash fees to small advertisers who mention the name of the large advertiser or show its logo in their ads. I know a woman who owns a small furniture store. When she mentions the name of a large mattress company in her ads, she receives a small sum of money from that company. Naturally, most of her ads mention the name of some large manufacturer that offers these coop ad funds.

This is worth looking into. It not only helps save money for entrepreneurs, but also lends credibility to their offerings by mentioning the name of a nationally known company. Some companies that offer these co-op funds insist they be the only company mentioned. Others don't care, just as long as you spell their name right. Still others demand that you include their theme line or logo in your ad. A smart entrepreneur, interested in saving lots of marketing money, will include the names of several co-op-oriented companies, thereby saving a large percentage of the ad cost — frequently more than 50 percent. This takes research and prearranging, but if you're interested in saving money, it's worth it.

Talk to your suppliers and simply ask them about their co-op program. If they don't have one, ask them to start one. One of my clients consistently has over half of his marketing costs covered by co-op funds. His business is video rentals; the co-op funds come from movie studios. Very few advertising agencies will help you obtain co-op funds, so it's your job as a guerrilla — and worth every minute you or your designated guerrilla devote to doing it because it significantly reduces your investment in marketing. Who says you can't get something for nothing?

I also suggest you *put forth the effort to set up a P.I. or P.O. arrangement with an advertising medium.* This is a rather common method entrepreneurs employ to save and make money. *P.I.* stands for "per inquiry" and *P.O.* stands for "per order". Here's how it works. You contact, say, a television station to see if it is interested in a P.I. or P.O. arrangement with you. That means that it gives you television time, and in return, you give it a prearranged sum of money per inquiry or per order.

P.I. and P.O.

Suppose you want to sell books for $10 a piece by mail. You strike up a deal with a TV station whereby the station gives you commercial time and you give the station, say, $3 per order. At this point, no money has changed hands. Okay. Now, the TV station provides you with the equipment to produce a commercial heralding your book. Normally, it might charge $100 to run a one-minute commercial, but it gives you the time for free. Then the commercial runs and fifty people order the book. That means the TV station receives $150 (at its $3 per order), which is a good deal for the station. You also come out very well, because you receive fifty orders ($500) and risk no marketing costs. Now, if you can make that same arrangement with other TV stations, you can clearly achieve very attractive profits without risking marketing outlay.

P.I. and P.O. arrangements are available with many magazines, radio stations, and television stations, more every year. I have never heard of this kind of deal being available with newspapers, but I imagine some far-sighted publishers would welcome the idea. All it takes is a letter to the medium of your choice, outlining the arrangement you're proposing. If the medium feels it can make money on your offer, you're in business. In this way, you can engage in quite a bit of high-level marketing with virtually no out-front costs to you, other than minimal production costs. Of course a TV station might put your commercial in a time slot after midnight, a time slot that couldn't be sold to another advertiser. But you can bet that the TV station wants to make money on the arrangement. Therefore, it will go all out. And if it makes money, you make money.

Many an entrepreneur has made many a dollar with this little-known method of saving marketing dollars. A client of mine sold $3000 worth of his newsletters through a P.I. arrangement with a magazine publisher. The publisher gave free ad space (a full-page ad usually sold for $900) in return for a $50 cut of a $100 subscription price. Thirty subscribers signed up. Result: $1 500 for the publisher and $1 500 for my client — the first year. Renewals will increase his profits.

The magazine wanted to repeat the ad — on the same P.O. basis. Naturally, my client declined the offer and paid the magazine full price for the full-page ad.

People enjoy being asked about themselves, enjoy talking about themselves. Take advantage of this human characteristic by *asking questions of your customers*. This can provide you with expensive research data for free. Prepare a questionnaire asking your customers all sorts of questions. Some will toss your questionnaire right in the wastebasket. Others will complete every question and provide you with a wealth of information. This research, if obtained through standard research-company channels, would cost you a fortune. But when obtained the way I've just described, this same information costs very little. More about this in the next chapter.

Free research

If you are a patient sort, you can save money, lots of it, *by taking advantage of "gang runs"*. Large printing companies often run huge amounts of full-color printing on large presses all at once. Sometimes they have an opportunity to run a bit more printing than is scheduled. If you are about to have something printed and wish to save money, let a large printer know that you are interested in being included in a gang run and are patient enough to wait until it happens. Then furnish the printer with the press-ready materials and the paper, and sit back and wait. Eventually, the printer will have that gang run and you will be the happy recipient of a mass of your full-color brochures, obtained at a fraction of the normal price. And all you had to do to take advantage of this money-saving opportunity was to be patient. I've seen clients too impatient to wait for gang runs. They paid five times the price they could have enjoyed if only they hadn't been in a hurry. And the sad thing is that often their rush was unnecessary.

Being in a rush is a deterrent to good marketing and to inexpensive marketing as well. If you wish to gain the maximum effect from your marketing and to save money at the same time, avoid rushes like the plague. With a solid marketing calendar, a program that is planned ahead for a year, it will be quite easy to avoid them.

Slow down

A key thought for you to remember if you wish to save money is that in marketing, there are three variables —

The three variables

quality, economy, and speed. You get to select any two of them. Guerrillas opt for the first two.

You can also save considerable sums of money if you realize that the cost of radio and TV time is nothing if not negotiable. Of course, prime time or drive time is hard to buy, therefore hard to negotiate. But understand that if radio or TV time is unsold, it is wasted forever. Therefore, stations will usually accept prices far below their normal rate-card prices. Deals abound.

To entice new advertisers — that is, entrepreneurs — TV stations will ordinarily offer even more attractive prices. Just knowing this will save you money. Large advertisers do know that rate cards are works of fiction. But small advertisers often believe what they read on rate cards. Don't you believe it.

An offer you Remember that you can save media money by making an offer
can afford you can afford. You'll be surprised at how many radio and TV stations will accept your offer.

While we're on the subject of radio and television and saving money, let me emphasize that a vast amount of research has proven that you can accomplish almost as much with a thirty-second commercial as you can with a sixty-second commercial. So save money by cutting the verbiage and saying your message in half a minute. Think hard and you can even do it in less time than that. In 1991, over 80 percent of national TV commercials were less than thirty seconds long. Some are so short, they're termed "electronic billboards" instead of TV commercials.

You can save money by applying this same truism of brevity to your print efforts. Unless it is necessary for you to look important by running large, expensive newspaper or magazine ads, you can attract business just as well by running
Ad size small, inexpensive, but consistently run newspaper or magazine ads. You may not look as important as the purchasers of full-page ads, but you'll end up making more money. Don't forget: as I emphasized in chapter 3, consistency is the one of the most important factors in marketing. And you can gain that

consistency with small ads as well as large ones. Largeness does not produce the consumer confidence that comes with consistency — a truth that can save you impressive sums.

It is axiomatic that shoddy production gives you a shoddy image. Therefore, when running print ads, especially newspaper ads, it is usually silly to save money on production by **A silly saving** having the newspaper or other medium design your ads. Instead, you should have a professional do that work.

There are basically two types of professionals: high cost and low cost. To save the most money and gain the best identity, hire a high-cost to lay out your first ad and create a visual format for you. Then hire a low-cost to do all of your follow-up ads, telling him or her to follow the format created in the original ad. This will not infuriate the inexpensive designer, who will probably be thrilled with the business. And it will not anger the expensive designer, who got a fair sum for the talent expended. The result will be that you will always have sharp-looking ads, even though you paid through the nose only one time. You get the best of two worlds: a classy look and format throughout the life of your marketing campaign, and a low price for the production of all the ads except the first. You shouldn't have to spend high production fees more than one time, but believe me, it is well worth it that one time. Ask any entrepreneur who has employed this tactic.

While we're on the subject of the cost of advertising time and space, we should take a look at one of the most efficient money-saving strategies in all of marketing — establishing a house advertising agency for yourself. Normal advertising agencies earn their money by receiving a 15 percent discount from publications and broadcast stations where they place advertising. If an ad or commercial costs an advertiser $1000, that same ad space or commercial time costs an advertising agency only $850. This is known as an agency discount, and advertising agencies are entitled to every cent of it. The advertiser would have to spend $1000 anyhow. So by utilizing an ad agency, the advertiser receives professional help at no extra cost, since the advertisement will cost $1000 with or without an agency. And the ad agency picks up $150 for its efforts.

But what if you're too small to require an advertising agency? What if you just plain don't want an advertising **You are the** agency? You should establish your own in-house ad agency. **advertising** To do this, you usually need do no more than tell the advertis- **agency** ing medium that you are an in-house or internal agency for your business. In some cases, the medium may require that you have a bank account in your agency's name (ten dollars in an account will do nicely). And you may need agency stationery. Again, this is no problem. If your business is called Atlantic Manufacturing, just call your agency Atlantic Advertising on inexpensive stationery you have ordered in the minimum amount.

With this bank account and stationery, you are now ready to be your own in-house advertising agency. And you can save 15 percent on almost all the advertising you place for yourself you can save on virtually everything but newspaper advertising, where you pay only the retail rate, which is low to begin with. It's so easy to set up an internal agency that I'm surprised more entrepreneurs don't do it. But you can.

TV production If you ever do use local television, start out with tight, well- **on a shoe-** planned scripts. Have a rehearsal session or two prior to the **string** shooting date, then try to shoot three or four commercials in one session. Although the average thirty-second TV commercial costs around $175,000 to produce (thanks to the soft drinks, beers, and fast-food chains), you can get that cost down to $1000 if you shoot several spots at once, work with thought-out scripts, and avoid paying high talent fees to actors and actresses. Once again, some difference! The difference is due to a variety of things. For one thing, full-scale TV productions usually involve large crews for lighting, props, make-up, hairstyling, and moving the camera around. That ordinarily involves union and inflated costs. Guerillas work with skeleton crews and do not work with unions unless absolutely necessary. They're not anti-union; they're pro-efficiency.

One of the highest costs in TV production, especially with videotape, is editing. With very well planned scripts, you will need very little editing.

Some advertisers feel that they must have a celebrity to hawk their wares. This adds from $5000 to $500,000 to the tab. Guerrillas rely on the power of an idea and save the cash.

Expensive production devices such as complex scenery, special effects, and ornate sets make commercials cost more than they should. Because many people are involved in the actual shooting, each scene may be shot four or five different ways, to stroke four or five different egos. Guerrillas shoot each scene one way and get their ego kicks by making sizable bank deposits.

In addition, TV professionals tend to shoot commercials to suit their own tastes and needs. They can spot flaws that most viewers would never see. So they reshoot and reshoot and reshoot. Guerrillas accept minor flaws and get on with the commercial.

All this adds up to a whale of a difference in money — but not in quality. I have a reel of commercials, each costing under $500. TV pros who have seen them have estimated that the cost of each spot was $10,000 or more. In my opinion, unnecessary TV production costs are murdering many large-company production budgets. The amazing thing is that they are easy to avoid. So avoid them.

In the final analysis, there are two kinds of advertising: **Two kinds of** expensive and inexpensive. The expensive kind of advertising is **advertising** the kind that doesn't work. The inexpensive kind of advertising is the kind that does work — regardless of cost. This chapter has suggested additional ways to save money with your marketing. But you'll save the most if you always make sure to run inexpensive advertising — the kind that gives you the results you want. And that has more to do with quality than cost.

8

Secrets of Obtaining Free Research

IT'S NOT DIFFICULT to turn up a marketing pro who will tell you that the three most important things to do to market anything successfully are to test, test, and test. That is pretty good advice. But it is unrealistic for those with resource poverty, who cannot shell out big bucks for sophisticated research.

The big secret is that you need not shell out any money to learn about your market. If you know what to look for and where to find it, you can obtain crucial information for nary a cent. Let's examine some of the things you might want to find out.

Ten crucial questions

1. What should you market - your goods, your services, or both?
2. Should your marketing feature some sort of price advantage?
3. Should you emphasize yourself, your quality offerings, your selection, your service, or merely the existence of your business?
4. Should you take on your competition or ignore all competitors?
5. Exactly who are your competitors?
6. Who are your best prospects?
7. What income groups do they represent?
8. What motivates them to buy?

9. Where do they live?
10. What do they read or watch or listen to in the way of media?

The right answers to these questions can prove invaluable to a marketing effort. The wrong answers, or no answers, can prove disastrous. Do what you must to get the right answers.

In most cases, great advertising is preceded by great research. There are three prime ways for you to engage in research that will provide you with the information that can make the difference between success and failure, yet not cost you much, if anything. The first is to go to your local library. The reference librarian will be able to steer you to just the books and other publications that contain a raft of money-making information for you. Some of these publications have market studies of your area, conducted by companies that paid impressive sums for the data. Others contain studies of products or services such as yours, and indicate the level of their acceptance by the public. Still others include census reports, research reports, industry studies, and more. Whenever I write a book, I find myself in libraries ferreting out information. And I am always dazzled by the expertise of the reference librarians, who not only know where to find information but also seem to delight in the finding. And all the information to which they lead you is free for the asking. The more customer information you have, the better equipped you will be to serve those customers. This is where inquisitiveness pays off big.

Enlist your library as an ally

A second, and commonly overlooked, way to obtain information is to ask your own customers. If you have a new business, I strongly suggest that you prepare a lengthy questionnaire for them. On it, ask them everything under the sun.

Your customers have the answers

Large corporations that enclose brief questionnaires with their manufactured items such as TV sets, electric razors, or hair dryers report that fewer than half the questionnaires are returned. These questionnaires consist of five or six questions, even fewer. On the other hand, I had a client who gave each of his customers a fifteen-question questionnaire. Seventy-eight percent of the forms distributed were completed and returned. It seems that many people enjoy providing personal information, just as long as they can remain anonymous.

Suppose you wanted to establish a company that provided auto mechanical services at people's homes rather than in a garage. You might prepare and hand out a questionnaire that asks the following of your prospects - namely, motorists:

A guerrilla *We are establishing an automotive service that makes "house*
questionnaire *calls". To help us serve you most effectively, please provide the following information:*

What type of car do you drive? ————————————

What year is it? ——————— What model? ————

How long have you owned it? ——————————

Who usually performs mechanical services for your car? ——
——————————————————————————

Would you want these services to be performed where you live? ———————————————————————

List the three main reasons you would want "house calls" made to service your car: ———————————————
——————————————————————————
——————————————————————————
——————————————————————————

Would you pay more to have "house calls" for your car? ——————————————————————————

What is your sex? ————— Your age? —————

Your household income? ———————————————

What newspapers do you read? ————————————

What radio stations do you listen to? ———————

What TV shows do you watch? ——————————

Which magazines do you read? ——————————

What type of work do you do? ——————————

Would you purchase products as well as service from a traveling automotive service? ——————————————

Who do you consider to be our competition? ————

Where would you expect us to advertise? _____
Do you have any other comments? _____

In this game of twenty questions, you always emerge the winner. By studying the *questions only*, you can easily see how much you can learn. Just think of how informed you'd be by studying the answers! This kind of questionnaire should be distributed for a number of months, and the answers should be studied each month so trends can be spotted after the business has been established. Notice that the questionnaire did not ask the name or address of the customer, so anonymity was preserved, enabling you to ask many personal questions.

Analysis of the completed questionnaires will show you the kind of people your prospects are, how to reach them through the media, how to appeal to them, and what kind of cars they drive.

What you'll learn

You can analyze the questionnaires by grouping the responses to each question. Perhaps you'll learn that the majority of people interested in patronizing your business drive foreign cars. That would alert you to the possibility of doing a mailing to foreign-car owners. Their names are available from mailing-list brokers.

It might be that your customers are owners of older cars. Again, you can reach these people with a targeted mailing. Also, the questionnaire will help you focus your advertising on the right people.

From the questionnaire, you can learn who your competition is by learning who usually performs mechanical services for your prospects. You can determine what it is you offer that is most enticing to your customers - again helping you choose the proper emphasis for your advertising. You'll discover the sex and age of your customers, and you'll learn exactly how and where to communicate with them once you ascertain the newspapers, radio stations, TV shows, and magazines that interest them. If your customers are primarily white-collar workers, this questionnaire will inform you of that fact, and you'll be able to tailor your media selection to that reality. You can find out which marketing vehicles will work most effectively for you. And you can obtain a report on your own service.

It is very simple to make this analysis, very useful in helping you determine your marketing thrust, yet extremely inexpensive for you. This information can be used to update or revise your marketing plan. And just think, the only cost was for duplicating the questionnaire - well under $100. This is free research at its best, and frankly, you're nuts if you don't take advantage of it ... then repeat it every few years to keep you abreast of your market.

The third way to take advantage of inexpensive research is to prepare a questionnaire similar to the preceding one, and hand it to people using the kind of services you provide. That way, you'll be researching serious, rather than potential, prospects. You'll receive fewer returns than the 78 percent my client enjoyed, but you'll learn something - which is a lot more valuable than you knowing nothing. Naturally, you won't hand your questionnaire to motorists if you are selling computer education. If that's your business, you'll want your questionnaires in the hands of people entering or departing computer stores. If you are a traveling hair-stylist who makes house calls, hand your questionnaires to people leaving beauty salons or barbershops. Whatever your business, you can find prospective customers somewhere: with their kids at the kiddie playground, at the beach, in the park; downtown; coming out of the hardware store; leaving the park. Chances are, you've already got a line on where they are. All you've got to do is go there and hand them your long list of questions.

How to get answers to your questions   How do you ensure that the prospective customers will return your questionnaires? Well, you can furnish them with stamped envelopes. You can tempt them with offers of free (but inexpensive) gifts. You can offer discounts to them if they complete and return your questionnaire. And you can use pure honesty by telling them, atop the questionnaire, exactly why you are asking so many questions. Just be sure to include your address, so that the questionnaires will be mailed (or brought) to the right place.

It helps if you have an introductory paragraph atop your questionnaire. It should say something like, "We're trying to learn as much as possible from motorists in the community, so that we can offer them the best possible service. We apologize for asking you so many questions in this questionnaire, but we're doing it so that you can benefit in the long run. We promise that your answers will remain anonymous (notice we are not asking for your name). And we also promise that we'll use the information to help you enjoy better automotive service." Such an honest introduction serves to disarm people who resent being asked so many questions; and it does explain exactly why you are doing it. Once again, you end up with valuable information. Once again, it costs you hardly anything. A true guerrilla will try *all three methods* of obtaining such free research. Then he or she will put the information to work to create a first-rate marketing plan, using reliable data that can aid in the selection of marketing methods, the evaluation of the competition, and the framing of the creative message.

These are not the only methods of conducting inexpensive research, simply the most common and effective. Also worth checking for important data are your local chamber of commerce, any industry organizations to which you belong, and any industry publications of which you are aware. You might also make a field trip or two to poke around and talk to people in your business but not your geographic area. Guerrillas abet their primary research with these additional sources of knowledge. They know, and so do you, that knowledge is the currency of the nineties.

More sources of inexpensive insight

When questioning your target audience, it might help to list some of the basic needs people have, and ask them to make check marks by those that pushed their particular buttons.

Most people will react to one or more of the following basic
needs (known as "appeals" in advertising lingo):

Achievement	Style
Pride of ownership	Social approval (status)
Convenience	Health and well-being
Comfort	Profit
Love	Savings or economy
Friendship	Conformity (peer pressure)
Security	Ambition
Self-improvement	Power

If you have had the feeling that people patronize you because
you offer convenience and economy, you may be surprised to
learn, via your questionnaires, that they really give you their
business because your work adds to their sense of security.

You can engage in more free research by conscientiously
studying the other advertising that is going on in your community - not only that of your competitors but that of everyone
else as well. Have frank conversations with your customers.
Talk with your competitors. If they're from a noncompeting
area, tell them about a marketing tactic that worked for you,
then ask about any that worked for them; most likely, they'll
talk their heads off because you're obviously a person who
understands them because you're in the same business. Guerrillas call this "sharing". The way it works is, the more you
give, the more you get.

Talk with other businesspeople in your community. You'll
find that these sources will provide you with useful information and won't charge you one cent for it. Research can help
you save a lot of money and earn a lot of money. Free research
can help you save and earn even more.

Section II
Mini-Media Marketing

IT IS IN MINI-MEDIA MARKETING that practitioners of guerrilla marketing have their chance to shine. For standard marketers rarely, if ever, resort to such teeny-tiny marketing methods as canvassing, writing personal letters, marketing by telephone, distributing circulars, posting signs on bulletin boards, running classified ads, using signs other than billboards, and putting the Yellow Pages to work. Fortunately, because the titans do not practice mini-media marketing, you'll come across very little competition in these arenas — except from fellow guerrillas. Be warned, there are more and more of them *daily*, and your close attention to the media will alert you to their presence — as well as educate you by their examples. Be prepared to respond. Giant companies aren't as quick on their feet as you, so you can respond faster.

Your mini-media marketing must still adhere to your marketing plan. It must still be accomplished with talent and style. It must still follow many of the fundamentals. But it gets to break many of the rules, too. For instance, you can make letters highly personalized. You can post one-of-a-kind signs. You can take advantage of the smallness of your business when making telephone calls. Make them personal, friendly, informal, yet professional.

I urge you to utilize as many media as you can possibly use correctly. And I especially urge you to use the mini-media to the max. Big companies don't. This will rarely put a strain on your budget. Production costs will be small. You'll have an opportunity to star in the mini-media more than in the maxi-media, where you can be outspent even if you're not being out-thought.

In the mini-media, your size will be an advantage, not a disadvantage. So I hope you'll put most or even all of the following marketing methods to work while you're still small. If you do, you'll know which to utilize when you're large.

Your small size enables you to offer advantages in the area of customer service. Your geographic proximity — including the fact that you're a true-blue local — if your market is your own locality, is a big weapon, possessed by few of the behemoths. You know folks on a first-name basis. You see them regularly. Chalk up one major advantage for your side.

You can provide extremely individualized service, tailored to the realities of your customers' budgets. Few big companies can match you in that area. By necessity, they're forced to run customer service by company policy, and that deprives them of flexibility.

As a guerrilla, you're reeking with flexibility — and it can be translated into service that customers crave. Another point for your team. The mini-media includes maxi-service. Used properly, they can make you a juggernaut. The nineties have brought a multitude of changes in the mini-media, all of which work to the advantage of the entrepreneur.

- Faxes allow you to render speedier service (but don't use faxes for marketing; people resent "junk faxes").
- Computer bulletin boards enable you to zero in on specific target audiences, then communicate by modem.
- Freephone numbers are less expensive than ever, so you can increase your response rates.

- Catalogues, newsletters, and brochures are simpler than ever to produce, thanks to desktop publishing.
- More newspapers than ever now offer low-cost zone editions that reach prospects in targeted neighborhoods.
- Computer technology allows entrepreneurs to tap into computer networks, communicate with many people at once, and keep more accurate databases.
- TV time, thanks to the growth of cable companies, has dropped in price to a point that almost any small business can (and should) consider it.
- Satellite TV transmission allows advertisers to home in on very, very specialized markets.
- Home shopping networks enable viewers to buy instantly, providing advertisers with instant gratification.
- Car phones and airphones offer more sophisticated communication options, saving time and opening the door to more personalized service.
- VCR penetration is nearing 80 percent, adding to the attractiveness of a video brochure.
- New breakthroughs in psychology are giving us a clearer view of human behavior, so that we can create more effective marketing.
- New media are springing up all over the place: in a sky full of advertising blimps, on airport luggage carousels, on jetplane movie screens, at grocery check-out counters, in postcard decks, integrated within major movies and TV shows.
- People are being marketed to while on telephone hold, and they actually appreciate the data while they wait.
- Special-effects TV technology allows small advertisers to get a big-advertiser look without spending big bucks.

I'm just scratching the surface of the new changes in mini-media that have taken place since the original edition of this book. Many of the maxi-media, once the domain of the big spenders, are now your domain, too. As a guerrilla, your eyes must be open to the marketing options of the nineties, and far more of them than ever before. New ones enter the marketing arena on a daily basis. These lovely marketing weapons and technologies are by-products of the age of the entrepreneur. Each one represents an opportunity for you.

Whether or not you capitalize on the opportunity is up to you; whether or not you learn of the opportunities is up to me. And learn you will as soon as you turn the page.

9

Canvassing: Marketing on an Eye-to-Eye Basis

Canvassing can be the most inexpensive marketing method of all. In fact, it can be free, except for the time you devote to it. And if you're just starting out, time is something you have a great deal of in your inventory. After all, canvassing is merely asking prospective customers for business. During a canvass, which the dictionary defines as "a soliciting of sales", you should engage in three separate steps.

The first step, called the *contact*, is when you first meet your prospect. That first impression counts like crazy. So make your contact friendly, upbeat, customer-oriented, honest, and warm. *Try to establish a relationship.* Smile, look directly into the person's eye, and if at all possible, *use the person's name.* You need not talk about business if you don't want to. And you really shouldn't. Some companies require that their salespeople ask at least three nonbusiness questions before actually getting down to business. You can talk about personal matters, about the weather, about a current event, about sports, or hopefully, about your prospective customer. That's probably his or her favorite subject.

First impressions count

The second step of a canvass is called the *presentation*. It usually takes longer than the other steps, yet it need take no longer than one minute. During the presentation, you outline the features of your offering and the benefits to be gained from buying from you. Some pro canvassers say, "The more you tell, the more you sell." I'm not sure about that. Depends upon what you are selling. If it is a home security system, your presentation might take fifteen minutes. If it is an offer to wash your prospect's car, the presentation might take one minute or less. Presentations to sell waterbeds take about forty-five minutes; presentations to sell home satellite systems take a day and a half, presentations to sell million-dollar computer switchers take up to a year and a half. The price of your product or service will dictate the time you have to spend on presenting it.

The most   The third step of a canvass is the most important part. It's
important step called the *close*, and it is that magical moment when you complete the sale. That happens when your prospect says "Yes" or signs on the dotted line or reaches for his or her wallet or merely nods affirmatively. If you are a poor closer, it doesn't really matter how good you are at the contact and the presentation. You've got to be a good closer to make canvassing work at all.

Before there were any other methods of marketing, canvassing existed. In fact, the very first sale in history probably occurred when one caveman asked another, "Want to trade me an animal skin for this fruit I picked?" No advertising was necessary. No marketing plan, either. Life has become far better since then. But far more complicated, too.

If you think that canvassing is like door-to-door selling, you're right only if you want to do it that way. You can canvass by going from door to door. You can do it in residential neighborhoods, you can do it in commercial neighborhoods, and you can do it at trade shows. Or, you can presell your canvass by first calling or writing to the people you intend to canvass. You have a choice of telling them you'll be coming around so that they'll expect you sometime, or actually setting up an appointment. When that happens, it's more like making a sales presentation than canvassing. For most guerrillas, canvassing is something done with little or no advance warning. Sure, it helps if you advertise so that the prospective customers have heard of you when you come calling. But you don't have to advertise. If you make a good contact, a crisp presentation, and a dynamite close, and if you are offering good value, canvassing may be the only marketing tool you ever need.

I mentioned that canvassing can be free, and I wasn't kidding. But canvassing improves when you do invest a bit of money in it. For one thing, you want to look good so as to inspire confidence. That means you should look the part. If you are canvassing store owners with the idea of getting them to sign up for your window-washing business, you need not wear a coat and tie. But it helps if you're wearing spotless work clothes, and even if you have a clean rag dangling from your rear pocket.

Canvassing with intelligence

The investment increases a bit more if you offer a business card to the person you are canvassing. The card establishes that you are for real and enables a person to give you business later, if not now. It also helps your referral business — if you do a good job. Your investment will be even greater if you decide to canvass using a brochure or circular. If you do produce such materials, either use them as sales aids while you are making your presentation or give them away after you have closed the sale. Don't expect a person to read your sales literature and listen to your sales talk at the same time. Generally I frown on giving out a circular during this contact, since it gives your prospect an opportunity to avoid buying by telling you he or she will "study" your circular, then get back to you. If they don't buy now, figure that they won't buy later. Most of the time, they won't. Another way to see it is that *someone will buy*. Either you'll buy their story about why they can't buy now, or they'll buy what you're selling. Some entrepreneurs give free demonstrations or samples while they canvass. Although this adds to your investment, it is often a smart addition.

Someone will buy

Once you learn the best way to accomplish your canvassing, you will be confronted with several choices. First, will you want to continue using this method of marketing? Second, are you doing it as well as it can be done? Third, should you be delegating the canvassing job to someone else or to several other people? To an organization of sales reps, called distributors? The advantages of canvassing are readily apparent. It doesn't cost much, if anything. It is a great way to get a brand-new business going. It strengthens your contacts, because looking a person directly in the eye is more personal by a long shot than writing a letter, making a phone call, or attracting attention with an ad. Canvassing is also a good way to learn the objections, if any, to your offering. It provides instant results and can be commenced instantly as well. And it lets you be sure that your message is being heard. Like television advertising, it enables you to demonstrate. Like radio advertising, it enables you to be intimate. Like newspaper advertising, it allows you to be newsy. Like magazine advertising, it allows you to involve your prospect. And like direct response marketing, it is geared to get you a direct response of the positive kind.

The success of canvassing depends upon you and you alone. You can't blame the media if you mess up. And if you succeed, you deserve to get all of the credit. Furthermore, canvassing is very accountable, meaning that you know darned well whether it's working or not. Results aren't always so accountable once you get into the more sophisticated media.

Let's say you have a brand-spanking-new home security company. You sell and install burglar and smoke alarms. You've named your company Always Alert, and you've printed up business cards, nothing else. Your marketing plan calls for you to spend the first two months canvassing for business. The first month, you'll canvass commercial establishments. The second month, you'll canvass homes. Then you'll decide whether to concentrate on businesses or homes, and you'll decide whether or not to continue canvassing for new business. Let's assume you're so short of cash that you

A canvassing campaign

cannot afford to run even one ad. I hope that is never the case, but right now, let's stack the deck against you.

Okay, you're ready to make your detailed canvassing plans. What to wear? As a general rule, dress exactly as your prospects dress, whether it be Levi's or a three-piece suit. If you're calling upon businesses, I'd suggest a dark business suit, whether you are male or female. The dark colors — navy blue, black, deep gray, or charcoal — lend authority to what you say. The suit itself implies professionalism. I'd stay away from any accessories that detract from the professional look you wish to convey. I'd also be sure that my hair was neat and my hands were clean, and that I had a handsome case to carry either samples or sales literature provided by the manufacturer. I'd feel so good that a smile would come easily.

Once you're properly attired, the next step is to decide what you'll say during the contact, that first precious moment. It is probably best to make a comment first about the store you are visiting: "I like your window display. It seems just right for this location. My name is Tim Winston. My company is Always Alert. We offer security systems to businesses such as yours. What type of security system do you have now?"

During this contact, you have complimented the prospect on his or her window display, thereby showing that you noticed it in the first place. I hope you were smiling and making eye contact as you announced your name and the name of your company. Finally, you qualified your prospect with one single question. By "qualified," I mean you determined your prospect's need for your product. If the prospect has a security system and tells you that it consists of both a burglar alarm and a smoke alarm, you can save time by making no presentation whatsoever, and go ahead on your way after first thanking the person for the information imparted. You might inquire if the person is happy with the current security system, and be sure to leave your card behind just in case he or she wishes to make a change later. But you'd be best off keeping the time spent with nonprospects down to a minimum. Once your prospect indicates that he or she already has what you're selling, you should save time for both of you.

At the next store, following a similar contact, the prospect may tell you that they have no security system. That's your cue to make your presentation. While giving it, remember that **Features and** *whenever you mention a feature, follow it with a benefit.* For **benefits** instance, "Always Alert features security systems that run on solar power. So they never need batteries. They use up no expensive electrical power. And they are maintenance free." The feature is the solar power. The benefits are freedom from purchasing batteries, from spending money for electrical power, and from taking up time maintaining the devices.

Continue your presentation, making it as long as it must be, yet as short as it can be. After all, both you and your prospect have other things to do. While presenting, be constantly on the lookout for closing signs. It may be that you have already made the sale and that the prospect wants to buy. But if you don't look for signs that you've said enough, you might end up losing the sale. As the topnotch salespeople say, *A-B-C — Always be closing.*

Ask and ye After you have made your presentation, try to close with a **shall close** question that requires more than a yes or no answer. Such a question might be, "Well, that about does it. Will it be better for me to install your alarm system Wednesday or Thursday?" Another closing question might be, "Do you intend to pay for your alarm system at the time of installation, or should I bill you?"

Many excellent books on salesmanship carefully dissect the sale, examining the contact, the presentation, and the close. For reasons of enlarging your bank account rather than catering to my ego, I recommend *Guerrilla Selling* by Bill Gallagher, Orvel Ray Wilson, and myself (Houghton Mifflin Company, 1992). If you're going to be a guerrilla, go all out; don't merely play at part of it.

Canvassing requires salesmanship. It requires a contact, a presentation, and a close. Furthermore, it requires just as much quality in that salesmanship as is needed for the sale of an expensive car or an item of furniture. And it requires far greater salesmanship in terms of quantity. A great car sales-man may make ten contacts, presentations, and closes in one good day. You may make ten in one good hour. To succeed at canvassing, you must have enthusiasm about your product, an honest enjoyment of people, and a load of determination.

But if you're to succeed as an entrepreneur, if you're to build your small business into a large one, you'll have to move beyond canvassing, even though it may continue to be part of your marketing mix. The disadvantages of canvassing are that it takes too much of your time, that you can't reach enough prospects even in one high-energy day, and that it is limited in scope geographically. Some of those disadvantages disappear when you start delegating the canvassing to others. But if you succeed at canvassing, you'll soon become itchy to reach more people.

Before we go into ways you can do that, let's try to make you the best canvasser possible. To do that, let's examine the contact, the presentation, and the close in a bit more detail.

First, realize that *somebody* is going to close a sale with your customer. It might be a competitor of yours. It might be a friend of the customer. But it *will be somebody*. That somebody can be someone else or you. While your customer is with you, you have a lot of control over who will close — the most control you will ever have. After you've left your customer, you have very little control, if any. *So while your customer is with you is the best time to close.* And remember: closing is really the name of the canvassing game. So even though you will need to make a contact and a presentation, you should be thinking "close close close" all along. By doing that, you'll be gradually closing all the time you're with your customer. And that's good. Still, in spite of the importance of closing, it is crucial that while you are making your contact, you think of *that* as the most important part. If you mess up on it, you may not have a chance to move on to the close. Do the

When you have a lot of control

contact well, and you may breeze right through to the actual close. That's how important the initial contact is.

If your contact comes from a "cold" call, and your prospect is a complete stranger, take steps to make that prospect a new acquaintance. If your contact comes from a lead — a recommendation from a friend, an answer to an ad you ran, or some other reason to make you believe the prospect can be converted into a customer — refer to that relationship, that bond between you. It will help break the barriers that much faster. You are no longer a complete stranger. Now you are at the very least, an acquaintance of an acquaintance. Here are a few tactics canvassing pros use:

Guerrilla tips about the contact

- Greet your prospect warmly and sincerely, using eye contact.
- Allow your prospect some time to get acclimated to being with you, some time to talk. Don't come on too strong. But don't waste your prospect's time, either.
- Engage in casual conversation at first — especially about anything pertinent to your prospect. Make it friendly and not one-sided. Be a good listener. But let the prospect know that your time is precious. You are there to sell, not to talk.
- Ask relevant questions. Listen carefully to the answers.
- Qualify the prospect. Determine whether or not this is the specific person to whom you should be talking, the person with the authority to give you the go-ahead, to buy. Try to learn, during the contact, what to emphasize in your presentation.
- Try to learn of your prospect's attitude toward your type of offering. Tune in on his or her fears, expectations, feelings — so that you can tailor your presentation to them.
- Learn something about the person to whom your contact's directed, so that he or she will feel like a person rather than a prospect. Make your prospect like you, for

people enjoy doing business with people they like. But don't be phony. Don't be syrupy. The best possible thing you can do is to make your prospect *feel unique* — proving that you recognized his or her individuality and needs.

- Be brief, friendly, outgoing, and truly inquisitive. But be yourself.

- If you're in a retail environment, one of the best questions to initiate healthy contact is "Mind if I ask what brings you into our store today?"

- Even though you are selling, don't think of yourself as a salesperson but as a partner to your prospect. This healthy mind-set improves both your perspective and your chances of closing.

Important elements of your contact are your smile, your attire, your posture, and your willingness to listen and look directly into the prospect's eyes. Your nonverbal communication is as important as your verbal communication. The impression you make will come as much from what you don't say as from what you do say.

It is often during the contact that the sale is cinched. This happens if your contact has truly opened up communications and you have convinced your prospect that you are honestly interested in helping him or her. During a successful contact, each party will have made a friend — and thereby paved the way to a sale, even continuing sales. The contact may be the shortest of the three phases of a canvass. But it does establish the basis for the presentation and the close.

When making your presentation, keep in mind that you are not talking by accident. You are there because of intent on your part. If your prospect is still with you and has not ended the canvass, there is intent on his or her part, too. And the intent to buy. Either you will buy a story about why a sale cannot be made, or your prospect will buy what you're selling. It truly is up to you. And don't forget: people do enjoy being sold to.

They do not like being pressured. They do like being persuaded by honest enthusiasm to buy. Here are some tips to make your presentations flow smoothly:

Guerrilla tips about the presentation

- List all the benefits of doing business with you, one by one. The more benefits a prospect knows about, the more likely a prospect will buy. When compiling your list of benefits, invite your employees and at least one customer. Customers are tuned in to benefits you offer that you may take for granted.

- Emphasize the *unique* advantages of buying from you. You should be able to rattle these off with the same aplomb you can state your own name and address. It is upon these competitive advantages that you should be basing your marketing.

- If your prospect has no experience with what you are selling, stress the advantages of your *type* of offering, then of your specific offering. If you're selling security devices, talk of the value of owning them, then of the value of owning *yours*.

- Tailor your presentation to information learned during your contact — and before. I hope you learned a lot before making any contact. Homework pays off bigtime to guerrillas.

- People do not like to be pioneers, so mention the acceptance of your products or services by others — especially people in their community. If you can mention names and be specific, by all means do so. The more specific you are, the more closes you'll make. But don't be tedious. You can't bore a prospect into buying.

- When you know enough about your prospect, you can present your product or service from his or her point of view. This ability will increase your number of closes dramatically. Emphasize what all of your product or service benefits can do for your prospect, not what they can do for the general population.

- Keep an eagle eye on your prospect's eyes, teeth and hands. If the prospect is looking around, rather than at you, you've got to say something to regain attention. If your prospect is not smiling, you are being too serious. Say something to earn a smile. Best of all, smile yourself. That will get your prospect to smile. If your prospect is wringing his or her hands, your prospect is bored. Say something to ease the boredom and spark more interest.
- A sales point made to the eye is 68 percent more effective than one made to the ear. So show as much as you can: photos, drawings, a circular, a product, *anything*. Just be sure it relates to your presentation.
- Sell the benefit along with the feature. If the feature is solar power, for instance, the benefit is economy. If the feature is new computer software, the benefit is probably profitability. Mention your past successes so the prospect will feel that the key to success is in your hands and there is little chance of a rip-off.
- Be proud of your prices, proud of your benefits, proud of your offering. Convey your pride with facial expression, tone of voice, selection of words. Feel the pride and let it come shining through. There are 250,000 commonly used words in the English language; there are 600,000 nonverbal methods of communications: stance, facial expression, hand gestures, eyebrow position, and 599,996 others. Learn them and utilize them. They're completely free, another example of pure guerrilla marketing. No cost. High payoff.
- Throughout your presentation, remain convinced that your prospect will buy from you. This optimism will be sensed by the prospect and can positively affect the close.

Despite the importance I have attached to the contact and the presentation, I still reiterate that all the marbles are in the close. Effective salespeople and canvassers are effective closers. Aim to be a dynamite closer and your income will reflect this. To close effectively, try to close immediately, rather than in a week or so. Also, remember these thoughts:

Guerrilla tips about the close

- Always assume that your prospective customer is going to do what you want, so you can close with a leading question such as, "Will it be better for you to take delivery this week or next week?" "Do you want it in grey or brown?"
- Summarize your main points and confidently end with a closing line such as, "Everything seems to be in order. Why don't I just write up your order now?"
- Ask the customer to make some kind of decision, then close on it. Typical points that must be agreed upon are delivery date, size of order, method of payment. A good closing would be: "I can perform this service for you tomorrow, the eighth, or the fifteenth. The eighth would be best for me. Which would be best for you?"
- Begin to attempt the close as soon as possible by easing your prospect into it. If that doesn't work, try again, then again. Continue trying. If you don't, your prospect will spend his or her hard-earned money elsewhere — and with someone else. Count on that. Remember: people *like* to be sold to and *need* to have the deal closed. They won't make the close themselves. So you are performing a service when you sell and close.
- Always be on the alert for signs that the time is right to close. The prospect will hardly ever tell you when the time has come. You must look for hints in the prospect's words and actions. A mere shifting of weight from one foot to another may be a signal to close.
- Try to give your prospect a good reason to close *immediately*. It may be that you won't be back in the neighborhood for a long time, or that the prospect will wish to use your product or service as soon as possible, or that prices are expected to rise, or that you have the time and

the inventory now but might not have them later.

- Let your prospect know of the success of your product or service with people *like* the prospect, with people *recently*, with people in the community — *with people with whom the prospect can easily relate.*
- Be specific with names, dates, costs, times and benefits. Evasiveness in any area works against you.
- If the prospect likes what you say, but won't close now, ask "Why wait?" The prospect may then voice an objection. And you may close by saying, "That's great, and I understand." Then you can solve the objection and close on it. In fact, one of the easiest ways to close is to search for an objection, then solve the problem and close on it.
- If you have not yet completed your presentation but feel the time may be right to close, attempt to close on the most important sales point you have yet to state.
- Always remember that a person knows what you want him or her to do, that there is a reason for your meeting, that your offering does have merit, and that at that moment, your prospect has your offering on his or her mind. Just knowing all these things will make it easier for you to close.
- When a prospect says "Let me think it over," that means "no".
- If you do not close just after your presentation, chances are you have lost the sale. Few prospects have the guts to tell you they will definitely not buy from you. They search for excuses. So do everything you can to move them into a position where they will buy from you. If you don't, a better salesperson will.
- Tie the close in with the contact. Try to close on a personal note. Something like, "I think you'll feel more secure now with this new security system, and that's important. Shall I have your smoke alarm installed tomorrow or the next day?"

Some canvassers are lucky. They get to talk only to people who are honest-to-goodness leads, who have demonstrated an interest in the product or service already. But most canvassers have to make cold calls. Brrr! A pundit once observed, "Throughout history, the most common debilitating human ailment has been cold feet."

But guerrillas are not troubled by this ailment. They thrive on cold calls. They need no introduction, referral, or appointment. They know the key to success is making the most of the short time they have to attract their prospect's attention. They also know six hot tips on cold calling:

Hot tips on cold calling

1. *Do your homework.* Learn as much as possible about the company you'll be calling upon. The more you know, the better you can tailor your presentation to the prospect.
2. *Start at the top.* Ask for and speak with the person in charge, the one who can say "yes". Do what you must to find out this person's name and title before you even begin. Anything extra you learn will prove extra helpful to you.
3. *Be brief.* Don't waste anyone's time. Keep your message concise. Brevity in cold calling primes you for success.
4. *Get to the point.* Tell if your offering does the job faster, easier, lasts longer, saves time, saves energy, or whatever. Zero in quickly on the prime benefits of your product or service.
5. *Give references.* Give names of satisfied customers, names that your prospect will recognize and respect. If he doesn't know the name, maybe he'll know the company.
6. *Close the sale.* Make an appointment. Schedule a full presentation or a demonstration. Know before you start exactly what you wish to achieve, and close on that objective. Whatever you do, ask for the order.

If you don't feel comfortable with A-B-C, "always be closing", at least learn to feel comfortable with A-T-C, which means "always *think* closing". If you think closing, your thoughts will carry over to your prospect. And you'll close more as a result. But eventually, you just may want to exercise your powers of selling on larger groups of people. One of the ways to do that is by writing personal letters. So we'll examine the art of creating them in the next chapter.

10

Personal Letters: Inexpensive and Effective

THE WRITING OF PERSONAL LETTERS — not direct mailings of large quantities of letters and brochures, but simple, personal letters — is one of the most effective, easy, inexpensive, and overlooked methods of marketing. Certainly the large corporations don't consider using this type of communication, because it doesn't reach enough people to enrich their coffers. But it's just the ticket for many an individual businessperson. If you can write clear English, spell properly, and keep your message short enough, you ought to be able to develop enough business through this mode of marketing so that you need not employ many other methods. Even if you're a dismal grammarian, professional typists can usually help put your ideas into acceptable form on the printed page.

The personal touch The primary value of a personal letter is that it enables you to convey a truly personal feeling and reach a special place in the mind of the reader. You can say specific things in personal letters that are just not practical in any other medium except for certain kinds of telephone marketing.

For example, you can say in your letter, "Mrs. Forman, your gardenias and carnations look wonderful this year. But your roses look as though they can use a bit of help. I can provide that help and bring your roses back to glowing health." That sure has more going for it than, "Dear Home Gardener, perhaps your garden isn't as beautiful this year as usual. We offer a full range of garden supplies and expertise to aid you."

The point is that in a personal letter you can, should, and must include as much personal data as possible. Mention the person's name, of course. But also mention things about the persons life, business, car, home, or — if you're in the gardening business — the person's garden. By doing so, you will be whispering into someone's ear rather than shouting through a distant megaphone. Naturally, you can't mention personal things unless you know them. So do your homework and learn about your prospective customers: their working and living habits, their hopes and goals, their problems, especially their problems.

Solving problems will be a growth industry in the next century, indeed, for ever. Businesses devoted to success are devoted to obtaining information about their prospects. You can get much of this information with the aid of a simple questionnaire, or by personal observation. Include your findings in your personal letter, and you'll be dazzled by the effect.

No matter how motivating your personal letter may be, you can double its effectiveness if you do one of two things — or preferably both: (1) Write another personal letter within two weeks; (2) Call the prospect on the telephone. **Doubling the effectiveness**

When you do the repeat mailing, your letter can be brief and for the most part a reminder of your original letter. However, it should also have new information in it, more reasons to do business with you.

When you make the follow-up telephone call, refer to your letters. Ask if the person read them. Talk about the high points. Take advantage of the fact that your letter has broken the "stranger barrier" and you are now on speaking terms with your prospect. Use the phone to develop a relationship. The stronger that relationship, the likelier the person is to do business with you. That relationship will intensify if your letter includes a number of personal references. That will prove beyond doubt that you have sent a personal letter and not a clever mass-mailed flier.

These days, with more and more advertising pieces being mailed, people are literally bombarded with letters. One way to make your letter stand out is by making it part of a two-, three- or four-letter campaign. Such multiple mailing campaigns are more expensive than single letters, but incredibly effective. Study after study confirms that people patronize businesses with which they are familiar. In the mid-1980s, a study was conducted to ascertain what factors influenced a buyer's purchase decision. Five thousand respondents indicated that confidence ranked first, quality second, selection third, service fourth, and price ninth.

Multiple mailings

But times have changed, and new research, conducted on the retail level, shows that price is now the biggest purchase motivation, quality the second, and environmental safety third. In another study of retail customers, price was first, selection second, quality third, location fourth, and service fifth. In a recession, when these 1990s studies were conducted, buying attitudes change. Confidence is not included on surveys. But be assured that people still won't buy the lowest-priced item if they don't trust what it buys.

The hot buttons of the nineties

The truth is that reasons for buying vary from industry to industry, from age group to age group, from target market to target market, from circumstance to circumstance. The leading appeal to a mother buying baby food would be different from the appeal to that same mother buying a sports car.

Forget personal letters altogether if you don't have a clear idea of the leading appeal to the people receiving them. Knowing it, along with as much personal data as possible, will enable you to gain the greatest benefit from your personal letter. And what might that be? It could be an order, a request for more data, a meeting with you. You've got to know what you want your personal letter to accomplish before you write it.

By sending out multiple mailings of personal letters, you build customer confidence through familiarity, paving your way to a relationship and a sale. Only an entrepreneur with a carefully targeted market can afford this luxury. A large company has too many prospects to engage in personal letter campaigns.

Understand that there is a difference between a personal letter and a personalized letter. The latter type is really a rather impersonal letter with a person's name in the salutation and within the body of the letter, along with some personal references. The personalization is accomplished by means of a word processor. A personal letter, on the other hand, is extremely personal. It is directed to one person and contains so many specific personal references and so much personal information that it cannot possibly be meant to be read by anyone but the person to whom it is addressed. It is signed in ink — smearable, fountainpen ink. It has a P.S., possibly even handwritten. Naturally, it has a greater effect on a reader than a mere personalized letter.

One good way to do a personal mailing is to *make it unnecessary for your prospect to respond.* Oh, your letter might have an address or phone number, but in this case it should not ask for a written reply or a phone call. It should not include a means for responding. It should whet the reader's appetite. However, it should also tell the reader that you will be telephoning within a week to set up an appointment or firm up a sale.

No response necessary

This accomplishes several things. It forces the reader to think about your offer — because it tells the reader that you'll be talking with him or her about it soon. It separates you from the many letter writers who leave everything to the discretion of the reader and require the reader to take action. You leave the reader waiting for you to take action, to provide the missing information. *And your letter prepares the reader for your phone call.* When you do call, you will not be a stranger but an expected caller.

This luxury of not including a response mechanism in your letters cannot be practiced by big firms, because it is too inefficient on a large scale. But it is the essence of guerrilla marketing, for it gives you an edge over mass marketers. And it goes to a unique extreme to gain attention.

The tone of your letter should incorporate business matters **Appeal to the** and personal feelings and should appeal to the reader's self-**reader's** image. If written to the president of a company, for example, **self-image** your letter should mention the responsibilities of a president, the importance of the job, and the problems encountered, and it should be well written, employing a relatively sophisticated vocabulary.

How long should a typical personal letter be? One page. But don't worry about going longer than that if necessary. Be sure to convey all the information you feel you must convey, but do it as briefly as possible. A good rule is to make your personal letter short unless it must be long. And when I say short, I mean one full page of warm, personal, motivating, enticing copy. Because it is a personal letter, it need not have a brochure or circular enclosed — although it may.

Your letter should give the reader relevant information, data that he or she might otherwise not have known. Occasionally, I will remind a prospective advertising client of an upcoming event or a promotion that worked well for another client. A gardener might alert a prospect to a coming season that is right for the planting of certain species. A tutor might talk of advances in education. What it comes down to is *giving something to the reader rather than merely asking for something or selling something.* The information you impart freely might impress a reader with your intelligence, insight, or personality. The prospect might also utilize it with no recognition to you. But the rewards are usually worth the risks.

The letter is It is crucial to remember that the letter should not be about **not about you** you, but about the reader. It should be in the reader's terms, about the reader's life or business. The letter should be loaded with potential benefits for the reader. The greater the number of benefits, the better. The classic advice about such letters is to remember the opera *Aida*. That's a memory crutch to remind you to get *a*ttention first, then *i*nterest the reader, then create a *d*esire, and finally make a call to *a*ction. But perhaps it's simpler just to remember to secure the reader's attention first, then state the benefits of doing business with you, and finally tell exactly what action the reader must take — make a phone call, write a letter, read page 15 of the Sunday paper, expect a phone call, anything, just as long as you say exactly what you want the reader to do.

From a purely technical standpoint, I offer these gems of personal-letter wisdom:

- Keep your letter to one page.
- Make your paragraphs short, five or six lines each.
- Indent your paragraphs.
- Don't overdo underlining, capital letters, or writing in margins.
- Do everything you can to keep the letter from looking like a printed piece.
- Sign your letter in a different-colored ink than it is typed in.
- Include a P.S. — and have it contain your most important point and a sense of urgency.

Personal letter wisdom

Studies show that when people receive personal, and even printed, letters, they read the salutation first and the P.S. next. So your P.S. should contain your most attractive benefit, or your invitation to action, or anything that inspires a feeling of urgency. There is an art to writing a P.S., and you should not sell such a brief comment short. Some personal letters contain handwritten P.S. messages. I recommend this. A handwritten P.S. proves beyond doubt that you have created a one-of-a-kind letter, that it is not a mailing piece that went out to thousands of people.

The potent P.S.

As with a great advertisement, a great personal letter should tell the reader what you are about to say, then tell what you want to say, and finally tell what you just said. This may seem repetitious, but believe me, it's practical in these days of mailboxes filled with direct mail.

I have written myriad personal letters. Probably five in ten get ignored completely. Probably one in ten results in business.

But the business from that one is usually so profitable that I can easily overlook the nine rejections. Ten percent is a great response rate compared with the 2 percent aimed for by many mass mailings. To give you some insight into how I create a personal letter, consider this one, to which I clipped a crisp one-dollar bill. I mailed it twelve times with zero business to me, then a thirteenth time that resulted in enough business to keep me grinning for months. It's over a decade old, yet versions of it continue to gain an impressive response. With the tactic of a million-dollar check by me (unsigned) instead of a buck, the letter pulled equally well. The gimmick is strong because it ties in with the letter's promise:

November 6, 1981

H. H. Thomas
Pacific Telephone & Telegraph
1313 53rd Street
Berkeley, CA 94705

Dear Mr. Thomas:

The dollar bill attached here symbolizes the thousands of dollars Pacific Telephone & Telegraph may be wasting by not utilizing the services of a prime quality free-lance writer.

During this year alone, I have accomplished writing projects for Visa, Crocker Bank, Pacific Plan, Gallo, Bank of America, the University of California, and the Public Broadcasting System. Although these companies do not ordinarily work with free-lancers, they did work with me.

In each case, the projects were completed successfully. In each case, I was given more assignments. There must be a reason why.

If you want to provide Pacific Telephone & Telegraph with the best free-lance writing available for any type of project — or if you have a seemingly impossible deadline — I hope you will give me a call.

I have enclosed a description of my background — just to inform you that I have won major writing awards in all the media and that I have served as a Vice-President and Creative Director at J. Walter Thompson, America's largest advertising agency. I guarantee you, however, that I am far more interested in winning sales than winning awards.

By your company settling for mere competent writing, or by having your writing assignments handled by traditional sources, you just might be wasting Pacific Telephone & Telegraph's money. A good number of companies have already figured that out.

Now, I look forward to hearing from you.

Very truly yours,
Jay Levinson

P.S. If you are not the person who assigns work to free-lancers, I would appreciate it if you would pass this letter (and this dollar) on to the person who does. Thank you very much.

It usually helps if you include a unique or informal enclosure with your letter. A newspaper article, a trade magazine article (especially in your prospect's trade), or a copy of your prospect's ad or a competitive ad helps a great deal, because the reader probably wants to read such material and will appreciate your sending it. In my case, the one-dollar enclosure served to separate my letter from the many others sent to the addressee. I'll bet many of them spent more than a dollar on a brochure. And I figure I'm the only one whose mailing piece was printed by the U.S. Treasury.

Would this letter be effective in the nineties? Judging by the way it has worked so far, it will be effective well into the

2000s. But I would make one change. After the fourth paragraph, I would write a separate paragraph, motivated by the recession, saying: "My fees are not low. But in a recession, you can't afford to take chances with less than the highest possible quality."

Timing   Timing is very important. Be careful you don't mail when everyone else is mailing. Try to time your mailing to coincide with a particular season or the advent of a new competitor, or when you hear word that your prospect may be in trouble and in the market for whatever it is you're offering. Marketing during a recession is very different from marketing during boom times.

During the bleak days of a recession:

Marketing in   1. Market more to your customers and less to your pros-
a recession   pects and the universe in general. Rely on love, and
                      make enticing offers to the people who have already
                      learned to trust you — your customers.

2. Use the telephone as a follow-up weapon. We're talking relationships here, and if you've got one on paper, widen it to include the telephone, a potent weapon in tough times. When the going gets tough, the tough make phone calls.

3. Eliminate any perceived risk of buying from you. Do it with a guarantee, a warranty, a deep commitment to service. Let the customer know *that the sale is not over until the customer is completely satisfied*. Now that is a risk remover, one guerrillas use to assuage skittish prospects.

4. Keep an eagle eye out for new profit-centers, fusion marketing opportunities, cooperative ventures. Because others are also suffering through the recession, there's a good chance they'll be willing to go along with your idea for a collaborative effort.

5. Instead of shrinking your offerings, go against the grain and expand them. Do what you can to increase the size

of your purchases, your selection of profit-producing
items, the services you offer.

6. Let your customers know that you are fully aware of the
recession and are basing your prices and offerings upon
it, making your business a more sensible place to
patronize than ever before.

It is important to mail your letter to the person who ought to
be reading it. Find out who that is by studying the appropriate
directories at your library or, better still, by phoning all the
companies to which you hope to mail. When in doubt, mail
your letter to the company president, who will either *be* the
person you want to reach or will see to it that the right person
does read your letter. It's worth a call to the company's phone
operator to find out the president's name and its correct
spelling. You can be sure that if the president asks a subordi-
nate to read something, it will get read.

With a word processor and laser printer you can send out
several thousand letters or more, all of which will appear to be
personal letters, for all can be personalized with appropriate
comments. But keep in mind that these are *not* personal letters.
Only a letter that is chock-full of personal references is really
a personal letter.

These you can send out in smaller numbers. And they will
give you, the entrepreneur, a big advantage over the huge
corporation. So take advantage of this valuable tool if you can.
If you do so, you will be practicing guerrilla marketing with
maximum skill.

11

Telephone Marketing: Dialing for Dollars

AMONG THE MANY FORMS of marketing is telephone marketing. In 1982, telephone marketing surpassed direct mail in revenues spent, and the gap has been widening ever since. In 1990, half of all goods and services sold were sold by phone. Telephone marketing is used both by the big guys and by budding entrepreneurs. *Forbes* magazine predicted that telephone marketing would be a prime marketing force in the latter years of this century, and they seem to be on the money.

Currently, there are three ways you can engage in telephone marketing. The first way is individual phone calls made by you or a member of your company. The second way is mass telemarketing, which is carried out by firms specializing in it or by dedicated telemarketing departments and is directed at thousands of potential customers at a time. The third way is by computer. Computerized calling machines actually call prospects, deliver tape-recorded sales pitches, and even pause during their messages so that prospects can answer questions and place orders. This method may be a bit impersonal, and many consider it an invasion of privacy, but it is commonly practiced. And for many a company, it works. Machines aren't hurt by rejection.

A telephone call takes less time than a canvass, is more personal than a letter, costs less than both (unless it's long-distance), and provides you with fairly close personal contact with your prospect. It is hardest to say no to a person's face. It is less hard to say no to a person's voice. And it is least hard to say no to a person's letter.

Guerrillas use telemarketing to make their ads and other marketing efforts work harder. They know that 7 percent of people hang up on all telemarketers, that 42 percent hang up on some telemarketers, and that 51 percent listen to all telemarketers. Bless that teensy majority. **What happens to tele- marketers**

What kind of companies use telemarketing? Mainly they are businesses that sell to other businesses, but often it is a business out to sell directly to a consumer. The ones that succeed plan the entire phone call: the objective, the words spoken, the mood and tone, and the follow-up.

As with advertising, telephone marketing should be part of an overall marketing program. And it should be a continuing effort. One phone call isn't enough. If a member of your company makes the phone calls, certain incentive policies should be instituted. For instance, you should always pay your designated callers both by the completed call and by the completed sale. Even if you use a salaried employee, add incentive bonuses to the salary.

No matter who does the calling, proper voice training is a good idea. Talk clearly. Use short sentences. Talk loud enough, but not directly into the mouthpiece; talking across the mouth- piece gives the most effective voice transmission. Your voice should project authority and warmth while instilling trust. Your message should be stated as concisely as possible. Whatever you do, don't read from a script. However, research shows that it's always a good idea to memorize a script, changing any words that feel "uncomfortable". The script must be so well memorized that the words sound as though you know them by heart. Don't use words that feel strange to say. Find words and phrases that come naturally to you. Guerrillas are in full control of their telemarketing and do not recite awkward speeches to their prospects. Doing so is bad **How guerrillas talk** business — more personal than a computer pitch — but still not worth doing if not done right.

Studies in varied industries consistently show that a memorized telemarketing presentation always produces better results than the same presentation from an outline. It may be more humanistic to let the caller use his or her own words, but few callers have the ability to summon the right ones. Gone are the days when it was recommended that callers use an outline, or "thought flow". Still, the more naturally conversant you sound, the more sales you'll make. And that takes practice.

Memorized words are best

If you are more comfortable using an outline to structure your phone presentations, be sure to heed the following guidelines. If the outline is longer than one page, there is probably too much in it and you should try to streamline it. An outline not only creates a structure for your thoughts and ideas, but also helps keep the call on track when the person at the other end redirects it. Even if you do work from an outline — against my recommendation — it's still a good idea to write a script of a phone call. Once you have written the script, you should do three things with it: (1) Record it. See what it sounds like. After all, you'll be using "ear" words that are heard, rather than "eye" words that are seen. There's a big, big difference. (2) Make sure the recorded script sounds like a conversation and not like an ad. Leave room for the person being called to respond. (3) Make it a point not to restate the script but to rephrase it. State the same selling points. Present them in the same order. But use words with which you are comfortable. Your telephone outline should be able to accommodate several situations. After all, if your prospect decides to buy just after you've started, you should be prepared to close the sale and end the conversation.

Your telephone personality

Notice how your friends, and probably even you yourself, assume different voice personalities when speaking on the phone. This is subtle, but it's there. Try to eliminate that telephone personality and bring out your most conversational qualities by actually practicing on the phone — talking to a tape recorder or to a friend. If you're going to do a good amount of telephone marketing, engage in role-playing, with you as the customer and a friend or associate as you. Then switch roles. Role-playing gives you a lot of insight into your offering and your message. Keep doing this until you are completely satisfied with your presentation.

Many telephone solicitations crumble when objections are made. These objections are really opportunities in disguise. Many successful telephone salespeople (and nontelephone salespeople) are able to close sales when handling objections. In fact, "close on the objection" is a sales credo for many pro sellers. One way to handle an objection is to rephrase it. Merely by doing that, you can sometimes dissipate it. "We're already buying from someone else," says the person at the other end. "Oh, you're completely satisfied with the price, quality and service you're currently receiving and feel there's no room for improvement?" By rephrasing the objection, you not only defuse it but create an opportunity for yourself. **The value of objections**

When calling a potential customer, try to establish a real relationship with that person. You may not ever speak to him or her again, but you should try to create a bond between the two of you. Do it with a couple of personal questions or observations. Ask the person about some non-job-related subject. Relate as human beings before you relate as salesperson and prospect. You probably have some interests in common. Meet on that common ground if possible. Even though the two of you should relate as people, make no mistake: your purpose in making the phone call is to make a sale. So go for it. As with the standard canvass or sales presentation think in terms of contact, presentation, and close. **Find the common ground**

Remember, your contact should be brief and warm. Your presentation should be concise, yet loaded with references to benefits. And your close should be clear and definite. Don't pussyfoot. There is nothing wrong in most instances with asking for the sale. Just don't do it in such a way that a yes or no answer can be given. Close by saying something like,

"What will be the most convenient way for you to pay for this, check or credit card?"

A script that worked The following script is from a telephone marketing program that was used in conjunction with a direct-mail program. This makes for a potent combination. These days, with direct-mail advertising growing so rapidly, it makes a lot of sense to follow up a mailing with a phone call. For guerrillas, it's almost mandatory with big-ticket sales. In this instance, the mailing was followed two weeks later by a phone call. A week later, another call was made. The program worked. Direct mail alone would not have worked.

The one-two punch Hello, Mr_____? This is _____. I'm calling for the Wilford Hotel in Los Angeles. Have you ever been to the Wilford? _____ When was the last time you were in Los Angeles? _____ Recently, we sent you an invitation. Did you receive it? _____ Are you the person who makes out-of-town meeting arrangements for your firm, or is it someone else? _____ Do you plan to take us up on our special offer now, or do you plan to request more information?

As you may recall, we are offering special prices and complimentary services to companies that hold meetings at the Wilford between April first and June thirtieth. Will your company be holding a meeting in Los Angeles during that time? _____ Did you like the special offer we made to you? _____ Do you have any questions about it? _____ Do you usually have meetings in hotels such as the Wilford? _____ What size meetings? _____ Where do you ordinarily meet? _____ I think you might be interested in holding a meeting at the Wilford. Don't forget, during the period from April first to June thirtieth, we're offering:

● Special room rates
● Complimentary meeting room
● Complimentary wine with dinner
● One free room for every fifteen booked

- A complimentary coffee break daily
- Discounts on audiovisual equipment
- Preregistration for your people
- A suite for the meeting planner

Doesn't all that sound good? _____ You get all these benefits with a minimum of only fifteen guest rooms.

Is there anything else we might offer you? _____ When do you plan to hold your next meeting? _____ When would be the best time to arrange a reservation for your group at the Wilford? _____ Would you like to make the arrangements right now or later? When? _____ Is there any other person at your company that you suggest I contact? _____ Thanks very much for taking this time to speak with me. _____ Good-bye.

As you can see, a good phone script calls for lots of questions, so that the person called will feel he or she is part of the process and will not feel "talked at". Whatever you say on the phone should be part of your overall marketing and creative plans, so measure your scripts against your marketing strategies.

The downside to telemarketing is that most calls are poorly scripted. It takes talent to create a good call. That means more than a way with words. A guerrilla telemarketing script helps telemarketers overcome employee turnover, despondent moods, lack of enthusiasm, and rejection daze. It keeps callers on track and ensures that prospects receive accurate data — all the while allowing for natural telephone conversation. It even raises and answers objections. **The downside of scripts**

Most scripts fail because they don't give enough credence to the very important human element, and because telemarketing is now regarded as suspicious by an increasingly sophisticated public. Be sure your scripts are tight, yet loaded with warmth. Hard to do? You bet it is. **The guerrilla script**

Be sure your script has tons of humanity built into it, with room for give-and-take. Let the telemarketer add his or her own words and phrases to the script. The more comfortable the telemarketer, the more relaxed the prospect. Relaxed prospects are good to have.

Keep your script to a maximum of one page, single-spaced. Paragraph one introduces the caller and the company. Paragraph two gives the reason for the call or makes the offer. Paragraph three highlights the benefits of the offer. Paragraphs four and five close the sale or set the stage for the next step, possibly a personal appointment.

Your script should contain a good reason for your call and a way to get through the secretary barrier. You have fifteen to twenty seconds to gain or lose your prospect's attention, so don't waste one second or one word. Guerrilla scripts contain about four interest-creating comments and flow directly to the benefits. They build rapport right off with questions.

Good scripts have systems to handle objections to the sale and to close the sale. You'll need a system to test and improve your script. More about this later.

Get set to be rejected
You've got to be prepared for massive amounts of rejection when you embark upon a telephone marketing program. For this reason, employee turnover in telephone marketing firms is tremendous. On the other hand, telephone marketing is so instantly effective for some companies that they set up what are known as boiler-room operations. In these operations, several people gather in one large room, which is often partitioned. Each has a phone. And each can see the others. Each person makes call after call, trying to make as many sales in as short a time as possible. When a sale is made, a signal is given, such as an upraised fist. Seeing this signal, the other phoners give a reciprocal signal to show that they recognize the success. This seems to give a lift to the group morale and helps the telephone salespeople deal with the horribly high number of rejections. It also seems to nourish enthusiasm.

The boiler room
You can set up your own boiler-room operation. Or you can hire one. Many telephone marketing firms exist — more now than ever, because just two decades ago none existed. These firms are permanent boiler-room operations. They operate

from their own facilities, using their own scripts, tailored for your needs, and their own telephone sales pros. They charge by the hour and by the call. And many companies find them well worth the expense. If you ever consider establishing your own boiler-room setup, first look into the economics of hiring an outside firm with a going operation. These firms can put their facilities to work for you or they can set up an operation for you, training your people to be masters at telephone selling.

One of the great advantages of telephone marketing is that you can obtain an instant response to your offer. You can deal with objections and overcome them. You can, by using a boiler-room operation, talk to literally thousands of people per day. In doing so, you can categorize the people you have called as customers, near customers, and noncustomers. In rare instances, you can accomplish all of your marketing by phone. Some companies do.

Such marketing works far better for businesses selling to other businesses than it does for companies selling directly to consumers. This is because consumers at home have little time for business, but businesspeople in their place of business do have a bit of time for business matters, even those that come by phone. High-ticket sales are one of the reasons for telemarketing success in business-to-business transactions. Whereas with individual consumers, profits tend to be far lower, making telemarketing to them less cost-efficient.

Be sure you don't expect telemarketing to do more than it can do. A financial organization mailed a letter to its prospects, offering a free gift to those who requested a brochure. Telemarketing to the brochure requesters netted many personal appointments. It was during these appointments that sales were closed. Although sales may be closed on the phone, often telemarketing is merely a crucial cog in a big machine.

To succeed with telemarketing, know which benefits turn on your prospective customers. Give prime emphasis to the benefits you feel have the most impact. Be sure you are **Succeeding on the phone** speaking with the right person. Make a specific offer — preferably a special offer that is not available to all people at all times.

The more people you call, the more sales you'll close. Of every 20 people you *call*, you'll probably make contact with only about five on your first try. The others will be busy, sick, away, on the phone, or otherwise indisposed. Of every 20 people you *reach*, you may close a sale with only one right there on the phone. So you can see that you'll have to make about 100 calls to close one sale. That might sound like a lot, but to a true-blue telephone marketing pro it means that a mere 1000 phone calls will result in ten sales. Figuring an average of three minutes per call (some will take up to ten minutes, but most will take less than one minute), this means that 50 hours of calling will result in ten sales.

This also means that you'll either spend one hard workweek on the phone, or you'll hire someone to be on that phone for you. If your profit per sale is great enough, you should give serious consideration to marketing this way. If ten sales aren't nearly enough, perhaps you should think about using other marketing methods. For some entrepreneurs, ten sales in one week means joy, wealth, and fulfillment. If that's you, and you feel telephone marketing makes sense for your offering, utilize it before your competitors discover its powerful capabilities.

If you have an in-house calling department, don't let them call for more than four hours a day. The rejection rate Is so high that it may cause death — for all I know. I do know that so much rejection dampens enthusiasm, sometimes permanently.

Three things to do   Three things that you must do is to test, to test, and to test. What I am referring to are your scripts, your callers, and your target markets.

Recognize that although you are pleased with the results of your telemarketing — and you will be if you combine it with other guerrilla marketing methods — it can always be improved. That's why guerrillas never stop testing their scripts.

They will constantly experiment with new words, phrases, and ideas. As a result, their response rates continue to rise.

This chapter has discussed only part of telemarketing, the part known as outbound telemarketing, where *you* make the phone call. An entire other part, inbound telemarketing — how you handle calls to you — involves proper telephone demeanor and is more in the domain of large businesses than guerrilla small businesses.

Telemarketing is a superb mini-marketing weapon, already doubling as a maxi-marketing weapon, and I encourage you to give it a try, especially if you're selling to businesses. In 1990, the average telephone transaction — contact to closed sale — worked out at higher than $300 per call when one business telemarketed to another. Maybe you can improve on that figure. This guerrilla sure hopes so.

12

Circulars and Brochures: How, Where, and When

LET'S GET THIS STRAIGHT right at the outset: There is not much difference between a circular and a flier, but a brochure is a different kind of animal. To me, circulars and fliers are short and single-minded; a brochure is longer and more detailed than either. My dictionaries don't shed much more light on the subject, so we'll have to live with my distinctions.

Distribution There are several ways to distribute circulars and brochures. They may be mailed alone or as part of a mailing package; placed in mailboxes; slipped under doors or windshield wipers; handed out at street corners, at trade shows, or wherever lots of prospects congregate; given to prospects and/or customers; placed in racks that say "Take One" or on counters for general distribution; or even dropped from airplanes. I don't recommend the latter.

If you're going to distribute many pieces, make them circulars, because circulars are less expensive per piece. If you are distributing relatively few pieces, you might opt for the more expensive brochures.

Form and content The simplest form of circular is a single sheet of paper, printed on one side. Printing on both sides makes matters and format a tad more complex. Printing on both sides of two pieces of paper — each folded in half — makes a booklet, which I call a brochure if it is loaded with information, printed or visual. If it isn't, it's not really a brochure, but a folded circular. Some brochures run as long as twenty-four pages. When planning to produce such materials, remember that when you fold a sheet of paper in two, you have a total of four pages (two on each side). So generally you must think in terms of four-page units. Brochures are ordinarily four or eight or twelve pages. Some brochures have panels that fold rather than pages that turn. Usually, these are six-panel brochures — three panels on each side. If you start with a standard A4 piece of paper (297 x 210mm), folding it twice makes it ready to become a six-panel brochure and the ideal size for a standard 110 x 220mm envelope.

The format isn't nearly as important as the content. And the content must be factual information, enlivened with a touch of style and romance. Unlike ads, which must flag a person's attention, a brochure or circular already has that attention. So its primary job is to inform with the intention of selling. Most brochures, and some circulars, use artwork. Sometimes this is intended to keep the piece visually interesting. But most of the time, its purpose is to explain, inform, and sell.

When writing a circular, think first of the basic idea you wish to express. Then try to marry a picture (art or photograph) to a set of words. After you've stated your idea as briefly as possible, try to explain more fully what you are offering. Always be sure to include information about how to get in touch with you: address, phone number, place to find you. **What's the big idea**

I know an entrepreneurial-minded contractor named George. He markets his services well, and decided he'd improve business even more by distributing a circular or a brochure. Here's the way he proceeded. Being no dummy, George started out with a circular to see how this marketing vehicle would work for him. If it worked well, he might upgrade it to a brochure. On the circular, he had a drawing done of a man (George) doing five tasks at the same time in front of a house. Above the drawing, he listed his company name, which, incidentally, made a dandy headline for his circular: Let George Do It. Beneath that headline and picture, he briefly **George's circular** stated his offering:

> George builds sun decks and patios.
> George installs skylights and hot tubs.
> George paints and puts up wallpaper.
> George does masonry and electrical work.
> George also designs and makes building plans.
> <u>LET GEORGE DO IT!</u>
> Call George at 555-5656 any time any day.
> All work guaranteed. Contractor's License #54-45673.

Not very fancy, but quite explicit. The cost for George to write this circular was nil. An art student did the illustration for $50. And the cost to produce about 5000 of the circulars, including paper, was another $100. So George ended up spending about $150, which comes to three cents per circular. Even if printing costs had been higher — and they are — George would have spent less than a nickel per circular. And without paying for color, George was able to get a colorful circular by the ingenious use of colored ink on a colored paper stock — dark blue ink on light tan stock.

George then distributed his circulars by several methods: He mailed 1000; he placed 1000 on auto windshields (he had a high school student do some of this for him); he distributed 1000 more at a home show in his area; he handed out 1000 more at a local flea market; and he held on to 1000 to give to satisfied customers to pass on to their friends and neighbors. Being bright as a penny when it comes to saving money, the enterprising George also asked each of his customers where they had heard of him. When they said, "I saw your flier," George asked where they got it. This way, he learned which of the five methods of circular distribution was most effective.

Now that's guerrilla marketing. Not expensive whatsoever. But very effective. One job could recoup for George his entire marketing budget for circulars. And since 5000 circulars were distributed, you have to believe that George got more than one job.

Perhaps George will decide to put out a brochure someday. As a first step in planning a good one, he'd think in terms of photography, so that he could show actual pictures of work he has accomplished. And because he has such a comprehensive offering, he'd figure that an eight-page brochure was needed to do the trick. He'd use a simple 148 x 210mm (A5) size, which is half the size of a standard A4 sheet of paper. Unless the brochure was full-color — a good idea because color increases retention rate by 57 percent and proclivity to buy by 41 percent — all type and photos would be in black ink. The paper stock, either glossy or not, would be white or some other light color.

George's brochure

He'd plan to use the same drawing on the cover that he used on his circular. After all, if it worked once, it ought to work again. And it makes good economic sense. So his cover would show his drawing, list his company name (which fortunately doubles as a headline and a brochure title), and maybe, but not definitely, list the other copy points from his circular. Let's say he does list them, since he wants to impart as much information as possible. *Repetition in marketing is far more of a good thing than a bad thing.*

Following his cover page, page one, his second page, might list a bit about George. It would indicate his experience, his training, and jobs he has accomplished, and would list his skills and offerings. It might even include a photo of him. It would lead up to the other things he is about to say.

Page three would show photos of a sun deck and a patio, and would give a description, about five sentences long, of George's capabilities in this area. Page four would show photos of a skylight and a hot tub that George installed. Again, five or six sentences would indicate his expertise. Page five would show photos of a room that George painted and another room that George papered. It would also include a bit of copy attesting to George's talent at painting and papering. Page six would feature photos of houses with masonry and electrical work by

George. One would be an exterior shot and the other an interior shot. Again, copy would describe the work accomplished. Each of these pages, by the way, would repeat the short copy lines from the cover. For example, the seventh page, showing a gorgeous room addition designed and built by George, would have as its headline, "George also makes building plans and building designs." A few sentences of copy would follow the photo. The copy would not have to be brief. Don't forget, the purpose of the brochure is to inform.

Finally, George's eighth page, the back cover, would give the name of his company, his phone number, his contractor's license number, and probably a repeat of the best photo from the interior of the brochure. Such a brochure might cost George as much as one dollar per unit. But it would be worth it, when you consider George's profit per sale.

A solar-heating company for which I created a brochure had a special problem. They realized that a brochure would help their business, but the technology in their industry was changing so rapidly that they were reluctant to commit themselves to producing one. Solution: I created an eight-page brochure with a pocket inside the back cover. Within the eight pages, the brochure dealt with all of the aspects of solar technology that were not changing: its economy, its cleanliness, its responsibility to the environment, its acceptance and success in all parts of the world. Within the pocket were inserted separate sheets dealing with specific equipment as technology marched forward, as it has. These could be replaced at will. Price lists, also replaceable at a whim, could be put there as well. This enabled the company to have a brochure and flexibility at the same time.

Let's look at another example. A jewelry-making firm in San Francisco manufactured beautiful but very expensive jewelry. To add an element of value, it produced a lavish brochure — full-color, glossy, and photographed in the most glamorous parts of San Francisco. Each two-page spread contained one gorgeous photo of the San Francisco area and one photo of an item of jewelry. This lent an air of value to each piece of jewelry that could not have been created with a single photo. It connected the jewelry store with San Francisco, where tourism is the largest industry. A brochure was just the ticket.

One of my clients sent a photographer on a dream assignment: to visit Mexico and shoot photos of a wide variety of villas and condominiums that my client was renting to people for vacation use. These photos were later made the basis for a colorful brochure. Without the photos, the brochure could only have dealt with villa and condo vacations in a theoretical sense. The photos brought the theory to vibrant life. The brochure helped the company quadruple its sales. Without a vehicle to show the many villas and condos, complete with beaches, pools, balconies, lush living rooms, and spacious bedrooms, the company could not have made its point. Less than a brochure could not have done the job.

Still another company was able to grow from tiny to tremendous merely by the proper use of a brochure. The company owned the patent on a new product that replaced the old-fashioned blowtorch. But it couldn't communicate all of the advantages of its product with ads or letters or phone calls. Personal demonstrations were impractical because of logistics problems. A brochure was the answer. It was incredibly detailed, listing all of the advantages of the product and all of the famous-name companies using it, and showing several exciting shots of the product in use. The brochure included a pageful of testimonials from satisfied users, and it described the technical data in such detail that even the most nitpicking engineer would be impressed. In addition, it was very handsome. This inspired confidence in the company, and it grew. To this day, the company's primary marketing tool is that brochure.

A brochure success story

And so it is with a number of other companies. They have a story that does not translate well in advertising but becomes brilliantly clear when the details, both verbal and graphic, are communicated in a brochure. If yours is one of those companies, you can afford to spend a great deal of your marketing budget producing a knockout brochure. The cost, including everything, runs anywhere from $500 to $50,000. But don't let the $50,000 figure dazzle you. That's only $4166.67 per month, a lot less than many companies spend on media advertising alone. Perhaps you won't even need the mass media. Perhaps a brochure will do the trick for you.

Although some businesses benefit almost every time they give away their brochure, there are times not to give one away. If you have a store and distribute brochures to your potential customers, that gives them an excuse not to buy. They can tell you that they want to look over your brochure before buying. I advise my clients, except those selling very expensive items, not to give their brochures to shoppers — only to people who have purchased or to people who are on their way out anyhow.

I also advise people who run newspaper or magazine ads that contain a lot of information to consider using those ads as brochures. Merely reprint them and add front and rear covers by printing on the back of the folded-in-half advertisement. Often the magazine will do this for you for peanuts.

Brochures for peanuts

If you don't have the budget for large ads, you might consider running small ads offering your free brochure. I know a man who earns his entire income (a six-figure income, I might add) by running tiny ads in myriad publications, offering his free brochure in each ad. The people who request the brochure are serious prospects. They took the time to write for the brochure. They are interested in what he's offering. My friend's brochure does his entire selling job for him. It describes his offer, gives the details, and asks for the order. His ads and his brochures are his only marketing tools, and he is very successful as a one-man show. This demonstrates how important a brochure can be.

A mighty important point: when printing your business cards, think of them as mini-brochures. On them print your name, address, phone number, logo, and theme line, of course, but also include brief body copy — as much as you can fit. Some clever entrepreneurs hand out double-size business cards, folded in half. The outside of the cards has the standard business-card information. The inside has a headline, beneath which are listed several features and benefits, products and services. These cards look like business cards but work like brochures. And brochures work well.

If anything does a brochure's job better than a brochure, it's an *electronic brochure* — a five- to nine-minute version of a printed brochure. The cost of duplicating videos is under $2 and falling. The cost of producing videos is $100 to $10,000 per minute. The lower cost is if you do it yourself — not recommended. The higher number is for letting a first-rate video production company handle it. Guerrillas find a happy medium somewhere between the two.

Electronic brochure

A *video brochure* will give more of an impression of worth and value than a printed version. Prospects will view it, then probably view it again with one or more people. They may give it to a friend or associate, not likely with a printed brochure. The purpose of such a brochure is just the same as a printed one — using words, pictures, music, emotions, intellect, demonstration, and believability to create a desire to buy your product or service, Don't let the medium create the delusion that you're now in show business. Guerrillas don't fall into that enticing trap.

The video brochure

Guerrillas do not send video brochures to people on a mailing list, such as huge corporations can and a few automobile manufacturers have done. One car maker sent a video introducing the local dealer's name at the beginning, starring the car with glitzy cinematography in the middle, then ending with *the recipient's name superimposed across the video image* — it was the first of many personalized video brochures. Guerrillas like the idea of personalization and are wowed by the potency of video information. Still, they send their video brochures *only to people who request them.*

By request only

People learn of videos through magazines, direct mailings,

trade shows, and other modes of communication. When they request one, it should be sent free, with no obligation. Whatever you do, send a personal letter along with it, just as you would with a printed brochure. Follow within ten days with a phone call or letter. A request for a video should be construed as the first step in buying. Be sure to follow up — don't lose the momentum you've created.

Maybe you don't require visual input to tell your business story. Perhaps you can do it with words. Put your words onto **The audio** tape and offer an *audio brochure*. A large number of people **brochure** commute for over half an hour at a time. Instead of listening to the radio, they'll probably listen to your five- to fifteen-minute tape. They know it's a way to learn while saving time.

Create a video brochure according to a strategy, just as you'd create a printed brochure. Only, say as much as you can visually. Realize that your visuals will communicate more powerfully than your verbiage, so keep the visual excitement to a maximum. Be sure the visuals pertain to your company and aren't merely special visual effects substituting for a solid idea.

A video brochure is jazzy and more dynamic than a printed piece, but its purpose is still to make a sale, either all by itself, in concert with a sales rep who is present while the tape is being shown, or in tandem with a direct-mail letter, card, or a phone call. In numbers there is strength. In visuals there is strength. As great as your video brochure may be, it is only as powerful as your idea.

Electronic and printed brochures can be expensive mistakes, so don't say anything you'll want to change within a year. Do it once and do it right. Then do your darnedest to follow up on everyone who requests any kind of brochure.

13

Classified Advertising Hints: Making Small Beautiful

WHEN YOU THINK OF CLASSIFIED advertising, you probably think in terms of finding a job, looking for a car, selling a sofa, buying a boat, or locating a house or apartment. Think again.

Classified advertising can also be used to support a business. And many a flourishing enterprise exists primarily on the pulling power of classified ads.

On a random weekday, my local newspaper featured classified ads for a ticket-selling firm, a number of attorneys, an advertising medium, a pregnancy consultation center, a credit association, a fortune teller, a job-finding service, several books, a game arcade, a psychic adviser, a rent-a-mailbox firm, a ghostwriter, several introduction services, a group of escort services, two full columns of massage businesses, one and a half columns of firms offering loans, unique telegram companies, hairstylists, barbers, moving companies, auto transport firms, travel agencies, calligraphers, dozens of home-service entrepreneurs, tropical fish stores, pawnbrokers, coin and stamp dealers, antique dealers, auctioneers, TV dealers, computer equipment stores, musical-instrument stores, a horse ranch, boat dealers, a flying school, two résumé writing services, loads of schools, tutors, employment agencies, auto and truck dealers, motorcycle dealers, hotels, rooming houses, bed and breakfast places, rest homes, guest houses, realtors, business brokers, motels, and mobile-home dealers. And this was a weekday, not even a Sunday. I wouldn't even attempt to list the entrepreneurial enterprises using the Sunday classified section. Do your own homework and see for yourself — in your own community.

If all of these entrepreneurs and/or businesses use the classified section, it makes sense for you to consider it, too. I notice that many of these advertisers have had ads in the classified section for more than ten years. And I know that they wouldn't spend their money there if they weren't getting handsome returns.

In my files, I have magazines with far more classified ads than are in the newspaper just mentioned. And I'm sure you know of newspapers — many of them, and the number keeps rising — that consist of nothing but classified ads. Obviously, classified ads work as a marketing medium. And if you can see any advantage for your company in using this medium, a bit of investigation and investment on your part is worthwhile.

Where to run your ads Generally, there are three places you can run classified ads: in magazines, in daily newspapers, and in classified-ad newspapers. If your offering requires proximity to your customers, forget the magazines. And if your offering is national in character, forget the newspapers. There is little likelihood that you'll want to run classified ads in both local newspapers and national magazines — unless the papers you select are in localities spread throughout the country, and you want to combine that advertising with national magazine advertising.

You are probably noticing that more and more magazines are offering classified advertising. They know that the many new small businesses just plain can't afford a display ad, and they have this deep longing for revenue. So they offer classified advertising sections for entrepreneurs. Look long and deeply into this because the cost is relatively low to get into a major magazine and because the classified section is generally at the back of the magazine.

Guerrilla hint: because many people read magazines from the back to the front, your economical classified ad will have a decent shot at being read.

As you may have heard, it doesn't cost an arm and leg to run a classified ad. And you'll usually be offered a frequency discount. This means that if your five-line classified ad costs you $20 to run one time, it will cost only, say, $18 per insertion if you run it three times, and only $15 per insertion if you run it five times. The more frequently you run it, the lower your cost per insertion. This is called a frequency discount. Classified ad charges are based upon the number of words, the number of lines, or the number of inches. It depends upon the publication. The cost of the ad is also based upon the circulation of the publication — both in quantity and quality.

How much it costs

Many people read the classified ads each day. Some read them to find specific bargains. Others read them merely to browse via the newspaper. And still others find them the most fascinating part of the newspaper. Check them yourself. See which ads draw your attention. Also notice which classified-ad categories catch your attention. By reading through the ads, you'll get a sense of whether or not your business can profit from this method of marketing. You'll also begin to learn, by osmosis, what to say in a classified ad and what not to say. Although classified ads are short, fraught with abbreviations, and devoid of illustrations, they are not as simple as they may seem. If you decide to give the classified-ad section a go, there are a few concepts that you should keep in mind.

For one thing, keep your headline short — and be sure you do have a headline, printed in all capital letters. Don't use abbreviations unless you are sure that people will understand them. While living in England, my wife and I searched for an apartment by scanning the classified ads. Many said that the rental included CCF&F. At first, we were completely thrown by that. Do you know what it means? Later, we learned that it stands for "carpets, curtains, fixtures, and fittings".

Writing strong ads

Don't use esoteric terms in your ads unless you're sure that most of your readers (99 percent) know the meaning. Write in short sentences. Try to sound more like a human being than a want ad. And be sure you include a way to contact you. More than once I've seen an ad with no phone number or address.

In most instances, publications have people who can help you word your want ads. I suggest that you use these people as guides but do not slavishly follow their advice. If they were brilliant writers, they'd probably be paid for their writing and not for taking want ads. If you are a good writer, write your own classified-ad copy. If not, go to a pro. Don't rely on the person who takes the ads to write your copy, but do rely on that person's experience.

Word your ad in such a way that it contrasts with other ads in the same section. And choose that section very, very carefully. Some newspapers have categories that do not appear in other papers. Such categories include: attorneys, announcements, Christmas items, computers, and so forth. Be sure that you advertise in the right category. Make that plural. You may want to place your ad in more than one category.

Strange as it may seem, classified ads often outdraw display ads. So don't think that just because an ad has no picture and doesn't cost much it's not going to be effective. Many companies run display ads and classified ads in the same newspapers on the same day. They claim that the ads reach different classes of consumers.

I earned about $500 per month for at least a dozen years working about half an hour per month. I did it with a classified ad. I ran the same ad, with minor changes in wording, all twelve years. After I had been working for a few years as a free-lance writer, I'd learned quite a few important things about free-lancing, things nobody had ever told me, things that weren't written in books. So I wrote a book and published it myself. I called the book *Secrets of Successful Free-lancing*. And although it had but forty-three pages, I priced it at $10. The reason I charged $10 was because I sincerely felt the book was worth it. The book cost me about $1 to print, including type and binding. Advertising ran about $3.33 per book. So I figured that I made $5.67 per book. Here's a sample of the classified ad I ran:

> I EARN MORE AS A FREE-LANCER THAN I DID AS A VP/ CREATIVE DIRECTOR AT J. WALTER THOMPSON. I loved my JWT days. But I love now more. I live where I want. I work only 3 days a week. I work from my home and take lots of vacations. To do the same, read my incisive book, *Secrets of Successful Free-lancing*. Send $10 to Prosper Press, 123 Alto Street, San Rafael, CA 94902. $11 refund if you're not completely satisfied.

A money-making ad

Notice how my ad used standard language rather than want-ad language. When I've run other classified ads using "people talk", I've also had good results. A regularly worded ad appearing in a sea of want-ad-worded ads tends to stand out.

The cost of the ad was $36 for one inch in the publication in which it originally appeared. And the entire ad fitted in one inch in the classified section. For every dollar I invested in the ad, I averaged $3 in sales, $2.50 in profits. It cost fifty cents to mail it, envelope included.

For me, the biggest challenge (and biggest problem) was to find enough places to run the ad. After all, everybody isn't a prospect for a book on free-lancing. I ran the ad in three advertising trade magazines, two art-director publications, two writers' magazines, the *Wall Street Journal*, and four opportunity magazines. Some of these publications drew a great response every time I ran the ad — and I ran it every three months. Others didn't pull well for me, so I discarded them from my schedule. But by sticking with the four publications that worked, I was able to bring in around $500 per month in profits — after paying for the ads, the books, and the mailing. I had all the orders mailed directly to a mail-order-fulfillment house that mailed out the books on the day orders were received, put the names of the people who ordered into a computer, and sent me the checks weekly — coded so that

I knew which publications were working best.

People in the mail-order book business report that a 5 percent request rate for refunds is about par for the course. My requests for refunds were 1.2 percent. And don't forget, I offered an $11 refund for a forty-three-page $10 book.

The half-hour per month I spent on this business was used to keep tallies on the pulling power of the various magazines and to fill out deposit slips for my bank. There was not a lot of money from this endeavor, to be sure. But $500 per half-hour isn't anything to complain about. And just think — my only method of marketing was classified advertising.

That book is no longer available by that title because I enlarged it to help more than just free-lancers. It is now available as *555 Ways to Earn Extra Money* published by Henry Holt and Company, updated in 1991. In fact, it was the response to that book that prompted me to write *Guerrilla Marketing* in the first place. Enough about me. Back to your marketing.

Many marketers use the classified ads only to check out the pulling power of products, claims, prices, copy, headlines, and appeals. It's an inexpensive way to gain valuable information. Once you have a proven winner, you can then put forth your message in display ads if you wish. But remember, classified ads sometimes pull better than display ads.

A friend who advertised his books in *Psychology Today* found that classified ads, at 25 percent of the price of display ads, pulled considerably better than display ads. The kind of **Classified** classified ad he ran is called a *classified display ad*, available **display ads** in most publications. This is an ad that appears in the classified section but has a box around it and features dark, large display type. It costs more than regular classifieds, less than regular display ads, and depending upon the offering, pulls better than both in many instances. They're worth checking into.

It is a false economy to keep your classified ad as short as possible. Don't use too many adjectives, but do use a lot of facts. Aim to be as clear in your message as you can.

Remember that your classified ad is really your sales presentation. So don't hold back on features if your offering has features to boast about. You may end up spending several dollars more because your ad is longer, but if it pulls in sales, this will easily outweigh the extra cost. *The cost of all advertising is measured not in dollars, but in response.*

When thinking about classified advertising, think first in terms of clarity, then in terms of reader interest. You've got to capture your readers' attention. Do it with a catchy word such as GHOSTWRITING! or with a cogent headline such as NEED EXTRA MONEY? Keep in mind that you have but a fleeting instant to gain attention. The way to get it is with your short headline. The rest of your copy should follow directly from the headline. The GHOSTWRITING! headline might be followed with this sentence: "A professional writer will write, rewrite, or edit your letter, essay, manuscript, or advertisement so that it sings." The NEED EXTRA MONEY? headline might be followed by copy that begins with: "Obtaining the extra cash you need is not as hard as you think." If I needed money, I'd read on. Wouldn't you?

The idea in your classified ad is to maintain the momentum created by the headline. Write copy as though you are talking to one human being and not to a mass audience. Although you should mention as many features and benefits in your ad as you can afford, you should also practice the selective withholding of information. Merely by omitting certain facts, you may generate phone calls, visits, or whatever type of response you desire. The information you withhold may be the price, the location, or some other data the reader needs to complete the picture. Just be careful not to withhold enough information so that you attract a horde of unqualified prospects.

Talking to one person at a time

A good exercise for classified-ad writing is to write your ad as though it were to be a display ad in a newspaper. Then start cutting copy to make the ad shorter and shorter. Finally, you will be left with the pure facts. But remember, shortness does not equate with quality. Pepper your facts with a few adjectives, with word pictures. "I can paint your house so that it gleams like the day it was built" sounds a whole lot more appealing than "House painting at reasonable prices."

Though classified ads need not be as short as possible, they must nonetheless motivate your prospective customers. They must create a desire to buy. One advertising genius who specializes in classified ads claims that the key to success in the classifieds is simplicity and tight copy. If you think that is easy to achieve, you are wrong. It's tough to be simple, tough to be brief. The writing of classified ads is a very special art. The ads must be well written or else they will not inspire confidence. Just because they're short does not mean they can be shabby.

To gain the greatest possible insight into writing successful classified ads, I suggest that you spend some library time. Look through current newspapers and magazines, studying the classifieds. Then look at one-year-old issues of the same newspapers and magazines. Check to see which ads are in **Study the** both the new and the year-old publications. Those must be **winners** winners, or the people running them would not be repeating them. By studying them, you can learn what it is that makes them so successful. Is it the headline? The offer? The price? The copy? Apply whatever you learn to your own business.

Many large businesses that run high-powered advertising and marketing programs, making use of TV, radio, magazines, and other publicity, still use the classified section. They recognize that there are some people who read classified ads when looking for, say, antiques or certain automobiles. So don't think classified ads are small potatoes. There are even advertising consultants who specialize in classified ads. You give them your ad copy and they give it back to you, improved, and with a list of publications in which it is likely to elicit a response. If you will be marketing a product or service nationally, consider not only national magazines but also newspapers in multiple markets.

If our friend George were to run a classified ad in a local

newspaper, he'd probably run it in the "Home Services" section, and it would say something like:

> WANT A SUN DECK? PATIO? SKYLIGHT? HOT TUB?
> Let George do it! George can give you those
> things plus masonry work, electrical work,
> and building plans. Free estimates. Call 555-
> 5656. All work is fully guaranteed.

Fact is, a person with an offering similar to George's did run such an ad. After it appeared only six times, he had to withdraw it because he couldn't handle all the work. I wish you the same success.

Remember that classified ads in newspapers allow you to home in on a local audience. Classified ads in magazines allow you to home in on a more widespread audience. And all classified ads allow you to test your strategy, your message and the advertising media you are trying out. They're glorious places to say that magic sentence: "Call or write for our FREE brochure."

Testing the waters

Remember: just because classified ads are small and inexpensive doesn't mean they're ineffective. A true guerrilla marketer tries to find ways to put the power of classified ads to work. Hardly any other medium enables you to talk to honest-to-goodness prospects and not just browsers. There's a huge difference between the two.

14
Signs: Big and Little

THINK OF SIGNS IN TWO WAYS: those that appeal to people outside your place of business and those that appeal to people within your place of business. The first category consists of billboards, which we'll discuss in another chapter, small signs on bulletin boards, which are discussed in this chapter, window signs, store signs, banners, signs on trees, and poster-type signs. Category two is made up of interior signs, commonly called point-of-purchase (P-O-P) or point-of-sale signs.

Whichever you use, or if you use both, be certain that your signs tie in as directly as possible with your advertising. The dictum, as stated by the late, great advertising pro Leo Burnett: "Plan the sale when you plan the ad." The dictum, as stated by the current, above-average advertising pro Jay Conrad Levinson: "Signs trigger impulse purchases; guerrillas are trigger-happy."

Signs trigger impulse purchases

Your ads will have made an unconscious impression on your potential customers, and your signs will awaken the memory of that advertising and result in a sale. Many people will patronize your business because of your ads. Your signs must be consistent with your advertising message and identity or those people will be confused. If the signs are in keeping with your overall creative strategy, consumers' momentum to buy will be increased. The Point-of-Purchase Advertising Institute tells us that in 1991, 74 percent of all purchase decisions were made right at the place of purchase. People entered a store with a vague notion of buying. They didn't solidify their decision until they were in the store. And what do you suppose influenced their decision? In many cases, a package. In many other cases, a sign.

Signs have exceptional power in the realm of malls, hyper-markets (a galaxy of malls), shopping centers, warehouses, supermarkets — large spaces where many businesses are competing for the eye and business of passers-by. Many smart retailers have used their signs and their decor to tie in with the times. The idea is to match confidence in the offering — accomplished with mass marketing — with a reason to make an impulsive purchase. This is, in part, accomplished by the use of a sign. Make that match and — bingo! — you've made a sale.

Most exterior signs are there to remind, to create a tiny impulse, to implant inclinations a wee bit deeper, to sharpen an identity, to state a very brief message. As a rule, exterior signs should be no more than six words long. Some successful signs have more than six words, but not many. Probably the most successful of all have just one to three words.

How many words on a sign?

Right now, since we're talking about the power of words — few words — let's examine some of the strongest words in the English language. Many are used in headlines. Many are used in signs. Almost all are used in advertising.

Psychologists at Yale University tell us that the most persuasive words in the English language are:

Sign language

you	results	love
money	health	discovery
save	easy	proven
new	safety	guarantee

To that list, I would hasten to add:

free	why	announcing
sale	yes	how
now	benefits	fast
secrets		

Now that you know these words, I'll bet you can come up with some dandy signs.

Frequently, motorists make abrupt decisions (and left turns) when they pass windows with huge banners proclaiming SALE! or FREE GIFTS! or SAVE 50%! As you probably know, it doesn't take many words to convince some people that they ought to buy from you — right now.

And many famous businesses were built with signs and signs alone. I instantly call to mind Burma-Shave (for which I had the privilege of writing two signs that were actually "published," or shall I say "roadsided"), Harold's Club in Reno, and Wall Drug Store of South Dakota. These are nationally famous businesses. Many locally famous concerns marketed their wares the same way. You can be sure that the Burma-Shave people, Harold, and Mr. Wall were all pioneer guerrillas, for they blazed trails that led directly to the bank. They also incensed coming generations of environmentalists, who claimed the signs were encroaching upon the beauty of America. Lady Bird Johnson spearheaded this movement and it's never going to die. So be aware of it, and don't put up exterior signs that will be picketed by planet-savers. As a guerrilla marketer, you must stay in touch with trends, and I, for one, am heartened by the nation's growing concern with the environment as indicated by new marketing strategies, use of recyclable materials, and production measures to guide our species toward cosmic sanity.

Mike Lavin, a true "green guerrilla", wanted one more unique way to promote his Berkeley business. A healthy mixture of environmentalist and capitalist, Mike was able to have his cake and eat it, too, by erecting, in a field, a large sign frame with no sign inside the frame. Beneath his see-through creation was a smaller sign that said "Scenery Courtesy of BERKELEY DESIGN SHOP."

Other exterior signs that usually work well are those that say such things as VOTE FOR LEVINSON, GARAGE SALE, FLEA MARKET, PARK HERE and GAS FOR LESS. Perhaps the most profitable investment a retail business owner can make is in a red neon sign that says OPEN. Not a lot of creativity in the copy for those signs, to be sure. Nonetheless, they work. Failure to make a sign investment early on may mean making a sign investment later on, investing in a GOING OUT OF BUSINESS sign.

Almost (but not quite) as important as the wording of the sign is the overall look of the sign. By this I mean the picture or pictures, the lettering style, the colors, and the design of the sign. A powerful graphic lends more power to the words. A sign that says FRESH DONUTS can be made doubly effective if it shows donuts growing in a meadow like flowers. If the sign says DELICIOUS DONUTS, it can be more motivating if it shows a picture of a grinning little girl holding a donut with a giant bite taken from it or a close-up of a donut in the process of being dunked.

Effective sign graphics

Usually, it makes sense to use very light lettering against very dark background colors or very dark lettering against very light colors. Using one type of lettering makes for easier reading than using more than one type. The words on the sign should be as large as possible while leaving room for the picture.

Keep in mind that although your sign should be expected only to remind, and not to make an actual sale, it will be better if you do go for the jugular and try like crazy to make the sale from the sign. Large advertisers with humongous marketing budgets can use signs for reminding only. But guerrillas have to get more mileage from their money. So although they know deep down that signs remind, they also realize that it is impossible to sell *some* people with a sign, and they go for the sale with the sign.

Consider also the "clutter factor". Are there many other

The clutter factor

signs nearby? If so, your sign should stand out. If not, you can approach the creation of your sign with a different mind-set. In England, when designing an outdoor sign campaign for a product that promised economy, we took the clutter factor into account and introduced black and white signs that contrasted with the surrounding sea of color signs. Our black and white beauties not only won awards but more important, won customers. Had we used color with the same words and pictures, we would not have enjoyed such a high level of success. Our uniqueness, which tied in directly with our promise of economy, helped us stand out and make our point.

A powerful visual image should be created if you are going to use many signs. The Marlboro cowboy comes to mind immediately. Because you want your sign to be instantly identifiable with you, a graphic identity is highly recommended. The look should be unusual, connected with your company's identity, and suitable for being maintained over a long period of time. Consistency. Remember?

The only punctuation mark with which you need be concerned is the exclamation mark. It lends a tone of excitement. Questions marks, while of use in print advertising, take too much reflection time to be utilized on signs. Stay away from them unless you have a good reason to break that rule. Commas and full stops usually are not necessary with six-word messages. And long words are to be avoided whenever possible.

Making a sale with a visual image plus five or six words calls for a lot of thought, a lot of creativity. As with all other marketing devices, a great sign starts with a great idea. If you lack the idea, your words and pictures will probably end up plain vanilla. But with the right words and the right pictures, along with the right idea and the right location, a sale can be made.

Little signs do a lot Guerrillas must fight their battles with every single available weapon. And small signs on bulletin boards have proven to be extremely effective weapons for many an entrepreneur.

I'm talking about signs on cars as small as 3 inches by 5 inches. Even business cards. A sign need not be big to attract customers. Little signs do the job, too.

What kind of businesses and individuals might avail themselves of this minor a medium? Tutors. Gardeners. Plumbers. Typists. Writers. Baby-sitters. House sitters. Movers. Accountants. Room renters. Music teachers. Nurses. Answering services. Pet groomers. Cleaning people. Painters. Astrologers. Mechanics. Printers. Seamstresses. Decorators. Tree pruners. Entertainers. And a whole lot more.

If your business has any prospects who have occasion to see bulletin boards, perhaps you should use small signs on bulletin boards to promote your business. You'll find such bulletin boards, as do countless eager board readers, on campuses and in libraries, cafeterias, dormitories, company rest rooms, offices, supermarkets, Laundromats, locker rooms, bookstores, pet stores, sporting goods stores, barbershops, hairstyling salons, toy stores, and sundry other locations. Most major cities have hundreds of such locations; many small towns have as many as five or ten.

You can either post the signs yourself or you can hire companies that specialize in posting the signs for you. In the San Francisco Bay Area, where I live, a local company called The Thumb Tack Bugle provides this service. In 1981, it serviced 80 locations; now it services almost every location in the Bay Area, a number that tops 600. Their chief rival is The Daily Staple, a company that was spawned by the obvious success of sign-posting. The point is — this is a growing medium, and guerrillas must be aware of it because of its efficiency and low cost.

In most instances, your sign must be replaced on a regular basis (monthly or weekly). But sometimes it can stay in place for years. In a few cases, you'll have to pay a tiny fee to post your sign, but often this method of marketing is free (if you do your own posting). The companies that post for you promise to place your sign on a guaranteed number of boards — a large number, I might add — and they'll also replace it on a regular basis. Unless you've got the time to check your signs, look into these posting services. If signs do work for you, consider allowing one of these companies to handle all of that work for you, so you can concentrate on your primary way of earning money.

No fancy lettering, please
A crucial point to remember is to keep the lettering on your sign very clear. Fancy lettering is a definite no-no. Typewriter type is fine. But clear, handsome hand lettering is probably best. If you haven't the proper calligraphic skills, ask a pro or a friend with immense talent to letter your sign for you. Remember to keep your copy short and to the point. Incidentally, it is okay to make copies of your signs. One original plus a slew of copies and enough drawing pins, and you've got the marketing tools to make yourself a success.

If George of Let George Do It posted bulletin-board signs throughout his area, they'd be very similar in wording to his circular. In fact, a sign for George might say:

LET GEORGE DO IT!
George builds sun decks and patios,
installs skylights and hot tubs,
does masonry and electrical work,
and designs building plans.

Call George at 555-5656 any time any day.
All work guaranteed. Contractor's License
#54-45673.

George probably wouldn't even need a 3 x 5 sign. Instead, he could post his circular. Circulars have a charming way of doubling as small signs.

Amazingly, there are some businesses that need only promote via this wonderfully inexpensive method of marketing. Perhaps you can be one of them. Although guerrilla marketers should utilize as many marketing methods as they can effectively, they should also save marketing money whenever they can do so intelligently. Promoting your business with 3 x 5 cards is a true saving of marketing money. In fact, if you do the lettering and the writing and the posting, it's free.

At this point, if you own and operate a computer, you're wondering if you can use desktop publishing to help you produce and design signs. The answer is that you certainly can — and should — if you've got the right software, skills, and taste.

Desktop publishing your signs

Armed with those weapons, you can use your desktop publishing prowess to produce newsletters, direct mail, brochures, and a host of other marketing tools. The technology is getting easier than ever. People are used to a higher quality of production in the marketing materials they are exposed to. The opportunities for a business with desktop publishing capabilities are endless. Just be sure you devote your time to the areas where it can most help your business. If that includes desktop publishing, great. If you love it, but should be doing something else, delegate it to someone else. A hallmark of the guerrilla is in the intelligent apportionment of time.

Ornate graphics are generally not necessary when marketing with small signs, though borders, typography, and little illustrations enliven most signs. If you post on a regular basis, it's a good idea to change the wording — but not the basic message — of your sign periodically. It's also a good idea to use different-colored paper so that your sign stands out from the rest. But be careful that your paper color does not impair the clarity of your ink color.

Green ink on green paper makes for a very green but very unreadable sign. If you use green paper, make it light green — and make your ink a very dark color. Don't forget: your major purpose is to motivate prospective customers, and if they can't read your message, they can't be motivated.

I suggest that you visit a few places where signs are posted in your region and notice the clever ways people are utilizing this unique marketing method. When I look at the galaxy of

Take a field trip

signs on bulletin boards, I get the feeling that many entrepreneurs are true guerrillas. Of course, that is not necessarily true. Merely using such a method does not make one a guerrilla marketer. But a guerrilla marketer does seriously consider such a method when developing an overall marketing plan. And a true guerrilla doesn't think it is at all silly to combine radio advertising, newspaper advertising, and bulletin-board advertising in his or her marketing strategy. Would General Motors consider such a tactic? Is the Pope Buddhist?

Be sure to make your headlines large. Make plenty of signs. In fact, it's a good idea to make about ten at a time and staple them together. Tack the whole packet to a bulletin board and carefully letter the words "Take One" atop your signs. This way, people can not only read your sign but the serious prospects can take one home with them for future reference — and to pass it along to someone who is looking for a product or service exactly like yours.

If you place signs on ten different bulletin boards, be sure you engage in the same kind of research you would employ if you were testing any other type of marketing. Ask your customers, "Where did you learn of my business?" When they tell you that they saw your sign, ask, "Where did you see it?" This way, you'll be able to pinpoint your best sign-posting locations. The more you can home in on your most productive marketing methods including such subtleties as wording, sign color, sign location, and lettering style — the more successful you'll be.

It won't hurt for you to call some of the people who have posted signs in your area and ask about their effectiveness. Ask how long they've been posting signs, where they post them, whether the one you saw was typical, which locations seem best, and what success stories they may have heard. People are surprisingly open with information like this, and many enjoy being singled out as experts.

Interior signs require far more creativity than exterior signs, and you are allowed to use far more words. In fact, you are encouraged to.

Point-of-purchase signs are considered by those who use **P-O-P** them to be extremely effective because they create impulse sales. They also put forth extra selling energy and cross-merchandising opportunities. A person comes in to buy a pen, sees a sign that says briefcases are marked down, and buys a briefcase, too. That's cross-merchandising.

P-O-P signs make it easier for customers to locate and select products. They serve as silent salespeople, as aids to the actual salespeople. They demonstrate product features. P-O-P signs give customers product information, reinforce the ad campaign at the retail level, offer premiums and discounts, and actually generate sales all by themselves.

Many manufacturers offer free point-of-purchase materials to their customers. If you purchase from a manufacturer, you should ask if P-O-P materials are provided. If not, request some. Most manufacturers are happy to comply. They'll set you up with signs, brochures, display racks, window banners, display modules, counter cards, window cards, Plexiglas merchandisers, posters, display cases, stand-up signs, and more. Just ask.

The growth of in-store signs is causing the giant advertising agencies to change their attitudes toward this nonglamourous medium. They can't help but notice that during the 1980s, in-store media expenditures doubled, outgrowing more traditional vehicles such as television and print. The in-store sign industry is growing.

New video technologies are creating opportunities for in-store marketers. TV monitors are cropping up over product displays and store shelves, at checkout counters, and even on shopping trolleys. This very definitely is a happening medium. As a guerrilla, you can get in on the new technologies while the big guys are waiting around to see how well they work. Many new marketing weapons are ideal for guerrillas because of their low cost, nontraditional nature, and ability to let guerrillas market like the big dudes (and dudettes) before the biggies even get started.

In the 1980s, telephone marketing was an emerging marketing force, according to *Forbes* magazine, and it was right on the button. In the 1990s, *Adweek* claims that P-O-P is the emerging force. The reason for P-O-P advertising's popularity is its ability to connect mass media marketing with the consumer at the time of purchase. This makes it cost-effective. To give you an idea of the growing size of this market, the Point-of-Purchase Advertising Institute estimates that in 1991, $7.5 billion were spent making P-O-P materials, compared with $5.5 billion spent in 1981. Some surveys indicate that in the near future P-O-P materials will make up 80 percent of many advertisers' budgets.

Plan the sale when you plan the ad As I mentioned earlier, the basic rule in creating any advertising is to plan the sale when you plan the ad. That means that you shouldn't think in terms of a person reading your ad or hearing your commercial. Instead, think of the person at the moment of purchase. Is your message designed to motivate the potential customer at that crucial moment? By nature, almost all P-O-P marketing materials are. P-O-P signs get to people when the getting is good. They are there. They are in a buying mood. They are thinking in terms of the type of merchandise or service you offer. P-O-P advertising gives them many reasons to buy, or at least it should.

Many a smart guerrilla has run an ad, then blown it up into a five-foot-high poster, mounted it, and used it as a sign — inside the place of business, outside the place of business, and in the window. This is a way to market intelligently while saving lots of money, and it ensures that the interior signs will tie in with the ads.

What signs can do Interior signs can be used to encourage customers to touch your offering, taste it, try it out, and compare it with the competition, and also to explain complex points by means of clear graphics. Remember: 74 percent of all buying decisions are made right in the place of business, but even half that number would be impressive. It should cause any guerrilla to take the use of signs very, very seriously.

The Institute points out that today decisions to buy are less casual than they once were, and that people need to be convinced right there, at the point of sale. If your business is in a location where your customers will come to browse or buy, the Institute says you should consider your aisles to be your "trenches" where the true battle for customer dollars takes place. Since many battles are won or lost in the trenches, your point-of-purchase materials should be as potent as possible.

While the other marketing methods and materials create in the customer a desire to buy, as well they should, point-of-purchase signs promise instant rewards. Americans love instant gratification, if not faster. True guerrillas recognize that people patronize their businesses on purpose, not by accident. And they capitalize on the presence of prospects by using motivating, informative signs. Some have lengthy copy. Some have brief copy. Some go into detail about product features and benefits. Some contain lists of satisfied-customer testimonials. Some display ornate graphics. Some point out advantages of related merchandise. But each is there to move as much merchandise or sell as many services as possible.

Whenever possible, signs should be employed to pull the trigger on the gun already cocked by aggressive guerrilla marketing.

15

The Yellow Pages: Making Them Turn to Gold

IF YOUR BUSINESS IS ALREADY up and running, you probably know quite a bit about the Yellow Pages, having learned it from the Yellow Pages sales representative, not to mention real-life experience. But if your business has not yet started, it's a great idea to name it something that will appear as the first listing in its category in the Yellow Pages. For example, a new storage company called itself Abaco Storage. It didn't advertise, except in the Yellow Pages. Success came to the company that first year, and phone inquiries resulting from the first listing in the Yellow Pages were clearly responsible.

Must you be in the yellow pages? The first thing to decide is whether or not your business is the type that can benefit from yellow-page marketing. Do most people look there, as they do for storage companies, to find a product or service such as yours? If you are a retailer, chances are that people will consult the Yellow Pages directory and find out about you. But if you're an artist or a consultant, people will probably find out about you through other sources. Once you've decided you should be in the directory, determine which directory or directories. Will one be enough? Or, as is the case in large metropolitan areas, will you have to be in five or ten? The answer may be clearer after you've considered these findings by the Small Business Administration:

- The average independent store draws the majority of its customers from not more than a quarter of a mile away.
- The average chain store draws most of its customers from not more than three-quarters of a mile away.
- The average shopping center draws customers from as far away as four miles.

Furniture stores attract business from an average distance of ten miles away. One of my enterprises, Guerrilla Marketing International, draws business from throughout the nation. How about your enterprise? If you think you should run Yellow Pages ads in a number of directories, decide whether the ads in other areas should be as large as or smaller than your primary area ad. Decide whether you should have an advertisement or a listing. Decide whether the listing should be in dark, bold type or in regular type. My publishing business is listed in but one directory, in normal type. It is not the type of business that attracts Yellow Pages searchers. But some of my clients have large Yellow Page ads in three directories, small Yellow Page ads in five more directories, and bold-type listings in six other directories.

The cost for a large number of listings is assessed monthly, and it's steep. Find out the names of other companies in your business category and try to learn what percentage of their business each month comes from people who have located them through the Yellow Pages. I have some clients who obtain 6 percent of their business from people who first learned of them by consulting the Yellow Pages. Others obtain 50 percent of their business that way.

You must do the groundwork to see how, where, and whether you should make use of a strong Yellow Pages program. Now you know some questions to ask and answer. Here's another: in which categories in your Yellow Pages directory will you list yourself? For example, if you run a sleep shop in which you sell beds and bedroom furniture, should you list your shop under "Furniture," "Mattresses," or "Beds"?

Where do you list yourself?

Can you do with one listing, or do you need to pay for several? Answer: you'll probably have to list where people look. And they look in all three categories. One of life's necessary bummers.

A prime advantage A prime advantage of listing in the Yellow Pages is that you can appear as big as your biggest competitor, as large as the largest business of your type in town, and as well established as the oldest business of your type in town. Although directories differ, usually the largest space unit you can purchase is a full page. Since these are also the largest ad spaces available to your competition, you can appear equal in size. And you can take advantage of this by running a more powerful ad than your competition.

Some bright entrepreneurs, who realize that a great deal of their business comes from people who consult the Yellow Pages, spend the majority of their marketing budgets on this medium. But here's a crucial truth: unless you totally dominate your section of the Yellow Pages — I mean run the only large ad and the only good ad — you should never, in your advertising on radio and/or television, when directing people to your store or phone number, say "You'll find us in the Yellow Pages." If you do that, you will be spending your media dollars turning people on to your direct competitors.

Never direct them to the yellow pages

Believe me, many people innocently do that. They run a fine radio commercial, tell listeners to find them in the Yellow Pages, then sit back while nothing happens. Why? Because in the Yellow Pages, the listeners learn of several other places they can buy the product or service being advertised. Nope. If you don't appear as the clear choice within your category of the Yellow Pages, steer people away from the Yellow Pages. Tell people, "You'll find us in the phone directory." There, in the peace and quiet of the noncompetitive white pages, listeners and viewers can learn your phone number, your address, and even how you spell your name. And they'll not be aimed in the direction of any of your competitors.

Now that that's understood, let's talk about how you

must think of the Yellow Pages as a marketing vehicle, an advertising medium, an opportunity to sell. Many people think the Yellow Pages are merely a place to put their phone numbers in large type. Silly thinking. The Yellow Pages are an arena for attracting the business of active prospects. They are a place to confront prospects on a one-to-one basis. You are selling. Others are selling what you sell. The prospect is in a buying mood. Understand that opportunity, and you'll be able to create Yellow Pages ads that translate into sales.

Readers are in a buying mood

If you decide to run one large ad in the Yellow Pages directory for your locality, you may decide to run smaller ads in outlying directories. So you may need a large ad and a small ad. Maybe even more. At any rate, it's too expensive to run Yellow Pages ads that are poorly written. And most of them are. By putting a bit of thinking into the content of your ad, you can greatly increase your Yellow Pages response rate.

I'm familiar with a local business that was attracting 2 percent of its sales with Yellow Pages ads. Two percent isn't all that good, but it does represent a fair sum of money at the end of the month. So the business couldn't eliminate that particular marketing tool. Instead, it changed its ad copy. That's all. The result was a 600 percent increase in business from Yellow Pages ads. The store now drew 12 percent of its sales from people who first learned of it through those pages of yellow.

What accounted for this dramatic increase? The owner of this store, which carried a goodly selection of beds — by no means the largest in the area but big enough to enable her to promote her products seriously — understood the mind-set of Yellow Pages readers. She realized that people who consult the Yellow Pages are actively looking to find specific information. But she also realized that you can usually motivate people more effectively if you get them to agree with what you are saying — to the point where they say yes to questions you are asking.

The bed store owner asked a question to which the person

looking in the bed section of the Yellow Pages directory would always answer yes. The question was, "Looking for a bed?" Naturally, the answer was yes, and the reader read on. Whatever buttons the reader had regarding beds were intentionally pressed by the ad. The advertiser did not feel self-conscious about putting forth a lot of information. She also recognized the nature of the medium and actively sought the business of her prospective customers.

The answer must be yes

LOOKING FOR A BED?

Find the bed you want at the price you want.
Get it all — selection, reputation, and
expertise — at Oysterbed Sleep Shop,
Bay Area bed headquarters since 1970.

[illustration of three beds, fanned out]

- One of the Bay Area's largest selections
- Frames to fit any decor, any budget, to save space, too
- Wide variety of bedroom furniture, solid oak beds
- Delivery, expert installation, conscientious service
- All accessories, including linens, pillows, and spreads
- Visa, MasterCard, instant financing available

Giant Showroom:
1849 17th Street at deHaro
San Francisco
Free Parking

OYSTERBED Sleep Shop
626-4343

. . . unique, desirable, affordable

| Innerspring Beds | Platform Beds | Folding Beds | Foam Beds |
| Four-Poster Beds | Waterbeds | Bunk Beds | Sofabeds |

See the two-column by five-inch ad as it appeared in the San Francisco Yellow Pages. That other advertisers in the same directory used the same space to list their names, phone numbers, and little else is a good indication that if your offering is suitable for Yellow Pages advertising, you have a splendid opportunity.

If you use the Yellow Pages, here are the do's and don'ts: **The do's and don'ts**

- Do list a whole lot of facts about yourself.
- Do make your ad look and "feel" classier.
- Do treat it like a personal communication, not a cold listing.
- Do let folks know if you accept credit cards or can finance.
- Do gain the reader's attention with a strong headline.
- Do let people know all the reasons they should buy from you.
- Don't let the Yellow Pages people write your ad.
- Don't run small ads if your competitors run big ads.
- Don't make your ad look or sound boring.
- Don't forget to use graphics to communicate handsomely.
- Don't list your business in too many directories.
- Don't treat your ad less lightly than a full-page magazine ad.
- Don't hold back on the data; people are looking in the Yellow Pages for information. Give it to them, lots of it.

Lucky for you, the Yellow Pages are a misunderstood advertising medium. The Yellow Pages deserve your careful attention. But there is absolutely no reason why you *must* advertise there. If in doubt, read the Yellow Pages where you live and see what your competitors think about the whole idea.

Section III
Maxi-Media Marketing

MAXI-MEDIA MARKETING refers to the mass-market media, such as newspapers, magazines, radio, TV, billboards, and direct mail. Mistakes cost dearly in this area. The competition may be able to outspend you dramatically. For instance, the average cost to produce a television commercial in 1991 was in the neighborhood of $180,000. Some neighborhood. And that's for a thirty-second live-action commercial. You've got to add to that the cost of running the commercial, and running it often enough.

Don't be put off by that high number. It's high because of the fast-food chains, beer and soft-drink companies that spend lavishly to create a desire for what they make. Still, you should not think of maxi-media marketing as expensive. That is not the case. Expensive marketing is marketing that does not work. If you run one radio commercial on one local radio station and it costs you only $10, but nobody hears it or acts on it, you have engaged in expensive marketing. But if you've shelled out $10,000 to run one week's worth of advertising on a large metropolitan area radio station and you realize a profit that week of $20,000, you have engaged in inexpensive marketing. Cost has nothing to do with it. Effectiveness does.

When a guerrilla marketer uses the mass media, he or she does what is necessary to make them effective, therefore inexpensive. A guerrilla is not intimidated by the mass media but is fascinated by them, finds ways to use them with precision, carefully measures the results, makes them part of an overall marketing plan, and realizes that using them calls for a combination of science, art, intuition, and business acumen. A guerrilla knows what maxi-media marketing is all about: selling and creating a powerful desire to buy.

Since I first wrote this book, a marvelous revolution has taken place in maxi-marketing: it is now more affordable and more sensible for teeny-tiny companies than ever before. Responding to the growing number of small businesses — which comprise 98 percent of all businesses — the advertising media have bent over backward to attract business.

They have done this by offering far lower prices than ever before. TV costs have plummeted to where even George of Let George Do It can afford to go on the tube. Magazines and newspapers are now available on regional and zone editions. Radio stations offer extremely attractive package rates. Postcard decks have made direct mail extremely affordable and attractive to right-thinking guerrillas. The maxi-media are not only within your reach, but right up your alley because you can do what the big guys do without spending big to do it.

In truth, these are the golden years for entrepreneurs. They get to compete in arenas where their presence used to be unknown. They get to take on the big players when it comes to attracting the attention — and the disposable income — of the public.

Technology has changed so that breakthroughs such as desktop publishing, laser printing, satellite TV, cellular telephones, fax machines, voice-mail, and electronic mail are now beyond the stage of guerrilla engineers and into the arsenals of guerrilla marketers. Be aware of these technologies. Embrace them before the big corporations do. You're a guerrilla, lithe and agile. Your big competitors may be bright and wealthy, but they're moving through the molasses of their big-company bureaucracies — meetings, committees, reams of memos, and layers of decision making make them clumsy.

Be known for your quality, innovation, flexibility, and responsiveness to customer needs. Be known for epic service. Enter with confidence the world of the maxi-media. There has never been a better time to be a guerrilla. So go get 'em while the getting's good.

16

Newspapers: How to Use Them with Genius

WHETHER YOU'RE USING the mini-media, the maxi-media, or no media, as a guerrilla you should be aware of the changes always taking place in the marketplace. Because of the baby boom from 1946 to 1964, the median age is moving steadily upward. Soon it will exceed thirty-six. People are living longer as well. In fact, *Newsweek* accurately predicted that in the 1990s, the second biggest job opportunity will be in the field of geriatric social work (the biggest will be in industrial robot production). In the market of today — and tomorrow — the old will be older than they used to be.

Marketers must be aware of these trends as they begin to consider newspaper advertising. In most areas, a large number of newspapers are available. They all reach specific audiences. Which newspapers, which audiences, are best for you? Since there are metropolitan newspapers, national newspapers, local newspapers, shopper-oriented newspapers, classified-ad newspapers, campus newspapers, business newspapers, ethnic newspapers, and daily, weekly, and monthly newspapers to choose from, you can see that your work is cut out for you. You must make your selection skillfully.

Which newspapers are for you

By far the major marketing method used by small business is newspaper advertising. Of course your type of business may not benefit from business advertising. But if you think it may, pay close attention.

Newspapers offer a high degree of flexibility in that you can decide to run an ad or make changes in it up to a couple of days before the ad is to run. Radio gives you even more flexibility in that regard, allowing you to make changes up to the day your spot is to run. Magazines and television marketing allow you the least leeway.

If you don't have a clear-cut favorite newspaper — favorite being defined as most local and most appropriate for your **A newspaper** ads — there is a test you should use. Remember that there are **test** most likely far more newspapers in your region than you ever imagined. Run an ad in as many of the newspapers in your area as you can — there may be as many as thirty. Use coupons in your ads. Have each coupon make a different offer, such as $5 off or a free book or a 15 percent discount or a free plant. In the ad, request that the customer bring the coupon when coming to your place of business, or mention the coupon when calling you.

By measuring the responses, you'll soon see which newspapers work, which don't work, and which work best of all. You don't have to run ads in all thirty newspapers to learn which is the best paper. Maybe you'll only have to test in three or five or ten papers. But you are nuts unless you test. And be sure to determine what generated the customer's response — the offer or the newspaper. You can do this by means of a second test. Make a different offer in the most effective paper. If it still pulls well, you've got a horse to ride.

Don't forget, we're talking about advertising in terms of a conservative investment. So don't waste your money advertising in a paper that you happen to read or that your friends happen to recommend or that has a supersalesperson selling ad space. The paper you eventually select will be the one in which you advertise consistently. That paper is the one to which you will commit your marketing program, your regularly placed ad, your money, your hopes. So select with the highest care possible. The paper must have proven itself in your coupon test. It should be the one read by prospective customers in your marketing area. A monthly paper is not preferable. Use it, if you wish, but make sure your major newspaper is at least a weekly, if not a daily paper.

Marketing is part science and part art — and the art part is very subjective. The artistic end of marketing is not limited to words and pictures but also involves timing and media selection and ad size.

The importance of your ad's appearance is not to be underestimated. Far more people will see your ad than will see you or your place of business, so their opinion of your business will be shaped by your ad. Don't let the newspaper people design your ad, and don't let them write the copy. If they do, it will end up looking and sounding like all of the other ads in the paper. Your competition is not just the other people in your business, but everybody who advertises. **Your real competitors**

You're out there vying for the reader's attention with banks, airlines, car companies, cigarette companies, soft-drink companies, and who knows what else. So give your ad a distinct style. Hire a top-rate art director to establish the look for your ad. Later you can ask the paper to follow the design guidelines set down by that art director. But at first, either you or a talented friend or a gifted art director should make your advertising identity follow your marketing plan — and do so in a unique manner. You won't win customers by boring them into buying. You've got to create a desire. And a good-looking ad helps immeasurably, even measurably if you do your tracking. **Create your desire**

I must caution you that perhaps one in twenty-five newspapers has a first-class art department that can design ads with the best of the expensive graphics companies. Put another way, twenty-four out of twenty-five newspapers have art departments that can help you waste your marketing money by designing ordinary-looking ads. The same goes for copy. Newspapers will help write your copy — because they want you to advertise. Give your marketing money to charity instead. Or spend it on a great ad writer who can make your ad sing, motivate, cause people to sit up and say, "I want that." If you have a winning ad, your marketing money can be safely invested in newspapers with the expectation of a high return.

Select the type used in your ad for readability and clarity. Don't use any type size that is smaller than the type used by the paper. In fact, even type that size is too small. Make it easy for the reader to read your ad. If you decide to make your ad look different by having it appear in black with the type appearing in white (a process called reversing the type), be sure that the black ink doesn't spill over into the white letters, obliterating them. It happens every day. Don't let it happen to you. Newspapers are notorious for making good-looking ads come out faint and unreadable as a result of their particular printing process. Be sure that you or your art director check out your ad with people from the newspaper's production department to see if the ad will print well.

The right Then there's the matter of size. Of course, a full-page ad is
size ad probably best. But you won't want to pay for a weekly full-page ad, so you must make do with something smaller. What size can you comfortably afford?

Newspapers charge you by the line or by the inch. There are fourteen lines to the inch. If the newspaper charges, say, $1 per line, you are paying $14 per inch. If you want your ad to be fifteen inches high and three columns wide, you multiply $14 by fifteen, coming out with $210, then multiply that by three, for a total ad cost of $630. If you run an ad that size weekly, it will cost $2709 per month. (I multiplied the $630 by 4.3, because that's the approximate number of weeks per month.) If that charge is too high, you can run a smaller ad, one you can afford. Some people can run a weekly ten-inch ad (two columns by five inches) all year every year and enjoy a 25 percent sales increase each year. Other people want more of an increase, so they run a larger ad and run it two times a week. A lot depends upon the cost of advertising in the particular paper.

Most full-sized newspapers are twenty-two inches high. If you can afford it, run an ad that is twelve inches high or higher. That way, you'll be sure your ad is above the fold. Most full-sized newspapers are six columns wide. So you can be certain of dominating the page with a four-column by twelve-inch ad.

Dominating the page

That's a great tack, and if you use it you won't be wasting your money. But you can save a bit of money if you run a smaller ad with a powerful and unique border. An ad does not have to dominate a page to be seen. It merely has to interest the reader, then create a desire, then motivate the reader to do something you want him or her to do.

If you run your ad in a tabloid-sized newspaper rather than a full-sized newspaper, you can save money by running a smaller ad. A ten-inch ad seems a bit buried in a large newspaper, but it stands out in a tabloid. Many Sunday newspapers have tabloid-sized sections, and you can save money by using them. But don't use them just for that reason. Be sure that your prospects read that paper and that section.

What are the best days to run your ads? It differs with different towns and different businesses. Ask your local newspaper's space salesperson for a recommendation. Generally, Sunday is the day that the most people read the paper and spend the most time with it. But can your business succeed by running ads on days your doors are closed? Some businesses can. If yours can, give a nod to Sunday.

Run it on the right days

Monday is a pretty good day if your offering is directed to males, since many males read the Monday papers carefully because of all the sports events that went on the preceding weekend. Saturday is also a fairly good day, since many advertisers shy away from it and you'll have less competition. Some papers make Wednesday or Thursday their food day, so the papers are loaded with food and grocery ads.

You'll have to observe the papers yourself, then ask the person who will be selling the ad space to you. That ad space comes a lot cheaper if you sign a contract for a given number of lines or inches per year. Ask about the discounts you can receive for volume usage. They are quite substantial — a fringe benefit of consistent advertising in the same paper.

The best placement   In most cases, the best place to have your ad appear is as far to the front as possible, on a right-hand page, above the fold of the paper. But few, if any, papers will guarantee placement unless you sign a King Kong-sized contract. The main news section is also considered to be an optimum place for an ad, because of high readership by a large cross-section of the paper's circulation.

Because of the nature of your product, you may want to run your ad in the business section, the sports section, or the entertainment section. Run your ad where competitors run theirs. If you have no competition, run your ad where services or merchandise similar to yours are being offered. Why? Because that's where readers are conditioned to look for offerings such as yours.

Incidentally, readers most likely will read your ad, because study after study shows that newspaper readers read the ads almost as intensively as they read the stories. Because of the power of graphics, some ads attract more attention than the actual news stories. Use graphics in your ad, but go easy. Generally, more than three or four pictures — whether art or photography — is too many. But that's a rule that is both useful to know and useful to break. I've broken it successfully more than once. I've also run very successful ads that have only one illustration or photo.

When selecting your newspaper, You of course want to know its circulation. And you also want to know if the paper's circulation is in your marketing area. Otherwise you'll be paying for wasted circulation. A good thing to keep in mind is that when you hear a circulation figure, you can multiply it by three and learn how many people are actually reading the paper. When a family has a subscription to the paper and two adults and three kids read each issue, that only gets counted as one subscriber. When a woman buys a copy of the paper to read on the bus on her way home and her husband reads it when she arrives home, that, too, gets counted as one reader, according to circulation statistics. So newspaper circulation figures are one of the few marketing statistics that are understated.

If you have a truly good ad — one that tells all the features and benefits of your offering — consider making multiple reprints of it and using them as circulars, customer handouts, mailing pieces, or interior signs. They cost very little, and most of their cost was spent when you had the ad produced. And remember, you can blow up the ad and make it into a poster.

Reprint your ade

Don't forget that many people newspaper shop before they buy. That is, they scan the papers before going out to purchase a product. Keep that in mind when running your ads. If your product is aimed at a particular group of people, such as businesspeople, consider running your ad in a business paper rather than a metropolitan paper. If your offering is geared to discount hunters, run your ad in shopper-oriented papers. If it will appeal to college kids, advertise it in the campus paper. A finished newspaper marketing plan usually calls for ads in a number of papers, some primary, others secondary. The combination you choose can be the key to your fortune. You want to obtain exceptional results from both primary and secondary newspapers. Exceptional results mean many sales. And many sales come from many inquiries, be they in the form of phone calls, visits to your place of business, or even letters.

To increase the number of inquiries you receive through newspaper advertising, first and always remember to put your name and primary message continually in front of readers. In addition, put the following tips into action:

Tips for succesful newspaper ads

1. Mention your offer in your headline.
2. Emphasize the word *free* and repeat it when possible.
3. Restate your offer in a subhead.
4. Show a picture of your product or service in action.
5. Include testimonials when applicable.

6. Do something to differentiate yourself from others who advertise in the newspaper. That means all others — not just your direct competitors.

7. Say something to add urgency to your offer. It can be a limited-time offer. It can be a limited-quantities offer. Get those sales now.

8. Put a border around your ad, if it is a small ad. Make it a unique border.

9. Be sure your ad contains a word or phrase set in huge type. Even a small ad can "act" big if you do so.

10. Always include your address, specific location, and phone number. Make it easy for readers to find you or talk with you.

11. Create a visual look that you can maintain every time you advertise. This clarifies your identity and increases consumer familiarity.

12. Experiment with different ad sizes, shapes, days run, and newspaper sections.

13. Consider free-standing inserts in your newspaper. These are increasingly popular and may be less expensive than you imagine.

14. Try adding a color to your ad. Red, blue, and brown work well. You can't do this with tiny ads, but it may be worth trying with a large ad.

15. Test several types of ads and offers in different publications until you have the optimum ad, offer, and ad size. Then run the ad with confidence.

16. Be careful with new newspapers. Wait until they prove themselves.

17. Do everything in your power to get your ad placed in the front section of the paper on a right-hand page above the fold. Merely asking isn't enough. You may have to pay personal visits. Be a squeaky wheel.

18. Don't be afraid of using lengthy copy. Although lengthy copy is best suited for magazines, many successful newspaper advertisers employ it.

19. Run your ad in the financial pages if you have a business offer, in the sports pages if you have a male-oriented offer, in the women's pages for household services and products, in the food pages for food products. The astrology page usually gets the best readership. But in general, the main news section is still the best location for ads.

20. Study the ads run by your competitors, especially their offers. Make yours more cogent, more concise, sweeter, different, better.

21. Keep close records of the results of your ads. Experimenting doesn't mean a thing if you don't keep track of the experiments.

22. Be sure your ad is in character with your intended market.

23. Be sure your ad is in character with your product or service.

24. Be sure your ad is in character with the newspaper in which you advertise.

25. Try to use short words, short sentences, short paragraphs.

26. Don't put your address on a coupon only. If you use a coupon, have your address appear on it and outside of it, so that if the coupon gets clipped, your address will appear anyhow.

27. Use photos or illustrations that reproduce faithfully in newspapers.

28. Always put the name of your company somewhere at the bottom of your ad. Don't expect people to get the name from the copy, the headline, the picture of the product, or the picture of the storefront. Still, putting your name into your headline is generally a good idea. At least put it in the subhead.

29. Say something timely in your ad. Remember, people read papers for news. So your message should tie in with the news when it can.

30. Ask all of your customers where they heard about you. If they do not mention the newspaper, ask them directly: "Did you see our newspaper ad?" Customer feedback will be invaluable for you.
31. Aim your ad, in most cases, to people who are in the market for your offering *right now*.
32. If you're not going to use newspapers solely as a support medium, that is, to support your other marketing efforts, be sure you use them weekly or stay away from them altogether. Occasional use doesn't cut it.

These tips, your common sense, the quality of newspapers in your community, the newspaper production department, the newspaper representative calling upon your business, and the presence or absence of your competitors in the newspaper should be prime considerations in your decision to include or exclude newspapers from your guerrilla marketing mix.

17

Magazine Advertising: Its Value to Entrepreneurs

WHOEVER HEARD OF A small-time entrepreneur advertising in well-known and respected national magazines? You have now. Magazine advertising has been the linchpin for many a successful small business. Remember, the single most important reason people patronize one business over another is confidence. And magazine advertisements breed confidence by instilling familiarity and giving credibility. *A properly produced magazine ad, preferably of the full-page variety, gives a small business more credibility than any other mass marketing medium.*

The credibility factor

Consumer confidence will not necessarily be gained from one exposure to your magazine ad. But if you run the ad one time, you can use the reprints of that ad for ever. One highly successful company ran a single regional ad in only a single issue of *Time* magazine, then used reprints of the ad (reprints are available at a fraction of a cent each) in its window and on its counter for more than fifteen years after the ad had run. Reprints were also sent in direct mailings. Even mailings in 1993 can contain an ad reprint saying "As seen in *Time* magazine" — heavy-duty name-dropping from an ad run one time back in 1973. Now that's getting mileage out of magazine advertising. Several bright entrepreneurs have run an ad one time in a regional edition of a national magazine, then mailed out reprints in all future direct mailings — each time gaining for their products the confidence that prospects ordinarily placed in the magazine itself.

You see, that's the whole point of magazine advertising for small businesses. It gives them a great deal of credibility. And credibility creates confidence, which translates to sales. And profits. If people feel that *Time* magazine is reliable, credible, trustworthy, and solid, they will feel those same things about the companies that advertise in *Time*. So if you wish to gain instant credibility, advertise in magazines that can give it to you.

If you run a small display ad for a mail-order venture in a national publication, you should do as much testing as possible. An inexpensive method of testing is to avail yourself of the split runs offered by many magazines. By taking advantage of them, you can test two headlines. Send your two ads to the publication, being certain to code each ad for response so that you'll be able to tell which of the two headlines pulls better, and ask the publication to split-run the ads. One headline will run in half the magazines printed; the other headline will run in the other half.

Test as you go with split runs

For example, a manufacturer of exercise equipment once ran a split-run ad with a coupon. One headline said STRENGTHEN YOUR WRISTS FOR BETTER GOLF! and the other said STRENGTHEN YOUR WRISTS IN ONLY 2 MINUTES A DAY! The coupon in the first ad was addressed to Lion's Head, 7230 Paxton, Dept. G6A, Chicago, Illinois 60649, and the coupon in the second ad was addressed to Lion's Head, 7230 Paxton, Dept. G6B, Chicago, Illinois 60649. Even though the coupons looked alike, it was easy for the advertiser to tell that the appeal of two minutes a day was far stronger than the appeal of better golf, even though the advertiser had guessed ahead of time that the golf headline would attract the better response. How could the advertiser tell that his guess was wrong? Because the responses to Dept. G6B ran four times higher than those to Dept. G6A. Incidentally, the advertiser could also tell by referring to those responses that they came from *Golf* magazine (G) and that they were in answer to an ad run in June (6). So the code allowed the advertiser to tell three things: the publication, the month run, and which of the two ads drew the best response.

Coding can be even more complex so as to tell you the year, the ad size, and other information. Some publications allow you to do a triple-split run and not just a double, enabling you to test three headlines rather than two. If you can test three headlines, do it. Let your audience make your judgments for you whenever possible. After you count up the coded responses, you will know which headline is best. And the cost of the test itself will have been minimal. The magazine's split-run capability will have saved money for you while giving you valuable information. Now you can run the successful ad with boldness and confidence. **Measuring by coding**

Don't count yourself out of advertising in national publications because of the cost. You can cut down on that cost by establishing an in-house advertising agency, by purchasing remnant space, and by purchasing a tiny space unit — say, one column by two inches. Or you can advertise in the classified section that is available in many national magazines. Also, many magazines offer enticing discounts to mail-order advertisers. And virtually all magazines offer impressive merchandising materials: easel-back cards, reprints, decals with the name of the magazine (for example, "as seen in *Time*"), and mailing folders. The magazine's advertising sales representative will be happy to tell you about all of the merchandising aids offered. Be sure you take advantage of them. They will be useful at your place of business, in your window (if you have one), and in other advertising you do. **Merchandising aids**

Your business will be helped if you simply mention "You've probably seen our ad in *Woman's Day* magazine." And these materials can be used as enclosures in direct mailings, as enclosures with personal letters, as signs on bulletin boards, as counter cards, as display pieces at trade shows, exhibits, or fairs, and as part of a brochure or circular. The cost of these powerful guerrilla marketing aids is ridiculously low, sometimes even free, so use them to the fullest extent. Magazines can help you market your offering immediately and well into the years ahead. It's the years-ahead part that's going to result in profitable business for you.

When the waterbed industry was in its infancy, growth was dramatically spurred when Chemelex, a manufacturer of waterbed heaters, ran full-page ads in *Time, Newsweek*, and *Sports Illustrated*. Chemelex then distributed reprints of the ads to retailers throughout the country. The retailers prominently displayed the ads throughout their showrooms, and the industry grew to the point where it turned from a hippie-image industry into a steady $2 billion per year furniture-image industry. One reason: the instant credibility gained by advertising in highly credible publications.

Magazine advertising offers other attractive advantages. **Target your market** You can target your market much better with magazines than with newspapers. Instead of reaching a general circulation, you can reach people who have demonstrated an interest in skiing, gardening, do-it-yourselfing, or you name it. This results in very little waste circulation. Everyone who sees your ad is a prospect. And one of the basic tenets of guerrilla marketing is to talk primarily to prospects and not to browsers.

A good guerrilla marketer also considers advertising in magazines other than consumer magazines. There is a whole **Don't forget trade magazines** world of trade magazines out there. Almost every trade and profession has its own publication or, more likely, group of publications. Because you want to home in on prospects, you should consider advertising in some of these trade publications, because they are subscribed to and read cover to cover by large numbers of prospective customers. This is especially true if your product is at all business oriented.

So go to your library, locate a copy of *Business Rates and Data* (also known as BRAD) and look through it. Try to find publications in which you might advertise your products or services. You'll find many, many magazines you've never heard of, and quite a few may be read by prospective buyers of what you sell. If you find a couple of magazines (newspapers are also listed) that might be right, send away for sample copies. I predict that you'll be pleasantly surprised at the large number of marketing opportunities available to you in trade publications. You may find entrepreneurs with whom you can team up for greater sales. You may realize that you ought to be advertising in some of these publications. And you will learn a lot of inside information about your type of business. Most likely, you'll want to subscribe to at least one trade magazine just to keep abreast of new developments in your field.

Another important advantage of advertising in magazines is you can use color much more effectively than you can in newspapers. If your offering is oriented to color — if you are marketing fabrics, for instance — consider advertising in magazines just to show off the hues and tones. Magazines are better suited to lengthy copy than any other medium. The reason is that people buy magazines with the idea of spending time with them, unlike newspapers, which are read quickly for news. Magazines involve their readers, and your ads may do the same.

The colorful guerrilla

It has been over twenty years that many major magazines have been available to minor advertisers, but most small business owners are oblivious to the fact. Guerrillas avail themselves of these major magazine opportunities and all of their merchandising aids as a key to successful marketing. For at the same time that it gives you credibility within your community, it gives you respect in the minds of your sales staff, your suppliers, and even your competitors.

If you're a thinking entrepreneur, you'll utilize magazines in several ways. You will advertise regularly in a magazine that hits your target audience right on the nose. You will advertise only one time in a prestige magazine, so as to use its merchandising aids. You will use the classified sections of national magazines if you are in the mail-order business. And you will use the display sections of national magazines if what you have to sell is too big for the classified sections or if your

Using magazines properly

chosen magazine runs no classified ads.

It may be that you want to advertise in a national magazine because of the status, the huge circulation, and the easily identifiable audience, but do not have the money for a large-enough ad. No problem. In that case, use a two-step process. You might also consider *marketing with your own magazine*. In a fusion marketing effort with three or four other companies with the same types of prospects, you can produce your own beautiful, glossy magazine, replete with elegant photos, stylish writing, and fancy paper stock.

Your own magazine

To make this magazine work for you and your marketing collaborators — who each have several full-page ads in the magazine and are the only advertisers — you must mail it to a carefully selected audience, consisting mostly of your customers and those of your fusion partners. Your identity will be impressively conveyed through the editorial material, the style, and the ads. The readers will develop a tighter bond with you, much tighter than if you had invested this money in mere advertising. The cost of this endeavor is high — nearly a dollar per reader. This figure is based upon 100,000 copies of the magazine, about $25,000 each for you and your three other fusion partners. The same reader that costs you one dollar by this advertising method costs you only half a cent for a full-color, full-page ad in a standard magazine. But that's like comparing apples with emeralds.

With your own magazine, you have total control of the editorial environment, can run as many ads as you want, and can eliminate ads by competitors. This idea is already being used by MCI, Federal Express, Benetton, and others. Is it cheap? No way. Is it guerrilla-like? If you do it with fusion partners, it is. You don't have to be a big guy to market with big ideas.

If you are practicing guerrilla marketing to the hilt, you will mention your nations magazine advertisements in the other media you use: on the radio, in your direct-mail advertisements, on your signs, in your Yellow Pages ads, in your personal letters, in your telemarketing — wherever you can.

Guerrillas excel at *doing the two-step*. Step one is to have a magazine (or any publication) run a small display (or classified) ad that hits the high points of your offering, then tells readers to call or write for *free* information. When they respond, send them your brochure and a motivating sales letter (step two). Follow up with still another letter if they do not order. Consider selling or renting their names to mailing-list brokers. These people buy and sell or rent names and addresses of many different types of consumers. Find them in your Yellow Pages under "Mailing Lists." The two-step process lets you tell your entire story but does not entail the high costs of large-space advertising. It also gives you a large number of salable names, and you can be sure these are valuable names for your own mailing list.

Do the two-step

This two-step process worked for an entrepreneur friend of mine after the running of a large ad failed. In the classified section of *Psychology Today*, he ran a classified display ad telling readers that they could earn a legitimate college degree — B.A., M.A., or Ph.D. — right from their homes. Then he told them that they could secure free details about the offer by writing to him. My friend later told me that he made a great deal of money with this two-step process, but that it was twice as much work as the one-step process that I was employing at the time to advertise the free-lancing book I had written and published myself. Soon he was able to employ someone to handle the detail work for him, and his two-step ads continue to run in *Psychology Today* as well as in more than thirty other publications. It has been over eighteen years since the first ad ran.

I tell you this story to emphasize that if you come up with a winning magazine ad, you may be able to run it in a multitude of magazines. The result of this can be a multitude of profits. You can run your proven money-maker for years and years in a wide selection of publications. To a guerrilla, few marketing situations are as delightful.

But the prime reason for using magazines is the lasting value of the ad. I recall placing a full-page ad in *Newsweek* for a client. After the ad was run, the client asked each customer where he or she had heard of his company. At the end of one week, only five people claimed to have seen his ad in *Newsweek*, where it had run only one time. At the end of one month, that number climbed to eighteen people. And after a full year, a total of sixty-three customers said they had first heard of the company through its ad in *Newsweek*. And that's not even the impressive part! The really significant aspect of this story is that the entrepreneur blew up a reprint of the ad to the size of an enormous poster — five feet high — then mounted it and placed it outside his place of business. Thousands of customers patronized his business because of that huge poster.

Newsweek turned out to be his most effective advertising medium that year — and yet he placed but one ad there. To make matters even more wonderful, the *Newsweek* page was purchased at less than half the going rate, because it was remnant space. The magazine had sold three full-page ads to regional advertisers and had one page left over — a remnant. So my client was able to buy the space for a fraction of its original price.

If you are interested in advertising in any particular magazine, call the representative of the magazine and say that you are definitely a candidate for any remnant space and that you should be phoned when it is available. You may wait a bit, but it will be well worth the wait. Do Coca-Cola and AT&T practice this tactic? No. But do successful guerrilla marketing people practice it? You bet their bank balance they do!

Most small-business owners never even consider advertising in magazines. That's because they don't know about remnant space, in-house agency discounts, the two-step process, and valuable merchandising aids. Now that you do know about these lovely aspects of magazine advertising, give serious consideration to the medium.

18

Radio: It Costs a Lot Less Than You Think

UNLESS YOU HAVE A GOOD friend who owns a radio station, most of your radio marketing will be of the paid, rather than free, variety, though remember, in 1991, 55 percent of all media was obtained via barter, according to the head of one of the nation's largest media-buying services. It is possible to have stories or interviews about your product or service on the radio, and it may be that those will cost you nary a cent. In chapter 26, we'll go into ways of obtaining free publicity on the radio and in other maxi-media. But as far as this chapter is concerned, you'll have to pay or trade for your radio marketing. For purposes of simplicity, let's talk paying.

Although newspapers are the primary marketing media for most small businesses, and direct mail has taken over second place, radio does come in a strong third. Radio advertising can be used effectively by a company with a limited budget. And radio can help improve your aim when you're trying to reach your target consumers. Radio helps you establish a very close relationship with your prospects. Because of its intimate nature, it brings you even closer to them than newspapers do. The sound of an announcer's voice, the type of musical background, the sound effects you use to punctuate and enhance your message — all of these are ammunition in your radio marketing arsenal. All can help win customers and sales for you.

Radio is intimate

Although it is true that you can, if you try, pay $450 for a single thirty-second radio commercial on a large commercial radio station, you can also, if you try, pay $5 for a single radio commercial on a smaller, less popular station. You'll certainly talk to far more people with the $450 spot. But you'll be talking to more than a few people with your $5 commercial.

Now don't think that you can spend $5 and feel that you are involved in radio marketing. But if you spend $5 times five spots per day ($25), and you run your spots four days a week ($100), three weeks out of four, you may be able to say that for $300 a month you are adequately covering the listener profile in the community that particular radio station covers.

Because radio listeners are notorious button pushers and change stations a lot, you're probably going to have to run radio spots on more than one station. This is a rule to know and to break. But make sure you know it. One station does not a radio campaign make.

How many stations? How many stations do you need? Well, you may really need only one. But you'll probably need three or four or five. It may also be that you have the type of offering that lends itself so well to radio that you'll need no other ad media and can dive headlong into advertising on ten stations. Some of my clients have. One of the advantages to being on so many stations is that by carefully tracking your audience response — that is, learning which stations are bringing in the business — you can eliminate the losers and narrow your radio marketing down to proven winners. You can also use the coupon-type testing we explored in the chapter on newspapers. That means you pick, say, five stations and run commercials on all five. In each commercial, make a different offer — money off, free gift, 50 percent reduction — and ask listeners to mention the offer when they contact you. By keeping assiduous track of the offers mentioned by your customers, you'll know which stations to drop (maybe all of them) and which to continue with (maybe all of them).

Unless you really keep track of all of your media responses, you are not a guerrilla. If you run your ads and keep selecting media on blind faith, you are closer to a lemming. You've got to make your marketing as scientific as possible. This is one of those rare instances where you can measure the effectiveness of your media scientifically. Avail yourself of it.

If you have salespeople, ask them to track responses. If you're the person taking orders from customers, then you must track responses. Ask the customers, "Where did you hear of us first?" If they say radio, ask, "Which station?" If they name a station that you don't use, ask, "Which stations do you ordinarily listen to?" If that doesn't net a solid response, prompt the customer, naming a few stations, one of which you use. It's a drag to do this, but it's a bigger drag to waste marketing money and bankrupt a business. Do everything you can to learn which stations are pulling in customers and which are not. After you've been marketing seriously for a year or three, you can cut down on your media tracking, though I do not suggest that you do. If you start learning for sure which stations pull best, you may feel that you need no longer ask. But until you are certain, you must ask. Because stations and people change, it is a good idea to keep track constantly.

There are many types of radio stations: rock and roll, rap, middle of the road, country, public, all news, talk show, drama, religious, black, top forty, bubble-gum rock, jazz, oldies, intellectual, avant-garde, local interest, farm-oriented, progressive rock, reggae. Which are most likely to be listened to by your audience? Although it is possible to divide radio stations into categories, as I have just done, it is first advisable to divide them into two categories — background stations and foreground stations. **What kind of stations?**

Some radio stations play *background* programming. That means they play music that is generally a background sound. People talk, converse, work, play, iron, cook, and do myriad other things with background radio sounds. The music does not get in the way, does not command attention, does not distract. Unfortunately, because people are not actively **Background vs. foreground radio** listening, the commercials are also in the background. Oh, sure, when a person is driving home with the radio on, all alone, the commercials — and the music — move up from the background. But in general, all music stations are background radio stations. And many music lovers have cassette tape decks in their cars, not to mention their homes.

All radio stations that are sports, religion, all news, or all talk are *foreground* radio stations. They are in the foreground of people's consciousness. They command attention. They do distract. They are poor stations to have on during a conversation, during work, during situations that require your concentration. As a result, the commercials that are broadcast on them are likely to attract more active listeners. These people pay **Active** closer attention to commercials because they are actively **listeners are** listening to the radio. They don't have it on some back burner **best** of their mind, as is the case with background radio. This is not to say that foreground radio is better than background radio for advertising. But I do want you to be aware of the difference between the two.

There are other differences as well. Talk radio is hosted by "personalities" more than music radio is. All music radio requires is a person to say what music just played and what music is about to play, though sometimes this is on tape. Talk radio requires more listener rapport, more informal chatter, more personal asides.

A guerrilla Here's a guerrilla tactic that works gloriously well on **radio tactic** foreground stations when it is appropriate. Suppose you have a new company that sells, say, computer instruction. Invite a talk radio personality to take a few lessons. Then buy time on that personality's station. Rather than give him a sixty- or thirty-second script for your commercial, which you might ordinarily do, give him an outline — and invite him to ad-lib as much as he wants. The result is usually a sincere commercial, far longer than the commercial for which you have contracted, that has loads of credibility. If your product or service is worth raving about, you can count on most personalities to give it their all. You only have to pay for a sixty-second spot, but you may end up with a three minute spot at no extra cost.

That is about the only instance in which I'd advise you to put your message into the hands of the radio station. In virtually all other instances, I suggest that you have the radio station play recorded commercials, which you can tape either at an independent facility or at the station itself. Don't make the mistake of furnishing scripts to the station. Although some of their announcers may do a great job of reading them, other announcers may make mincemeat out of them, reading them with no conviction, no enthusiasm, but with oodles of errors. Murphy's law has a way of asserting itself at radio stations: If the commercial can be messed up, it will be. Protect yourself by furnishing finished tapes only — unless you can get a personality to breathe true life into your script.

Just as it is bad business to let a newspaper write your newspaper ad copy, it is also a grave error to let a radio station write your radio ad copy. Most stations will be all too willing to volunteer. Don't let them. They will have the script written by someone not quite good enough to be paid as a writer, who will, by force of habit, make your commercial sound just like everyone else's commercials. One of the most asinine methods of saving money is to let the station write your advertising. They'll do a C+ job for you and, as a guerrilla, you need an A+ if you're going to commit to a medium.

Who writes your commercial?

If the station offers to produce your spot, that's a different story. Check out their equipment. Probably it is all right. Listen to their announcers. If you trust their equipment — as measured by the sound of finished commercials produced on it — and you like one or more of their announcers, let the station voice and produce the commercial on tape for you. Generally there is either no charge or just a tiny charge for this service. And in most cases, but not all cases, it is worth the price.

Should you run thirty-second spots or sixty-second spots?

Thirties and sixties

A thirty-second spot is usually far more than 50 percent of the cost of a sixty-second spot. But in most instances, what you can say in sixty seconds can also be expressed in thirty seconds. So go with the shorter spots even though they are not great values. In the long run, they'll give you more bang for your budget. If, however, you have a complex product or service, you'll just have to run a full sixty-second spot. Some advertisers achieve superb results with two-minute commercials. So take as long as you must to state your message; but make it thirty seconds if possible.

A long-time radio pro once told me that if he had to cut 33 percent of his radio advertising budget, but could spend that 33 percent on a music track for his commercials, he'd gladly **Music hath** do it. He believes that the presence of music lends a powerful **charms** emotional overtone to the commercial. And I agree. Music can convey what words frequently cannot. And music can be obtained very inexpensively. You can rent it from the station's rights-free music library. You can have a music track made by hungry musicians who will record a track for very little money, appreciating the exposure they will receive. Or you can purchase an expensive music track — made expressly for you or taken from a hot record — and use it so much that the amortized cost is mere peanuts.

I know an entrepreneur who made a deal with a composer who had recently released a record album. The entrepreneur, upon learning that the cost of the particular music he liked was $3000, said that he'd pay the composer $100 per month for a full year. If, at the end of that time, he was still in business and wanted the music, he would then pay $3000 in addition to the rental fees he had paid. If he had not made it in business, he would merely be out the rental fees and the composer would still have the music. It sounded like a fair deal for both parties, so the composer agreed. At the end of one year, the composer did receive his $3000, in addition to the $1200 he had earned for renting out his music. His total gain was $4200. The entrepreneur, who at the time could barely afford the $100 rental, later could easily afford the $3000. Result: everyone came out a winner.

If you have to use announcers and musicians who are members of the various unions, such as equity, be wary. Union costs and paperwork are overwhelming, and you might be better off doing all in your power to avoid unions. I only work with unions when I absolutely must. And when I do, I have all the paperwork handled by an independent party. Unions and guerrillas mix like gasoline and fire.

As music adds new dimensions to your selling message, so too do sound effects. Use them when you can, and remember that radio stations (and most production facilities) have libraries of them and rent them at nominal costs. Just be careful you don't get carried away with their use.

When writing your commercials, keep in mind that you have but three seconds to catch and hold the attention of the listener. So be interesting during those first three seconds and say what you have to say, lest the listener's attention stray elsewhere. Be sure you use "ear" words rather than "eye" words, and whatever you do, repeat your main selling point. Also, repeat your company name as many times as you comfortably can.

Three crucial seconds

A successful way of putting together radio commercials is to put the president of the company into a recording booth and interview him or her. Let the interview go on for twenty or thirty minutes, or even longer. Then use small sections of the interview as ingredients — sound bites — in future commercials. Sound bites are ideas expressed, simply and briefly, in a short time. The concept was spawned for the political process by public relations pros, who themselves are named "spin doctors" by the media. This is based upon their ability to give the proper "spin", or public perception, to the activities of the firms they represent. Spin doctors can create the perception that an oil company is a group of ardent environmentalists. As a guerrilla, you can be your own spin doctor, selecting your own sound bites from the interview for your

marketing. It's important to remember that trust is the key —
you never want to be *perceived* as a spin doctor; you only want
to put the right "spin" on your marketing. Your use of selected
interview sound bites must come across as different, believable, and best of all, allow the president of the company (you?)
to go out on a limb publicly — a good idea.

A rich, meaty spot that worked The following script is reprinted not because it won Radio
Commercial of the Year honors in Chicago, but because it
successfully sold dog food at a not very generous savings. It
is a sixty-second spot and cost very little to produce.

ANNOUNCER:	Ladies and gentlemen! The makers of Perk dog food — the rich, meaty, energy-giving, delicious dog food — now bring you one minute of rich, energy-giving, delicious ... *silence.*
SOUND:	(*Five seconds of silence*)
MAN:	(*Whisper*) Aren't you going to say anything about the big Perk sale?
ANNOUNCER:	(*Whisper*) Shhh! This is supposed to be silence!
SOUND:	(*Four seconds of silence*)
MAN:	(*Whisper*) Won't you even remind people that if they buy three cans of Perk dog food during the sale, they get five cents off?
ANNOUNCER:	(*Whisper*) Quiet!
SOUND:	(*Four seconds of silence*)
MAN:	(*Whisper*) But this is important! Aren't you —
ANNOUNCER:	(*Whisper*) Will you be quiet!!
MAN:	(*Whisper*) Yes, but —
ANNOUNCER:	(*Whisper*) I mean now!
MAN:	(*Whisper*) Yes, but the big Perk sale! You've got to say something about how now is the time to stock up on Perk because people can get five cents off when they buy three cans!
ANNOUNCER:	(*Whisper*) I'm not going to say a word! Now quiet!

MAN:	(*Whisper*) Then I'm going to say something —
ANNOUNCER:	(*Loud whisper*) Keep away from that microphone!
MAN:	(*Loud whisper*) Listen, everyone ... (*Louder*) Perk is having a big sale, and —
SOUND:	(*Scuffling and fighting sounds. Man yells "Oof!"*)

That was a humorous commercial and the humor worked to gain attention. In a more serious vein (and even more economical because it uses one announcer instead of two), here's a straightforward spot as it might be broadcast, in thirty seconds, for a service-oriented entrepreneur:

MALE VOICE: (*Over music*) If you dislike the inconvenience of driving your car to a mechanic, you'll like the convenience of having the Mobile Mechanic drive to your car and fix it while you're relaxing at home. If you're not happy with the price of having your car tuned up at a garage, you'll be very happy with the bargain price of having your car tuned up at home by the Mobile Mechanic. Keep your car in top shape, conveniently and economically, Call the Mobile Mechanic. Find him in your local phone directory. The Mobile Mechanic. Call him.

Although most announcers can easily fit seventy words into a thirty-second spot, studies indicate that people listen more attentively if the announcer talks faster and crams more words into a short space. Thank Columbia University for making that study and giving speed talk a shot in the arm, and remember it when making your commercials. A few radio hints for guerrillas:

Speed talk

- Save money by running ads three weeks out of every four, not all four.
- Concentrate your spots during a few days of the week,

Radio hints for guerrillas

such as Wednesday through Sunday.

- The best time to run radio advertising is during afternoon drive time, when people are heading home. They're in more of a buying mood than during morning drive time, when work is on their minds.

- When listening to the radio commercials you have just produced, be sure you listen to them on a car-radio-type speaker, not on a fancy high-fidelity speaker like those production studios use. Many an advertiser, dazzled after hearing his commercial on an expensive speaker system, has become depressed when hearing what the commercials really sound like on the type of sound system most people have in their cars.

- Consider radio rate cards to be pure fiction. They are highly negotiable.

- Study the audiences of all the radio stations in your marketing area. Then match your typical prospect with the appropriate stations. It's not difficult.

How much can radio do? Unless you simply cannot see your way to using radio, do give it a try. You'll appreciate its flexibility, its ability to allow you to make last-minute changes, and the way you can home in on your prospects on the basis of station format, time of day and day of the week. I have a client, very successful, who owns a furniture store. Although he uses many marketing media — newspapers, Yellow Pages, billboards, point-of-purchase signs, and direct mail — he spends 90 percent of his marketing money on radio advertising. With such a high concentration of dollars in just one medium, does he qualify as a true guerrilla? He sure does!

He has learned through the years that radio reaches his exact audience and motivates them to come into his store. He runs his commercials on anywhere from six to ten stations, and he often runs the same commercial fifteen times in one day. What's more, he's never off the radio, using it fifty-two weeks per year. Because he has learned how to use this medium to the benefit of his bottom line, he is a true guerrilla marketer. After experimenting with all kinds of marketing mixes, he finally decided that radio was the medium for him. He uses it a lot. He uses it with music. He uses it consistently. And he makes so much money that he is now able to live a luxurious life in Hawaii while his business, located in the Midwest, continues to flourish. Although many factors are responsible for his success, he gives most of the credit to radio advertising. He is living proof that you can prosper in style even as a one-medium guerrilla. But things rarely work out that way.

19

Television: How to Use It, How Not to Abuse It

ALTHOUGH TELEVISION IS THE MOST EFFECTIVE of all marketing vehicles, the undisputed heavyweight champion, it is also the most elusive and easiest to misuse. It is elusive because it is not as simple as it seems, because it requires many talents, because it is not normally associated with small business-people, and because it is dominated by giants who give entrepreneurs a mistaken impression of how it should be used. Just remember: you cannot use TV as Coca-Cola and McDonald's use it unless you have their money. But you can use it. It is easy to misuse because it does seem straightforward, because almost anyone can afford to run one or two television commercials, because it is readily available, because it is the medium that strokes the entrepreneur's ego the most tantalizingly, and because it requires a whole new discipline. Television is not, as some believe, radio with pictures.

But television has changed in many ways, all of them favoring guerrillas. The cost has plummeted to where a thirty-second commercial in prime time runs around $20 even in major markets. The targeting ability has improved to where you can run commercials in specific regions. The options have broadened to where satellite and cable TV let you pick TV channels that hit your audience smack-dab in their viewing patterns. Using a big dish called an uplink, satellite TV is broadcast upward to one of twenty-three communication

The plum-
meting cost
of TV

satellites. The satellite then sends the TV signals down to earth where it is picked up on home satellite dishes and by cable stations.

Whether your interest is education, international news, movies, adult programming, network TV, kids, business, information, shopping, religion, sports, travel, weather, or a skyful of other topics, chances are that it's on satellite.

Cable stations select their programming from both local sources and all these satellite options.

As TV technology, cable systems, satellites in orbit, and videocassette ownership — now approaching 80 percent — have changed, so have viewing patterns. Guerrillas know that the ten prime uses of TV sets are: **What folks watch**

1. Network television
2. Local television stations
3. Public Broadcasting System
4. Playing rented tapes
5. Recording on-air programs for later viewing
6. Cable movie channels
7. Other cable channels
8. 24-hour music videos
9. Video games
10. Monitor for a home computer

Guerrillas also know that some uses of TV have died down while others have become growth areas. Right now, the eleven *fastest growth areas* for TV set use are, in order:

1. Playing rented tapes
2. Public Broadcasting System
3. Cable movie channels
4. Other cable channels
5. Recording on-air programs for later viewing
6. Local television stations
7. Viewing home movies

8. Playing video games
9. 24-hour music videos
10. Monitor for home computer
11. Network television

When you were a kid, network TV ruled the roost. Today it is hanging in there, but not enjoying a growth spurt.

The sophisti-cated viewer

TV viewers are now more sophisticated than ever. They've been around the block when it comes to TV advertising spots, and they have opinions about the spots that you should know: 31 percent find TV advertising spots to be misleading; 24.3 percent find them offensive; 17 percent think they are informative; 15.9 percent think they are entertaining.

Awesome power, teensy prices

Never before has TV been more available and desirable to owners of small businesses. Guerrillas in droves are, at this very moment, discovering the awesome power of TV, and I suggest that you do the very same.

What TV can do

You'll find that TV can do many things the other media cannot. It allows you to demonstrate, to act, to dance, to sing, to put on playlets, to show cause and effect, to create a lively identity, to be dramatic, to reach large numbers of people, to home in on your specific audience, to prove your points visually and verbally — all at the same time, No other medium provides so many advantages to the advertiser at one time.

Of the various times you can advertise on the tube, unless you're going to economize by running on cable channels, steer clear of prime time — the 8.00 p.m. to 11.00 p.m. period when so many people are watching. You can realize better values more viewers per dollar — by using fringe time, the time before and after prime time, especially on local affiliates of the big networks. You might also look into daytime TV, which attracts many women viewers. The audience size is smaller and so is the cost. The time period past midnight, when few people are watching, is very inexpensive and can prove a springboard to success. Some postmidnight shows have ratings so low they are unmeasurable. That also means, happily, that they are inexpensive.

If you truly want to advertise on television, find out what shows your prospects watch, then run commercials on those shows. Many of the shows are available on cable. For example, when the solar energy industry was in its infancy, aggressive marketing people soon learned that the same people who watch Star Trek tend to buy solar energy units. They also learned that men who watch science-fiction movies, not sports, have a proclivity toward solar power. Some solar energy companies went to the bank as a result of that fascinating information. Even though Star Trek was in its tenth series of reruns, it still proved to be a marvelous and inexpensive vehicle for solar heating marketers. Talk shows, which frequently attract an older audience, were determined to be poison for solar energy sellers. Their product simply did not appeal to seniors — at least at first it didn't. Today it does, as solar energy becomes more and more acceptable as an alternative source of power, and as media coverage of solar applications becomes generous, appealing to our increasing number of environmentally aware citizens.

To get the most out of TV, keep in mind that TV rate cards, like radio rate cards, are established as the basis for negotiation and are not to be taken as gospel. In fact, if you're going to go on to television, you should retain a media-buying service to make your plans and buys for you. They'll charge about 7.5 percent of the total for their services, but they'll save you more than that. Many small businesspeople make their own buys, thinking they are getting good deals. But the media-buying services, which purchase millions of dollars' worth of TV time monthly, obtain bargains that would shock the small businessperson.

Media-buying services

Another warning about buying your TV advertising directly: TV salespeople have a powerful way of putting the egos of their commercial clients to work for them. Some convince an advertiser that he or she would be a terrific spokesperson. The advertiser, enjoying the strokes to his or her ego, then goes on TV and presents the commercial in person. Sometimes, but rarely, this is effective. Generally, the advertiser loses as many sales as he or she gains. Frequently the advertiser becomes a laughingstock but continues to present the ads because his or her TV salespeople wouldn't dream of risking their sales by telling the truth. Don't let your ego get in the way of your TV marketing when it comes to buying the time or presenting the information. If you've watched enough TV, I'm sure you get the gist of what I'm saying.

Cable is able I strongly suggest that you look into cable TV. It just may be that you can afford to market your offerings on television because of the new cable availabilities. Instead of going on TV and reaching the 90 percent of the audience who are out of your marketing area, you can telecast *only* to people within your marketing area. As cable (and satellite TV) is making TV more and more affordable to more and more small businesses, the networks are losing their shirts. In 1991, they lost $625 billion to cable. And TV is still in a state of flux — all favoring the guerrilla. So be one! And get yourself onto the tube.

Also, videocassette recorder sales are skyrocketing — nearly 80 percent of Americans have access to one at this writing, compared with 45 percent in 1984 — letting audiences view postmidnight programming anytime the next day. Stay tuned. These are very interesting times from the standpoint of television.

If you do decide to invest in television marketing, there are many methods by which you can cut down drastically on the cost of producing TV commercials. Truth is, you can turn out a very good thirty-second spot for about $1000. And even that figure can be reduced as you increase your TV savvy.

How to First of all, let your TV station provide all the *production* **produce a** assistance. Not the writing. Let *them* put up the equipment and **TV spot** furnish the camerapeople, the lighting experts, the director, the all-important editor. Don't let them write the spot. If you do, it will look like all their other homegrown TV commercials. Instead, either you or a talented individual you coerce, barter with, or hire should write a tight script. The left side of the sheet of paper upon which the script is written is reserved for video instructions. On that side, describe every single action the viewers will see, numbering each one. The right side of the script paper is for the audio portion. These are the sounds the viewers will hear. Again, number each audio section, matching it up with the appropriate video section so that the audio and video make a team.

If necessary, and it usually is not necessary, make a storyboard. A storyboard is a pictorial representation of your script. It consists of perhaps ten "frames", or pictures. Each frame contains a picture of what the viewers will see, a description of what will be happening, and the message that will be heard while the action is taking place. Storyboards tend to be taken too literally, however, and do not allow you the leeway to make changes during production. Those little changes are often the difference between an ordinary and an extraordinary commercial. Most (but not all) people have the imagination to understand a commercial from a script alone. If the people you are working with don't, you just may have to resort to a storyboard.

While working in major ad agencies, I had to prepare a storyboard for every commercial I wrote. And I know that I wrote over a thousand. Many art directors enjoyed gainful employment because of my active typewriter and the traditions of advertising agencies, which called for storyboards. Since I've been working on my own, I have written well over a thousand commercials, and only five or six required storyboards. Yet the commercials were no less successful than those I made using storyboards that swelled the budget.

You can also save money by having intense preproduction meetings with all who will be involved in the production of your commercial. Meet with the actors, actresses, director, lighting person, prop person, everyone. Make sure everyone

Intense preproduction

knows what is expected and understands the script. Make sure the timing is on the button and not one detail is unexplored. Then hold at least one tightly timed rehearsal. Have the people involved go through the motions before the cameras are running. By doing so, you'll be able to produce two commercials in the time usually necessary to produce one. You'll even be able to fit three commercials into the same production time, if you're good enough.

To keep the cost down, which is one characteristic of a guerilla, you will have to avoid expensive union talent and crew whenever possible, get everything right the first time as a result of well-planned rehearsals and preproduction meetings, and plan the editing when you plan the spot. Editing videotape can be very expensive so plan your shooting so that little editing will be necessary. And know that most experts tell you that it's in the editing room that the commercial is really made. So make it a point to be there watching — and opening — when the editing takes place. It's an important process of guerrilla learning.

Film or tape   Whether you shoot with film or tape usually won't make much difference in your final cost. Film allows you to use more special effects, has more of a magical quality because it has less "presence" than tape, and allows for less expensive editing. But with film you have no feedback. If someone goofed, you won't know it till the film is processed. With tape, you can replay what you have shot immediately, and if anything is wrong, you can redo it. No processing is necessary. As to which is better, there is no correct answer. Both can be ideal, depending upon the circumstances. But if you are planning to have the station help with production, better plan on videotape. Stations don't usually film for you. That's okay; guerrillas seem to opt for tape.

What makes a great TV commercial? Well, Procter & Gamble, one of the most sophisticated advertisers in the United States, frequently uses "slice of life" commercials, which are little playlets, the type that seem boring and commonplace. But with the big bucks P&G puts behind them, they work extremely well. And many companies have made a bundle copying this format. So don't knock them if you are considering TV as a marketing vehicle. You can learn plenty from P&G. I certainly did.

There are a few guidelines that will help you regardless of the type of commercials you wish to produce:

Remember always that television is a *visual medium with audio enhancement.* Many ill-informed advertisers look upon it as the opposite. A guerrilla marketer knows that a great TV commercial *starts with a great idea.* Try to express that idea visually, then add the words, music, and sound effects to make it clearer and stronger. Try viewing your commercial with no sound. If it is a winner, it will make its point with pictures only.

Where a great TV spot starts

Again, go with thirty-second spots rather than sixties, and if you are using TV for direct response, such as for ordering by Freephone number, try two-minute spots. They're very effective. Say that phone number at least three times.

Keep in mind that, as with radio, you have three seconds to attract the viewers' attention. If you haven't hooked them right up front, you've probably lost them. So say what you have to say in a captivating manner at the outset. Say it again, in different words, in the middle of your spot. Say it a final time, again in different words (or maybe even in the same words), at the end. Don't fall into the trap of making your commercial more interesting than your product. Don't allow anyone to remember your commercial without remembering your name. There are bushels of sob stories about commercials that won all sorts of awards while the products they were promoting died horrible deaths. You want sales, not awards, praise, or laughs.

When you can, *show your product or service in action.* People's memories improve 68 percent when they have a visual element to recall. So say what you have to say verbally and visually, especially visually.

Communicate to their eyes

The following thirty-second commercial not only won first

prize at the Venice TV Film Festival but caused the advertiser to withdraw it from the air because he was unable to keep up with the demand for his product. The basic idea to be conveyed in the commercial is that this particular cookie, known as "Sports" and manufactured by a company called Carr's, has more chocolate on it than any similar cookie, Simple enough? Here's the script:

VIDEO	AUDIO
1. OPEN WITH TWO SLAPSTICK CHARACTERS FACING THE CAMERA. ONE IS TALL AND ONE IS SHORT. TALL ONE SPEAKS.	1. (Tall man) Good evening. Sidney and I would like to prove that Carr's Sports have the most chocolate - by showing you two ways to make chocolate cookies.
2. SHORT MAN SMILES WHEN HIS NAME IS MENTIONED, BUT LOSES THE SMILE WHEN HE HEARS THAT HE IS A COOKIE.	2. Imagine Sidney here is cookie.
3. TALL MAN LIFTS HUGE CONTAINER MARKED "CHOCOLATE" AND POURS REAL CHOCOLATE FLUID ONTO SHORT MAN.	3. Now take your cookie. Cover it with chocolate.
4. CAMERA TILTS DOWN TO SHOW POOL OF CHOCOLATE AT SHORT MAN'S FEET.	4. Effective, but not much stays on. Carr's makes Sports a better way.
5. CUT TO TWO MEN. TALL MAN NOW CARRIES SHORT MAN, HOLDS HIM ABOVE A TUB MARKED	5. Pop the cookie in chocolate.

"CHOCOLATE." TALL
MAN THEN DROPS
SIDNEY INTO THE TUB.

6. CUT TO SHORT MAN'S
   HEAD SURFACING FROM
   THE CHOCOLATE. AS
   IT SURFACES, MORE
   CHOCOLATE IS POURED
   ON IT.

6. Top it up, and when it is
   set . . .

7. DISSOLVE TO SHORT MAN
   NOW ENCASED IN CHOCO-
   LATE AS HE IS LYING
   DOWN. TALL MAN STANDS
   PROUDLY ABOVE HIM.

7. . . . you have your cookie
   with all your chocolate on it.

8. TALL MAN HOLDS OUT A
   CARR'S SPORTS PACKAGE
   AS CAMERA ZOOMS TO
   CLOSE-UP OF IT.

8. That's how Carr's makes
   Sports.

9. HAND SETS PACKAGE
   DOWN NEXT TO SHORT
   MAN, STILL ENCASED IN
   CHOCOLATE. MAN LOOKS
   AT PACKAGE.

9. Carr's Sports - the bar of
   chocolate with the cookie
   in the middle. Right,
   Sidney?

The commercial, which cost about $1500 to produce, including everything, states the premise right up front. In the beginning the two characters are whimsical, so the viewer's attention is caught. The commercial is very funny. But the product is always the star. All the talk is about the product. The theme is chocolate. And the viewer makes a clear connection between Carr's Sports and chocolate, which was the basic idea all along. Viewers are told in frame one that the product has the most chocolate. In frame seven, the point is made again. In frame nine, it is made one more time. Even if there were no words, viewers could tell what the commercial is all about and could understand the connection made between Sports and chocolate.

The commercial uses no music, has ninety-three words instead of the pedestrian sixty-five, and employs humor to make its point. Humor, often referred to as the most dangerous weapon in advertising because it is so frequently misused, works well here, selling a product that retails for about seventy-five cents. And the spot makes full use of television's ability to demonstrate product advantages. Best of all, the commercial is so much fun to watch that viewers could watch it several times without becoming bored with it. They must also have remembered the name of the product, in view of the sales that resulted.

This just goes to show that you don't need a huge budget and a fancy jingle to make a successful commercial. As a marketing man, I am far more proud of the sales than of the awards won by this commercial.

Because so many people, estimated now at 70 percent, have remote controls with both their TV sets and their VCRS, there's a big chance, estimated at 67 percent, that your commercial will get "zapped" — either shown at fast forward, or muted, with the sound off. Does this steer guerrillas away from television? No, it does not.

Overcoming zapping   Instead, guerrillas take heed of this ugly reality by working with it, not against it. They make their commercials remote-proof by telling their stories visually, using words and music, but not really requiring them because their pictures make their point. They show their names — often throughout the commercials — by superimposing them in the lower corner of the screen, à la CNN.

And they show their commercials enough times to their target audiences that they begin to see the results of this ultra powerful guerrilla marketing after a few months. A few months? Why not instantly? Because TV, as high potency as it is, does not bring about instant results unless you are having a limited time sale, making a limited-time offer, or using TV as a direct-response medium, providing viewers with a toll-free number and enough information to make the decision to buy from you.

You're going to be a happy guerrilla if you *lower your expectations for TV in the short run.* Over time, TV will work **TV miracles** its miracles for you. Only they won't be miracles. They'll be the result of your patience combined with your knowledge that no medium does as much to sell your offering as television

Yet, even with your newborn confidence with this medium, keep in mind that you've got to have a great product or service for TV to do its job for you. You've got to be aware that the 1990s are shaping up into a decade that responds most to the basics. The hot buttons of this decade are the functionally elegant, the plain and simple, what is healthy and sensible, what is politically correct, what is environmentally responsible, what is good for America, and what is solidly positioned as mid-price.

Once you've got offerings that live up to those consumer demands, that's when TV can be most effective for you, the guerrilla. That's when to use and not to abuse TV.

20

Outdoor Advertising: What It Can and Cannot Do

OUTDOOR ADVERTISING CONSISTS of billboards, bus ads, taxi signs, painted walls, and outdoor signs. Let's deal with billboards first. Rare is the entrepreneur who can survive on billboard advertising alone — although it can be done. We have already chronicled the successes of Harold's Club, Wall Drugs, and Burma-Shave, but these enterprises really used outdoor signs, not billboards. Billboard advertising — and to use the term advertising is somewhat of an overstatement — is really reminder advertising, for the most part. It works best when combined with advertising through other media.

Each year, an Iowa entrepreneur I know runs a month-long one-cent-sale promotion on the radio and in newspapers. He supports the radio and newspaper advertising for a month each year with billboards, too. His sales rise an average of 18 percent. With billboards alone, this would never happen. But the billboards add an important ingredient to his marketing mix. He uses them only once a year to promote his furniture business. And they work wonderfully.

But billboard advertising doesn't have to be strictly re-minder advertising. In some instances it can lead directly to **Two magic** sales. In regard to this, let me stop right here and tell you the **words** two most important words you can use on a billboard. They are not at all like the high motivation words we discussed several pages back — not at all that obvious. The two magic words that can spell instant success for you if used on a billboard are *next exit*.

If you can use them on your billboard, it may do a full-blown job of marketing for you. For example, a new store in the San Francisco Bay Area that did not have enough money for most marketing could afford one billboard. And that billboard, fortunately, was able to display the words *next exit*. Success came rapidly and overwhelmingly. Of course, the store had to do everything else right to succeed, and it did. But the billboard must get the prime credit. If you can't use those two words, these three also work well: *two miles ahead*.

Most of the time, you cannot buy just one billboard. Usually you've got to rent ten or twenty billboards at once. Some are in all winning locations. Some are sure-fire losers. You must take the bad with the good. But sometimes, through cogent arguing or through some loophole in the billboard firm's policies, you can lease just one beautifully located billboard. If ever you can, do it. Otherwise, be careful. Consider using billboards if you have a restaurant, tourist attraction, garage, gas station, motel, or hotel. But look with disdain upon billboard advertising if you've got a business that will not have instant appeal to motorists. If you have a car wash that really is at the next exit, a billboard might just be the ticket. If you have a computer-education firm, forget it. A billboard can, however, help you maintain your identity — if your identity's already established.

When to use billboards

The Marlboro cigarette company is able to maintain its cowboy identity with billboards. It wouldn't even have to use any words, though it does. But if you are thinking about using billboards simply as reminders and haven't invested a lot in your identity, as Marlboro has, scratch that idea from your marketing plan.

To ascertain whether or not you want even one billboard, find out how many cars pass the billboard site each day. This is known in the business as the traffic count. Billboard firms have that data at their fingertips. Find out also the type of traffic passing by. Trucks won't be able to patronize your car wash. On the other hand, homeward bound affluent suburbanites may be interested in your take-away restaurant.

When planning a billboard, keep the rules for outdoor signs **Six words** in mind. Rarely use more than six words. Remember that **only** people are probably driving around fifty-five miles per hour when they glance, if they glance at all, at your billboard. Keep it simple for them. Give them one large graphic upon which they can concentrate. Be sure the type is clear. Be sure the words are large. If the traffic count remains more or less the same at night, be sure your board is illuminated. That costs more than a nonilluminated board but may be worth the extra bucks.

Billboard companies are open to price negotiation, although they may not appreciate my putting that down in print. They are also amenable to location negotiation. Once I wanted a specific location and was told that in order to get it, I'd have to rent nine other billboards — all in dismal locations. I said I was not interested. A couple of weeks later, I was offered the billboard along with only four other locations, also dismal. Again, I said no. Finally, I received a call from the sales rep saying I could have the one location I wanted, but the price would be significantly higher than originally quoted. It would have been a good deal, and I wished I could have said yes. But by this time, my client's monies had been committed. So we all lost out. Too bad the rep hadn't made me the same offer in the beginning. I could have used "next exit" on the billboard and had one more success story to report here.

In addition to attracting direct sales on occasion, billboards help guerrillas in three other instances:

1. When you are new to an area and want to make your presence known
2. When you want to tie in with a unique advertising campaign or promotion
3. When you have an idea that translates ideally onto a billboard, and you can rent just one board

An example of the third instance is a roadside cider stand that sells cherry cider grown from trees visible from the highway. A gutsy entrepreneur might display a billboard with the entire center section cut out so that motorists can see right through the billboard to the cherry trees. A simple line of copy at the top (or bottom) might say: CHERRY CIDER FROM THESE TREES — NEXT EXIT. I know it is seven words long, but it's okay to break the rules occasionally, just as long as you know them and have a good reason for breaking them when you do.

One of the more attractive aspects of billboard advertising is that if you supply the design, the billboard company will produce the billboard for you. That means the company will handle blowing the artwork up to a size that will fit on the billboard. Billboard sizes are measured in sheets, with one sheet approximating the size of a large poster. The usual size is a 24-sheet. Whatever you do, make sure your billboard fits in with the rest of your advertising campaign. The Iowa man was able to present his message in six words on his immensely successful billboard only because the message had been explained more fully elsewhere. A guerrilla uses billboards like darts. A guerrilla either says "next exit," "two miles," or "five minutes ahead", ties his or her billboard in directly with a strong campaign, or uses a single billboard with surgical precision. No guerrilla uses a "next exit" billboard for the usual one month or three months. After testing the merits of a billboard, a guerrilla signs a one-year, three-year, or five-year contract for such a board. A guerrilla contracts with a billboard company to erect a billboard in a place where "next exit" can be used, if one does not yet exist there. And a guerrilla still realizes that a great billboard isn't much more than a great reminder.

Producing your billboard

I would suggest that you avoid the use of billboards unless there is a compelling reason to use them. Drive around your community and carefully note the local companies that use billboards. Then talk to the owners of those companies and find out if the billboards work. Unless you are in a business that competes with theirs, you'll probably get a straight answer.

Sometimes a guerrilla can get several fellow guerrillas to collaborate on a billboard. This brings the cost of the board down considerably and puts it within range of many an entrepreneur. If two or three companies share a board, the cost may be low enough to enable each of them to use the board on a full-time basis, as part of their overall marketing plan.

Call the billboard representatives in your area and listen to their sales pitches. Perhaps they can enlighten you as to special opportunities, new boards to be erected, chances to go in on billboards with other companies. Chances are, you won't be persuaded to put even the tiniest billboard into your marketing plan. But you've nothing to lose by talking with them. So do it. Better yet, listen to them. If you have a well-known theme, billboards might be for you. As with many other marketing media, it may be worth your while to test their efficacy. Different towns respond in different ways to billboards. Maybe you live in a town that gets motivated by billboards. Los Angeles seems to be the billboard capital of the universe, with a multitude of ornate moving billboards in high-traffic locations — all heralding movies, stars, shows — but never Preparation H. Maybe you are located near a street that is ideal for a billboard. If that's the case, I recommend testing. If you test a billboard for a month or two and nothing happens, you're not out all that much money. But if you never give it a try, and then your biggest competitor tries billboards and goes to glory with them, you'll kick yourself from now till Sunday.

Share-of-mind advertising   Billboard marketing is, almost without exception, *share-of-mind* advertising. Share-of-mind advertising is advertising that attempts to win sales down the road by implanting a thought or establishing an identity. It tries to win for you a constantly increasing share of the minds of the people in your marketing area. It does not normally prove effective in a hurry, cannot be translated into results, and is only profitable in the long run, if ever. *Share-of-market* advertising, on the other hand, is advertising that attempts to win instant sales. It tries to win for you a constantly increasing share of whatever market your offering belongs to. Share-of-market advertising is the kind of advertising that is the most effective, the most instantly translated into results, and the most profitable in the short run. Most entrepreneurs are a bit too concerned with cash to worry about shares of minds. They want increased shares of markets, and they want them right now. So consider using billboards, but don't expect to attract highly motivated prospects through them.

You can expect about the same, perhaps a little more, from bus signs, both interior and exterior, and interior or exterior taxi signs. These may be employed as part of a marketing plan that calls for the use of signs in targeted urban areas. These moving signs are seen by many people, a lot of whom may be serious prospects. Taxi signs are seen by people throughout the metropolitan area. Bus signs are usually seen by the same people — bus riders and people who live along the route. Of course buses don't always travel the same routes taxis do. But this should be kept in mind if you're thinking about using both bus signs and taxi signs.

Buses and taxis

A client of mine enjoyed a great deal of success attracting temporary office workers with signs placed inside buses. The client was an agency that provided these workers to large employers, and the signs were designed to appeal to both the workers and the employers. If your product or service is located near a bus line, you should consider placing signs on that particular bus line — on the exterior of the buses. Such signs will not serve as a complete marketing plan, but they can be an effective part of one.

Learning where your prospects go will help you determine the best location for outdoor advertising, whether it be placed on a billboard, a bus, a painted wall, or a sign on a barn. For example, if you sell a new type of tanning oil and a paintable wall is available near a sunbathers' beach, grab it. If you market agricultural products or services and a paintable roof is available on a well-traveled country road, rent the space and paint it with your message. Give serious thought to placing a sign outside your own place of business. A good sign often results in good business. A poor sign invites disaster.

A bad sign What makes a bad outdoor sign? Lack of clarity. Lack of uniqueness. Fancy lettering. Bland colors. Tiny words. Improper placement. What makes a good outdoor sign? Readability. Warmth. Good location. Uniqueness. An identity that matches that of your business. Clarity from afar, from moving vehicles, on dark nights. Good colors. Make certain that your sign communicates what your business is all about. For instance, "Moore's" tells us a lot less than "Moore's Stationery." To gain community acceptance, try to have your sign designed in such a manner that it fits in with the character of the community. Garish signs may be dandy in some locations and horrid in others. Conservative signs may be just the ticket on some streets, and a ticket to doom on others. Be sensitive to the tastes of your community.

Always be on the lookout for potential sign locations. I know a guerrilla marketer who could not secure a billboard near his place of business. But he was able to persuade the owner of a drive-in located within one mile of his business to sell him space on the back of the drive-in screen. It's no accident that the back of the drive-in screen faced a heavily traveled freeway.

Successful guerrilla marketers tell me that one of the most **A neon** important signs they have is the neon one that says OPEN. Some **money-maker** remind me that the high cost of neon signs prevents a few business owners from using them, necessitating instead the eventual expense of a GOING OUT OF BUSINESS sign.

Don't allow yourself to be hemmed in by a small imagination. But remember that advertising seen by speeding motorists has less impact than advertising seen by relaxed prospects — the type that might take the time to read a direct mailing from you.

21
Direct-Mail Marketing: Pinpointing Your Prospects

ATTENTION ALL GUERRILLAS! Direct marketing is where it's at. Direct marketing is the name of your game. Direct marketing has a built-in mirror that reflects the true effectiveness of your advertising message. A other forms of marketing have much to be said for them. All other forms of marketing can help you immensely, but direct marketing can help you more.

Direct marketing refers to direct-mail, mail-order, or coupon advertising, to telephone marketing, direct-response TV, postcard decks, door-to-door salespeople, home shopping TV shows, or any method of marketing that attempts to make a sale right then and there. It does not require a middleman. It does not require a store. It requires only a seller and a buyer. And because of that, much unnecessary game playing is removed from the marketing process, leaving only accountable results. Let me repeat that word: *accountable*. When you run a radio commercial or a newspaper ad, you do all in your power to make sure that it works, but you don't really know if it does. But when you engage in direct-mail advertising, the form of direct marketing upon which we'll concentrate in this chapter, you'll know clearly whether or not your mailing worked. Either it did or it didn't. If it worked, you'll know how well it worked. And if it failed, you'll know how dismally it failed.

Accountability is all

Direct-mail advantages   Along with its all-important accountability, consider some of the other advantages of direct mail over other advertising media:

1. You can achieve more accurately measured results.
2. You can be as expansive or concise as you wish.
3. You can zero in on almost any target audience.
4. You can personalize your marketing like crazy.
5. You can expect the highest of all response rates.
6. You can use unlimited opportunities for testing.
7. You can enjoy repeat sales to proven customers.
8. You can compete with, even beat, the giants.

Along with those eight advantages come eight rules of thumb:

1. The most important element is the right list.
2. Make it easy for the recipient to take action.
3. Letters almost always outpull mailing packages with no letters.
4. The best buyers are those who have bought by mail before, a rapidly growing number.
5. Do anything to get your envelope opened. (A list of hints is coming up later in this chapter.)
6. Keeping good records is paramount.
7. Testimonials improve response rates.
8. Remember that *nothing is as simple as it seems.*

How guerrillas gain response   In true guerrilla fashion, I also offer you eight tips for gaining the response rate you want with direct mail:

1. Ask for the order in the headline of your brochure.
2. Always tell the person what to do next.
3. Blue is a dandy second color, but red with black is generally the best-pulling direct-mail combination.
4. Don't overuse red; use it primarily for highlights.
5. Experts say the four most important elements in direct

mail are the list, the offer, the copy, and the graphics. Guerrillas pay close attention to each.

6. The fastest-growing segment of the direct-mail industry is nontraditional mailers — those who haven't used direct mail in the past.

7. Direct-mail success comes with the cumulative effect of repeat mailings. Make them repetitive, yet different from one another.

8. Direct-mail spending by consumers tripled between 1980 and 1990; expect more growth in the current decade.

Guerillas realize that when it comes to determining the normal percentage of return on direct mail, there is none. You'll have to determine your own, then go about improving it — the name of the game in direct mail. **The normal response rate**

Right now, about 40 percent of direct mail is from national advertisers, 25 percent from local advertisers, 20 percent from mail-order firms. The average U.S. household receives an average of 104 pieces of direct mail each week. To a guerrilla, this means a slimmer chance than ever for a great response rate amid a more acute need than ever for true creativity in your mailings. Keep in mind that more money is spent on direct mail than on magazines, radio, or TV. Remember also that over 95 million Americans responded to direct-mail pitches in 1991, that one in six Americans purchased six or more items via this maxi, medium, that older people want less mail while younger folks want more, and that nonprofit groups use direct mail to raise up to 90 percent of their funds. Finally, keep in mind that with postal rates rising, amateurs are being forced away from direct mail, leaving a lush new universe for guerrillas.

Those same guerrillas are grateful that direct mail is the least expensive method of marketing — on a per-sale basis. The overall cost may be high, but if it works for you, it is inexpensive marketing. There are many books, many articles, **The least expensive method** many chapters devoted to enlightening marketers on the intricacies of direct-marketing. Read them. Keep reading. For a guerrilla, marketing is part art and part science. Direct mail is more science than art. This is not to downplay the art of creating a successful direct-mail package. But for now, let's focus on the science, the things we already know.

Test, test, then test

For instance, we know that the three most important things to do if you are to succeed at direct marketing are to test, test, and test. If you know that and do that, you are on the right road. If you play it by ear, you will probably fall on your ear. Direct marketing is growing faster than any other type of marketing. More and more people trust it. More and more people enjoy the convenience of being able to shop and buy by mail. More and more people want to be spared the lack of parking places, high fuel costs, irritable sales clerks, and crowded stores. They turn, therefore, to companies that make their products or services available through direct mail. In 1991, 94 percent of Americans purchased something by mail. They obviously appreciate the convenience and the saving of time. With a mailing, *you have a good chance of getting through to people.* Studies show that 60 percent of people say of direct mail, "I usually read or scan it"; 31 percent say, "I read some of it, don't read some of it"; 9 percent say, "I don't read any of it." The bottom line: you have a shot at reaching 91 percent of your audience. That's a healthy number.

The 60-30-10 rule

More on the science of direct mail is embodied in the *60-30-10 Rule*. Sixty percent of your direct-mail program depends upon your using the right list of people; 30 percent depends upon your making the right offer; 10 percent depends upon your creative package. You can make it extra creative if you take to heart these three tips:

- Brightly colored envelopes grab attention. Although red and blue are time-honored direct-mail colors, the nineties are proving that yellow, orange, and pink merit consideration, too. But white is always a safe, good bet.

- Oversized addressing stimulates the unconscious pleasure people gain from seeing their name in print. The larger, the better.
- A white business-sized envelope with a first-class stamp and no return address is especially intriguing and gets rave notices when it comes to response rates. Look into it (that's a guerrilla hint to test it).

The complete honesty that results from direct-mail marketing is invaluable. Because it is so *accountable*, it lets you know if you have done a good job making your offer, pricing your merchandise, constructing your mailing package, writing your copy, timing your mailing, selecting your mailing list. Soon after you have accomplished your mailing, you learn whether it worked or failed. That's what I mean by accountability. During the past few years, more of my work than ever before has been in the area of direct response. That is because companies are moving rapidly into direct-response marketing. They are learning that the feedback is instant and accurate when they employ this marketing vehicle.

But before studying the secrets imparted in these pages, you must honestly ask yourself whether or not your product or service lends itself to direct marketing. If you have a product or service, or are trying to select a product or service, to market through direct-mail or mail-order marketing, you should first consider several factors. You automatically consider them when asking and answering these questions:

- Is there a perceived need for the product or service?
- Is it practical?
- Is it unique?
- Is the price right for your customers or prospects?
- Is it a good value?
- Is the markup sufficient to assure a profit?
- Is the market large enough?
- Does the product or service have broad appeal?

Checklist for direct marketers

- Are there specific smaller segments of your list that have a strong desire for your product or service?
- Is it new? Will your customers perceive it as being new?
- Can it be photographed or illustrated interestingly?
- Are there sufficient unusual selling features to make your copy sizzle?
- Is it economical to ship? Is it fragile? Odd-shaped? Heavy? Bulky?
- Can it be personalized?
- Are there any legal problems to overcome?
- Is it safe to use?
- Is the supplier reputable?
- Will backup merchandise be available for fast shipment on reorders?
- Might returns be too huge?
- Will refurbishing or returned merchandise be practical?
- Is it, or can it be, packaged attractively?
- Are usage instructions clear?
- How does it compare with competitive products or services?
- Will it have exclusivity?
- Will it lend itself to repeat business?
- Is it consumable, so that there will be repeat orders?
- Is it faddish? Too short-lived?
- Is it too seasonal for direct-mail selling?
- Can an add-on to the product make it more distinctive and saleable?
- Will the number of stock-keeping units — various sizes and colors — create problems?
- Does it lend itself to multiple pricing?
- Is it too readily available in stores?
- Is it like an old, hot item, so that its success is guaranteed?
- Is it doomed because similar items have failed?

- Does your mother, wife, brother, husband, girlfriend, boyfriend, sister, or kid like it?
- Is direct mail the way to go with it?
- Does it fill an unfilled niche in the marketplace?

These questions were posed by Len Carlson, who for thirty years has sold about 10,000 different items from a direct-marketing company called Sunset House. They were listed in *Advertising Age*, in an article written by Bob Stone, president of Stone and Adler, a direct-response firm in Chicago.

You've got to ask yourself these hard questions and come up with answers that please you — and if you can't, either you've got to discard the idea of direct mail for your particular product or service, or you've got to make some major changes in your offering. If as few as five of your answers to these thirty-seven questions are not the right answers, you may be going in the wrong direction. This checklist can serve as a handy guide to direct-marketing success. Luckily, you have these questions to save you from spending money unwisely.

Only after you are satisfied that you ought to proceed into the world of direct marketing should you take the next step — which is to understand the relationship of direct-response advertising to non-direct-response advertising. Rather than giving you my words about that relationship, I would like to quote from a speech made to the Direct Mail/Marketing Association's 65th Annual Convention by David Ogilvy — the head of a major advertising agency that has offices worldwide. Keep in mind that David Ogilvy's agency is a standard agency, not a direct-response agency, although it now has a branch called Ogilvy and Mather Direct. Here is a portion of Mr. Ogilvy's talk:

Direct is different from indirect

> In the advertising community there are two worlds. Your world of direct-response advertising and that other world — the world of general advertising. These two worlds are on a collision course.

You direct-response people know what kind of advertising works and what doesn't work. You know to a dollar.

You know that two-minute commercials are more cost-effective than thirty-second commercials.

You know that fringe time on television sells more than prime time.

In print advertising, you know that long copy sells more than short copy.

You know that headlines and copy about the product and its benefits sell more than cute headlines and poetic copy. You know to a dollar.

The general advertisers and their agencies know almost nothing for sure, because they cannot measure the results of their advertising. They worship at the altar of creativity. Which means originality — the most dangerous word in the lexicon of advertising.

They opine that thirty-second commercials are more cost-effective than two-minute commercials. You know they're wrong.

In print advertising, they opine that short copy sells more than long copy. You know they are wrong.

They indulge in entertainment. You know they are wrong. You know to a dollar. They don't.

Nobody should be allowed to create advertising until he has served his apprenticeship in direct response. That experience will keep his feet on the ground for the rest of his life. The trouble with many copywriters in ordinary agencies is that they don't think in terms of selling. They have never written direct response. They have never tasted blood.

Until recently, direct response was the Cinderella of the advertising world. Then came the computer and the credit card. Direct marketing exploded. You guys are coming into your own. Your opportunities are colossal....

Ladies and gentlemen, how I envy you. Your timing is perfect. You have come into the direct-response business at the right time. You are on to a good thing. For forty years I have been a voice crying in the wilderness, trying to get my fellow advertising practitioners to take direct response seriously. Today my first love is coming into its own. You face a golden future.

David Ogilvy's speech was considered so important that he was the keynote speaker, and yet his entire speech was delivered on videotape. Goes to show that it's the content that counts. And the words just revealed to you are loaded with meaning. I hope you heed them. I hope you realize the enormity of Mr. Ogilvy's truth: if you don't know about direct-response marketing, you don't know about marketing.

According to technical experts in the field, direct marketing is not a fancy term for mail order. It is an interactive system of marketing that uses one or more advertising media to effect a measurable response and/or transaction at any location.

Marketing is all the activities involved in moving goods and services from seller to buyer. Direct marketing has the same broad function as standard marketing but also requires the maintenance of a database. This database records the names of customers, prospects, and former customers. It serves as a **The database** vehicle for storing, then measuring, the results of direct-response advertising. It also provides a way to store, then measure, purchasing performance. And finally, it is a way to continue direct communication by mail and/or telephone.

Risk-wary advertisers are shying away from the mass market media, choosing instead to target their prospects directly. These advertisers might have invested 50 cents a person to reach a general audience in the past, but in the 1990s, they're putting up $1 for someone whose demographic and economic profile indicates they're predisposed to making a purchase. From Waldenbooks' Preferred Reader Program to Liz Claiborne's store-based computers to Hyatt Hotels' Gold Passport program to the myriad of frequent-flier programs, retailers and advertisers are hoarding information on exactly who their customers are, what they bought, and what they are likely to buy in the future.

Scads of information pulled from scanners, coupons, and even a check-cashing card pinpoint exactly where a person lives, how many people they live with, how much they earn, what they drive, read, and eat, even what kind of toilet paper they use. Every right-thinking guerrilla is building a database because so few markets are growing. Companies are desperate to hold on to their current customers.

Interactive TV Looking into the future consider interactive TV as an up-and-coming selling device. This device, already in use in test markets and in the many home shopping shows now on cable TV, lets shoppers see items on TV, then order them immediately. Eventually, interactive TV will probably be the major vehicle employed by large users of direct marketing.

The value to you is potentially enormous. You get to home in on your prospects with amazing accuracy. You can be selective in regard to age, race, sex, occupation, buying habits, money spent on past direct-mail purchases, education, special interests, family composition, religion, marital status, and geographic location ranging from state to county to town to post code to block. Expensive? Yes. But it's the real cost to build lifetime customer loyalty.

Prodigy Services, a computerized on-line information and interactive shopping service, listed 1.7 million subscribers in 1992, proving that people will happily shop from their easy chairs. According to a survey by Simmons Market Research Bureau, 65 percent of Prodigy's subscribers graduated from college, and nearly half live in households earning $75,000 or more. Nearly 200 advertisers currently allow people to buy from them through Prodigy. Because the company has sunk at least $1 billion into its business, it has no serious competitors in the on-line consumer market. But this is still the wave of the future and not the present.

Home shopping networks Video shopping networks are already with us, as you gleaned from the chapter on television. In the US in 1992, video home shopping sales topped $2 billion. A whopping 70 million people watch Home Shopping Network; 28 million watch Cable Value Network; 18 million watch QVC Network. And those numbers are growing, along with the mailing lists compiled by the home shopping networks.

If you have the soul of a guerrilla, you will have been compiling your own mailing list from the day your business began. The list should naturally start with your own customers. From there, you can expand it to include people who have recently moved into your area, and people who have recently been married or divorced, or become parents. You can eliminate people who have moved away. **Your customer mailing list**

You might engage in a simple direct mailing of postcards to customers, informing them of a sale you will have the next week. They will appreciate the early notification and might show their gratitude by purchasing from you. You might also engage in a full-scale direct mailing, using what is now known as the "classic package", which consists of an outer envelope, a direct-mail letter, a brochure, an order form, a return envelope (maybe post-paid, maybe not), and often even more.

Whatever you do, the process begins when you decide exactly what it is you wish to offer. How will you structure that offer? Then you must select your mailing list. If you haven't got the names already, you can purchase them from a list broker (look under "Mailing Lists" in your Yellow Pages). Take care. Be sure you buy a clean, fresh list. The broker (and the price) can give you clues on this. You must be certain that you know all the costs involved: postage, printing, writing the mailing, artwork, paper, personalization (individualizing each letter by name and address, rather than saying "Dear friend" or the like), and repeat mailing costs. Your gross sales, minus these costs and your production, handling, and shipping costs, will constitute your profits. Be sure you make financial projections and know your break-even point.

According to Lynn Peterson, a former direct-mail executive in the direct-response arm of a major advertising agency who helped mastermind mailings for some of the nation's

Secrets and errors largest direct marketers, the three biggest secrets that can be disclosed to a direct marketer are:

1. Pick your list with the utmost care.
2. Structure your offer in such a way that it is extremely difficult to refuse.
3. Plan your projections so that you earn a profit.

Ms. Peterson was also asked to describe the three biggest errors made by direct marketers. Never one to be inconsistent, she said they were:

1. Failure to pick the right list or lists.
2. Failure to structure an offer properly.
3. Failure to plan projections with enough foresight.

Guerrilla direct-mail gems Along with her insights into making direct mail a money-maker for your company, I offer these gems:

- Printing your most important sentences in a second color will increase sales enough to warrant the extra money. Be sure you choose a bright, pleasing color.
- If you've got a two-page letter to send, use two pages. Printing on both sides of one page is a false economy and gets you right where it hurts — in your response rate.
- Restate your main offer on your response form. The repetition will be good for you as well as motivating for the reader.
- Illustrations or photos incorporated in your letter will also improve your response rate. Just be sure that the graphic element adds to the offer or the promise.
- The worst months for direct mail are June, March, and May. The best are January, February, and October.
- Guerrillas juice up their offers — and response rates — with free gifts for ordering, a photo of the free gift on the envelope, or a free trial of their product or service.

As you are learning, something free always aids in marketing.

In the old days, a direct-mail campaign meant a letter. Today it means a letter, two or three or five follow-up letters, perhaps a follow-up phone call or two, and finally, one more direct-mail letter. Many entrepreneurs engage in weekly or monthly direct mailings.

These are not the old days

There are a multitude of decisions for you to make when you embark upon a mailing, so it is crucial that you know the right questions to ask. In addition to deciding about your mailing list, your offer, and your financial projections, you'll have to decide whether to mail first class or third class. Will you personalize your mailing? Will you have a Freephone number available for ordering? Which credit cards will you accept? Will you need to alter your pricing because you'll be selling direct? This seemingly simple subject becomes more complex as you learn more about it.

The envelope for a direct mailing merits a chapter of its own. Executives should not be sent envelopes with address labels. For maximum response, their names must be typed on the envelope. And for selling stationery, feminine products, or political candidates or causes, a handwritten envelope provides a wonderfully personal tone. Envelopes can be standard size or oversize (6 inches by 9 inches), manila, covered with gorgeous art, foil-lined, or window-type. They can have a return address, or, to pique curiosity, omit the return address.

Getting them to open the envelope

One of the best devices you can use on an envelope is a "teaser" — a copyline that compels the recipient to open the envelope. Examples of successful teasers are: "FREE! A microcalculator for you!"; "Want to get your hands on $10,000 extra cash?"; and "The most astonishing offer of the year. Details inside."

As you can see, there are myriad ways to get a person to open an envelope. And that is the purpose of the envelope —

to interest the recipient so that he or she will open it and read the contents.

Guerrillas know that people read the addressee name first, then they look at the teaser copy, and finally they read to see who sent it. Was it the Office of the President? The Awards Committee? The IRS? If it has the name of the person's bank, it always gets opened. No teaser is needed. I doubt if the IRS needs one either.

When planning your own envelope, determine the needs and wants of your target audience. Remember that you can always use the back of the envelope and that 75 percent of the people holding it will read it. Figure that you've got three seconds to get them to open it. So say something enticing to motivate that action. Examples:

- Free gift enclosed
- Money-saving offer inside
- Wealth-building secrets for the nineties
- Private information for your eyes only
- Did you know you can double your profits?
- What every business like yours needs to know . . .
- How to add new profits for only six cents a day
- See inside for exciting details on (virtually anything)
- Read what's in store for you — this week only!

The idea of teaser copy is not to be cute, clever, or fancy. The job is to be *provocative*, to entice the recipient into opening the envelope. Sure, it's only an envelope, but guerrillas know that it's often the key to a successful or a failed mailing.

Always end with a P.S. You should almost always include a P.S. in your letter. They get read with regularity, far more than body copy. Many direct mailings now include what are known as lift letters — little notes that say things such as "Read this only if you have decided not to respond to this offer." Inside is one more attempt to make the sale, probably a handwritten message called a "buck slip", signed by the company president.

Be sure you guarantee what you are selling, because you are not as "In touch" with customers as you would be with a storesold product or service, and they will want the reassurance of a guarantee.

The most effective direct-mail efforts allow people to buy with credit cards. "Bill me" also works well as a rule. An element of urgency, such as "offer expires in one week", increases the response even more. Guerrillas always put a time limit on their direct-mail offers.

Whatever you do, make your offer clear, repeat it several times, keep your message as short as possible, and ask for the order. Don't pussyfoot around. Ask people to do exactly what you wish them to do. Then ask them again.

I also recommend Freephone numbers, which can triple the response rate. Every day, three-quarters of a million Americans order $225 million worth of merchandise by phone. **Let them order by phone**

When you create a direct-mail ad with a coupon, make the coupon a miniature version of your ad, complete with headline, benefit, and offer. In short, make it a brief summary of the advertisement. Some direct-mail pros write their coupons or response devices before they write their ads. This is called "working backward" and guerrillas see the wisdom in it. Working backward helps you immensely when you write the letter or brochure — because it helps you remember what you want the recipient to do.

Where should your mail-order ad appear in a publication? The best place, although relatively expensive, is the back page of a newspaper or magazine — where response can be as much as 150 percent greater than from the same ad inside the publication.

And while considering direct marketing, always consider including an insert with your bill. People certainly open bills, so that means they'll probably see your insert. And you'll get a free ride because the bill's paying the postage for the insert. Another type of insert is the free-standing type that often appears in newspapers or magazines. These are known to be very effective. So check with your newspaper or magazine rep to find out about their services with regard to inserts.

Freeman Gosden, Jr., president of Smith-Hennings-Gosden in Los Angeles, has come up with a direct-mail marketer's checklist. He offers these points for consideration:

- Look at the mail as your reader will.
- Keep your primary objective foremost in your mind.
- Does the number-one benefit hit you between the eyes?
- Does the number-two benefit follow close behind?
- Does the message of the mailing package flow?
- Does the outside envelope encourage you to open it — now?
- Is the letter the first thing you see upon opening?
- Does the letter discuss the reader's needs, product benefits, features, endorsements, and ways to respond?
- Do graphics support the copy?
- Does the reply card tell the whole offer?
- Is there a reason to act now?
- Is it easy to reply?
- Would you respond?

The almighty catalogue Catalogues are a whole different ballgame, part of direct mail, to be sure, but a very different part. As your business grows, you will probably require a catalogue to spur your direct marketing. When you do decide to market with a catalogue, be absolutely certain that your catalogue has the right positioning, the right merchandise selection, the right kind of merchandise, the right graphics, the right use of color, the right size (thirty-two pages is considered optimum), the right headlines, the right sub-heads, the right copy, the right sales stimulators, and the right order forms. Also be sure that you have formulated your projections correctly. Other than that, direct marketing with catalogues is a piece of cake.

If you run a mail-order business, your catalogue will be the heart of your business. It will be a mighty contributor to your bottom line. The success of your mail-order catalogue will be contingent upon your having customers who have already had one or more satisfactory transactions with you. That means that when they receive your catalogue they will trust you and will have confidence in your offerings. It also means catalogues are not for people just starting a business.

Be prepared to invest in your catalogue. A friend of mine who ran a successful mail-order company ($2 million in sales, with $500,000 in marketing expenses) spent 50 percent of his marketing money on direct mail, 30 percent on catalogues, and 20 percent on mail-order ads. Does it sound as if he believed in catalogues? Well, he didn't believe enough. Later he changed his marketing budget so as to spend 15 percent of his marketing money on mail-order ads, 20 percent on direct mail, and 65 per cent on catalogues. He had learned that his catalogues were the most important selling tools he had. In fact, he used to say he was in the catalogue business rather than the mail-order business. My friend became a millionaire in the business, so take heed of his words.

Think of your catalogue as a specialized form of direct mail. It is like a store on paper — a complete presentation of your merchandise. The items within your catalogue should reflect the interests of your audience and should be similar in nature. If you sell outdoor equipment, your customers won't want to buy gourmet foods from you. They look upon you as a specialist, and your catalogue must nourish that belief.

To print a catalogue you should have about 25,000 customers. That's a lot. But if you want to earn a whole of a lot of money, you'll have to start developing a customer list that long. The money — the truly large sums — will come to you when you send those customers your catalogue. What if you don't have 25,000 customers? Create an inexpensive catalogue, perhaps a mini-catalogue of eight pages, with just black and white photos.

Preparing a catalogue is quite a serious project. Once designed, it can be printed for 5000 customers or 5,000,000 customers. But the amount of work required to get the catalogue ready for the printer makes it cost-ineffective unless you print up 25,000 copies. That's just a rule of thumb, but it's a good one.

Catalogue costs   With your first catalogue, breaking even isn't too bad. It builds business. And the next year, when you have 50,000 customers, most of your catalogue work will already have been accomplished. You can pick up most artwork and copy from the first catalogue, and your in-the-mail costs will be substantially reduced. Therefore you ought to make a very impressive profit on your catalogue the second year, even more the third year, and still more each succeeding year. But as with all other forms of guerrilla marketing, you must be patient, must not expect miracles, must consider your expenditures as an investment, and must remain committed to your catalogue marketing program.

Up till now, we've been talking about mailing your catalogue to your own list of customers. If you purchase outside lists, even exceptional ones, you should not figure on a return that is more than 85 percent of that realized by mailing to your own list. So test other lists very carefully before plunging in and mailing a million catalogues. Whatever you do, you must mail your catalogue for Christmas. People want to buy at that time, and you've blown an important opportunity if you do not mail to them then.

Catalogue pointers   A few more pointers about catalogues: Work with your printer to determine the optimum number of pages, the paper stock, the format, and the print run. Naturally, your printer must be experienced in catalogue production to do this. Find one that is. Also, don't produce full-color catalogues until you can mail 200,000 or more of them. Use the front and back covers of your catalogues, along with your order form, to sell merchandise. They are very effective. Stay away from group-item shots. Display your merchandise item by item and don't try to be artistic. Instead, be clear. Steer clear of models, because they can increase your costs more than is necessary.

If you sell clothing, it's almost impossible to avoid using models, but do so if you can. Also, it is not a good idea to mix photos with illustrations. Choose between the two and stay with your choice.

Your copy should be simple, straightforward, and concise. Forget cleverness and give the facts, along with the benefits. Better to give the features and the answers to any questions that may come up than to be too brief. If you can possibly write the copy yourself, do it. You have a feel for the merchandise, or at least you should.

By all means, bind an order form into your catalogue. And offer some merchandise on that order form. Bribe people to order more than they ordinarily would. For instance, tell them that if they order $25 or more in merchandise, they will receive a free gift, and if they order $50 or more, they will receive a better free gift. And promise them a gift if they order $100 or more. Try it. People just love free gifts. Don't you? Also include on your order blank a brief letter from you to your customers. Make it warm, personal, and not too long.

Bind in an order form

Guerrillas do the whole job, which starts with *giving people what they want*. What else do people like about catalogues?

1. 36 percent say convenience is what they like most.
2. 19 percent give the nod to more variety.
3. 17 percent like low prices (hard to find in my Tiffany catalogue, and it's quite a successful one; has been for a long time).
4. 6 percent say they go for the high quality offered.
5. 22 percent list the inevitable "other" or list nothing.

What people like about catalogues

After the 78 percent who have good things to say about catalogues finish reading or ordering from them, what do they do with them? Forty-two percent save them; 41 percent toss them; 10 percent pass them on; 7 percent say "it depends".

If you're thinking of mailing a catalogue, follow these guerrilla guidelines:

- Set specific objectives on what the catalogue should do for your business.
- Define your audience so that you know who will receive your catalogue; that helps in creating and producing it.
- Preplan all the elements of your catalogue before going into production: products, prices, fulfillment, and more.
- Make all the hard decisions up front: which products to include, which to exclude, how production will be handled.
- If possible, group your offerings into clearly defined groups so that the catalogue is not a hodgepodge.
- Make a rough outline of the contents of your catalogue, including everything you wish to have in it — everything.
- Determine the exact format you want: size, typeface, color or not, paper stock, binding.
- Make a layout that is organized, logical, and pleasing to the eye of your target audience. Think of their eyes only.
- Plan, write, and perfect the copy. Then set up a time table and stick with it.

As you can tell, the business of producing and mailing catalogues is complex. But after the first year, it is exceptionally profitable — if you do it right. If you think you might ever offer a catalogue, start putting your name on as many catalogue mailing lists as possible. Then you can expect your mailbox to be filled with informative examples every day but Sunday. Mine is.

Keep it in mind that the number of Americans ordering at least one thing from a catalogue is fast approaching 95 percent, and the percentage continues to grow. There must be a reason.

Even if it isn't practical for you to use catalogues, I hope you'll try direct mail if it is at all feasible for your business. If you do, you will get a head start by using the major marketing method of the future.

Try a small number of mailings first. Test always. Learn from each test. In truth, if you break even while testing, you are doing fine. The goal is to come up with a formula that can be repeated and expanded. If you ever obtain a publicity story about your business, consider enclosing reprints of it in a mailing.

Breaking even is fine

In my own experience as an entrepreneur and as a direct-response specialist, I have found that envelopes with teaser lines get a better response than those without. I have found that short letters work better than long letters, that long brochures work better than short brochures, that postcards often make superb mailers all by themselves. I have learned that it is worth the time to check out many lists before selecting one, and that one's own customer list is a gold mine when it comes to direct mail. I know that a single mailing isn't nearly as effective as a mailing with one, two, or more follow-ups, and that a mailing with a phone follow-up is frequently best of all.

A guerrilla will either realize that direct marketing is not the way for his or her business to proceed, or will utilize direct marketing with intelligence, reading books about it, talking with direct-marketing pros, and making it his or her most cost-effective marketing method. Strange as it may seem, the majority of people like to receive mailings from businesses; so don't feel self-conscious, and put the Post Office to work for you.

Section IV

Non-Media Marketing

NOW THAT YOU KNOW YOU can market your products and services through mini-media and maxi-media, you should also know that you can succeed without using media at all. You can invite groups to your place of business to hear speakers. You can put on programs for these groups if they won't come to you. You can stage exhibits at fairs. You can display your offerings in model homes or auto showrooms or restaurants or other non-media places where groups of people will see them. You can talk with fellow merchants and entrepreneurs and arrange to exchange information, assistance, and ideas with them when possible. You can hold sales training sessions for your own people. You can ask the manufacturers that supply you for their aid in marketing. You can develop incentive plans to spur your people to greater heights. You can hold open houses and parties. You can create dazzling window displays.

Coming up are even more ways that successful entrepreneurs can promote their businesses without using the media — at least not directly. Some of these methods ought to become part of your marketing plan if you are serious about success. They are hard to develop. They require painstaking detail work. They are far more complex than they appear. But they are worth your time and effort, and for many a guerrilla they pay off handsomely.

Is it possible to succeed using only non-media marketing? Yes. But it is easier to succeed with a combination of mini-media, maxi-media, and non-media marketing. There are far more non-media media marketing opportunities available to you than there are media opportunities. *Use as many as you can.*

The way you answer the phone has a powerful influence over how people will feel about your company. Either an untrained, unfriendly voice will turn off a potential or, worse yet, a current customer — or a warm, welcoming voice will make the caller want to do business with a company such as yours. Is this media? No. Is this marketing? It is. So are the neatness of your premises, the smiles prospects receive upon entering, the respect for their time displayed when they place an order or make a request. If you know the name of your customer and use it, that's personalized marketing on a face-to-face basis. Guerrillas know the importance of eye contact in non-media marketing such as trade shows and of greeting people who visit their business.

Let me give you a prime example of non-media marketing that is so unusual it doesn't fit into any chapter. Although it's unique, it is the spirit of common sense. This guerrilla marketing technique helps you obtain the names of prime prospects, a noble endeavor. To do it, guerrillas invest in high school students on bicycles. The roofing guerrilla pays a student $1 for the address of each home in the community that needs a new roof. The gardening guerrilla pays $1 for the address of each home that could do with some quality gardening. The paving guerrilla pays for the address of each home that needs work on its driveway.

These guerrillas know that they will get only about thirty to fifty new addresses a month, not a lot. But at each address is at least one human being who needs a new roof or a manicured garden or a smooth driveway. And that person is probably soothed by the fact that you're a local business. Guerrillas write to them, pointing out the problem and offering a solution. Then guerrillas use the mini-medium of a personal letter to make everything happen (as is so often the case). I predict that you will get a lot of mileage from the non-media weapons you employ — in the form of PR, reprints of PR, and a warm, cozy relationship with your entire community, if not the entire planet.

Non-media marketing also includes your own attitudes. Your willingness to abide by guerrilla marketing principles indicates the right spirit of competitiveness. Your belief in the benefits of your product or service is manifested in the enthusiasm that spreads from you to your employees to your customers. These attitudes are non-media marketing in that they influence people, but don't cost you a cent for media. Combine them with media and get ready to soar.

22

Advertising Specialties and Samples: If You've Got It, Flaunt It

ADVERTISING SPECIALTIES ARE ITEMS on which the imprinted name (and sometimes the address, phone number, and theme line) of the advertiser appears. Examples of advertising specialties are ball-point pens, note pads, briefcases, calendars, key chains, paper-clip holders, caps, T-shirts, pins, playing cards, shopping bags, belt buckles, banners, lighters, bumbags, and more, lots more.

Consider these specialties to be the equivalent of billboards. That means they are great for reminder advertising. They are usually terrible as your only marketing medium. They do, however, put your name in front of your prospective customers. And your prospects don't even have to leave home or office to see them. As part of a marketing mix, that's a very good thing. As you well know by now, familiarity is one of the keys to success. And there is no question that ad specialties breed increased awareness.

Yet that's just the tip of the advertising specialty iceberg. Those free gifts — and that's the whole idea — to give them away gratis — can be used to leverage many a sale, and our nation abounds with billionaires who realized the power of something free. Procter & Gamble is famed for its generosity with free samples. **Everyone loves free gifts**

Advertising specialties make your prospects and customers feel good about you, especially if the specialty items are valuable. I remember that a businessman buddy of mine was ecstatic upon receiving a digital clock-pen. He spoke with reverence of the supplier who gave it to him, and he continues to show his loyalty to the firm. A specialty item with a high perceived value does breed a sense of unconscious obligation, to be sure. And if you can purchase a breakthrough type of inexpensive product for your deserving prospects *and customers*, by all means give it serious consideration. There are no particular industries or businesses that benefit more than others by this marketing medium. But if, for example, you come across a unique and advanced measuring device, and your prime prospects are contractors and carpenters, you'd be well advised to give it a shot. Be proud to put your name on such a gift. Guerrillas never put their names on anything shoddy, anything that will break at a dirty look, anything that doesn't make them proud to give it away.

Give away a sample Be proud to use sampling, too, if you sincerely believe that by providing exposure to your product or service you will win loyal customers. Choose sampling over advertising specialties every time, if it comes to making a choice. Both involve giving something away. Both win friends and create favorable associations. But sampling accomplishes these things by means of freebies that are more pertinent than advertising-specialty items, valuable as they may be.

I strongly suggest that you examine the use of ad specialties if they seem to lend themselves to your type of business. If, for example, you are a mobile auto mechanic, it's a dandy idea to give your customers and prospects key rings (for their car keys) with your name and number on them. On the other hand, if you are a computer consultant, handing out key rings makes no sense whatsoever. But handing out small guides to software makes a lot of sense.

Selecting the best ad specialities I have gained a wealth of information from the following tactic. I would consider my line of merchandise or services very carefully, then look in the Yellow Pages under "Advertising Specialties" and pick out the best ad — judging it by the amount of information it gives and its credibility. I'd call the rep listed in that ad and ask him or her to pay me a visit. While still on the phone, I'd tell the rep who my target audience was and ask the rep to recommend specialties that have worked for others in my line. I'd also ask about new ad specialty items that haven't yet been tried. Each year, a plethora of new items come onto the market, and a good rep regularly alerts his clients to the new ones. When the rep paid me a visit, I'd take the time to look through his or her pleasantly cumbersome catalogue of available specialties, and perhaps I'd get ten ideas that hadn't occurred to the rep.

I'd also ask the rep to tell me about upcoming specialties, gift ideas, and specialties that I might recommend to my own clients. I might decide that none of the specialties are for me. But at least I'd know a lot more about what is available, what certain specialties cost, and what use other companies have made of this method of non-media marketing. Perhaps I wouldn't want to use a specialty item now but would want to use one later.

I must admit to a prejudice toward calendars as an advertising specialty. I'm not talking about ordinary calendars. I'm referring to gorgeous calendars that most people will happily hang in their homes or offices, then look at almost every day. I have such calendars in my own home, and I have patronized the companies that gave them away. (I'm not really sure whether my business was instigated by the calendars; probably not, but one can't be too sure of one's unconscious thought processes.) And I have recommended the use of handsome calendars to my clients. They have used them and continued to use them. One of the reasons I like calendars as ad specialties is that people tend to look at them a lot. One of the reasons I do not like, say, playing cards, is that people tend not to look at them a lot, and when they do, they look at the side without your name and logo.

Marketing daily with calendars

If you do decide you want to distribute calendars, you've got to make that decision in the summer, at the very latest, so that the right calendars with the right inscriptions can be in your hands at the right time — probably in early November.

Put your name on their note pad
You might also consider note pads. Imprinted note pads have become very effective lead-generating gimmicks for salespeople, I'm told. What you do is pay a printer to stick a photo, your name, address, phone number, and theme line on a sheet of paper, then print up a bunch of sheets that are made into note pads — or Post-its — each sheet of the pad an ad for you. Next, distribute those pads — free, naturally — to your prospects. Either hand them out or mail them. People tend to keep such pads by their phones or on their desks. They use them to write notes to themselves. Every time they look at one of the scraps of paper, they see the name of your offering. Of course even the hottest offer will not motivate them to pick up the phone and order whatever you are selling unless they need it. But when they do need what you have to offer, chances are your name will come to mind first. And that's a big help to any guerrilla.

As with other types of marketing, the key here is repetition. Because it takes time to become known in a community, it's important to keep circulating new note pads.

I know of a real estate salesman who estimates that he earns between $15,000 and $20,000 in commissions per year from listings generated by his note pads. He sounds like a real guerrilla in that he obviously tracks his sales leads like crazy, and then even translates them into dollar figures.

There are no hard and fast rules as to who should use ad specialties, when they should be used, or how they can be used best. But your ad specialty rep probably has many tips for you. If George, of Let George Do It, were to consider advertising specialties, he might like the idea of calendars and rulers, maybe ball-point pens, and possibly even note pads. Or George might let his altruism come shining through by giving away auto litter bags with his name on them. But George would probably not get involved in giving away freebies until his business was well established.

The cost of an individual advertising specialty is tiny. But the volume in which you must order each specialty is not tiny. I once gave away felt-tip pens for a business I was running. The cost of each pen was less than a dollar. But I had to order 300 pens before the manufacturers would put my name on them. At the time $300 sounded like a lot.

A client of mine who is very successful at fund raising for public schools gives away pens with his name, company name, and phone number on them. His costs are even lower than mine were, because he orders so many pens. His pens, by the way, are neither felt-tip nor ball-point. Because he's a real guerrilla, he gives away a new type of pen. People perceive it to be a breakthrough product, and they associate him with innovation.

His company achieved tremendous profitability by using advertising specialties as a key ingredient in its marketing mix. Prospects were sent a letter or postcard with a color picture of a free gift such as a microcalculator or a quartz desk clock — both available for under $2. The teaser said "A free gift for you!" and the recipient, being of the human race, would open the envelope and learn that merely by requesting more information, the gift would be given without obligation. From this point on, the company gave the gift, paid a personal call, telemarketed, sent another letter, made a phone call or two or three, and prospered to a point where it was one of the 100 fastest-growing companies in America. All because of advertising specialties? Of course not. But they did a bang-up job of getting that door open, never an easy task.

Free gifts as door openers

In regard to the copy on your ad specialty, don't make the mistake of leaving it off entirely. I suggest that you include your name, address, phone number, theme line, and as much copy as will tastefully fit on the item. Not much will fit on a key ring or a pen. A bit more will fit on a calendar. But use restraint and remember that people won't hang a calendar if it looks like an ad. Nonetheless, it is possible to convey more information than the usual name and address. A guerrilla markets at every opportunity. Still, I caution you to use good taste more than hard sell.

A final hint: talk to people who give away ad specialties themselves. Ask if they consider them effective. Ask them to recommend a good rep. Ask about cost-effectiveness and how long they've been using ad specialties.

New ones every year I'm knocked out at each year's crop of new advertising specialties. Several are exciting and economical inventions. Clock-pens, solar calculators, Lucite-framed quartz desk clocks for a buck — don't let any winners pass you by. If there is any potential reason for you to invest in this low-cost marketing method, see to it that you find out about the new specialties each year. They can't help you all by themselves — but they won't hurt you either, unless they break on day one.

If you're considering using advertising specialties as a guerrilla marketing tool, you should have an idea of what your target market might want in the way of a free gift. The October 1992 issue of *Business and Incentive Strategies* magazine **Insights into** reported on a survey conducted to see what sorts of incentive **sales** items people most like to receive from their employers for **incentives** special performance. Say what you will about stereotypes, but when merchandise incentives were offered, men preferred electrical gadgets while women chose clothing. For merchandise incentives worth over $1000, men went for big-screen TVs while women selected a new wardrobe. In travel incentives, women's top choices for vacation activities were relaxation, sightseeing, and culture. Men opted for relaxation, sports/outdoor activity, and sightseeing. For an overseas travel destination, both men and women picked Australia and New Zealand as their top choice. The favorite incentive for both men and women (as if you didn't know) was money preferred by 51 percent of the men and 56 percent of the women. One thing about crisp cash: you don't have to question its quality.

If you're giving out free samples, the quality of your offering is as or more important than with a free gift. Sampling can help you all by itself if the quality's there. And it can kill you if your product or service is at all shoddy. Guerrilla marketing can hasten the failure of your business by letting more people know faster about the faults of your offering.

I consider sampling to be the most effective marketing method. Of course I am assuming that you have an excellent product or service. If your product is wonderful, sampling will help it take off in a hurry. You've got to have the ability to service the people you sell, and you've got to offer true quality. But if you do, sampling works wonders.

One of my marketing idols, Procter & Gamble, spends a fortune on sampling. So do other large, successful, sophisticated marketing concerns. But that does not rule out guerrillas. In fact, before this chapter ends, you'll know of six instances where sampling helped small-businesspeople realize healthy profits.

You'll have to examine your offering to see if it lends itself to sampling. Most offerings can be sampled. The first one that comes to mind is a car. You certainly won't want to give away a sample car. But almost all auto dealers offer free test rides. That's a sample. And it succeeds. Usually, and especially when you are offering a service, your sampling must be offered to one person at a time. But if you are offering a product, perhaps you can give away several of your items as free samples.

At my current address, I've received in my mailbox free samples of toothpaste, detergent, shampoo, cigarettes, and chewing gum. I continue to use the toothpaste. And we buy the new detergent. I doubt if any other marketing method would have persuaded me to switch brands so quickly. In time, more sampling will probably woo me from the brands I currently use. Like most Americans, I'm a fickle consumer, though I've driven my Buick GS-400 convertible 325,000 miles with the same engine and transmission. (When it had 300,000 miles on it, I took a photo of it, with its fancy new gold paint job, and sent it to Buick, along with a letter thanking them for making such a grand car; a month later I received a two-line form letter signed by a machine. I'm ashamed of such an unguerrilla-like response from the city of my birth.)

Naturally, it costs a bundle to give away free samples. But if you can look upon the cost as a conservative investment, you might be tempted to engage in sampling rather than radio advertising. It's worth thinking about. I cannot think of a more **That's the** guerilla-spirited marketing method. It is the essence of hon- **spirit!** esty, since it forces you to offer quality, and people will appreciate you for it. What's more, your competition probably doesn't do it. Not for the lazy or unimaginative, it is an optimum marketing vehicle for guerrillas.

Examples of Now here are the six examples I promised you on how **samples** sampling works:

In the early days of waterbeds, people considered the beds to be a fad, a mere offshoot of the counterculture. To overcome sales resistance to the new product, a retailer offered a free thirty-night sleeping trial: He would deliver and install the beds, then make a phone call thirty days later to see if his prospects wanted him to pick up the beds or were willing to pay for them. Ninety-three percent of the people were willing to pay for the beds. Sampling paid off.

Another entrepreneur was launching a newsletter. He advertised in magazines. He engaged in direct mail. Both got mediocre results. Then he mailed free sample copies to prospects. Instant success. Sampling came through. Incidentally, it cost him a total of $500 to try the sampling; he realized $7000 in profits from the attempt.

A third guerrilla was marketing a large-screen television set of his own design. Very few people took the time to visit the showroom in which it was displayed. So he took out ads offering free home trials. Soon he had to discontinue the ads because the response was so great. And even better than the response to his trial offer was the fact that 90 percent of the respondents purchased from him after sampling. That is the main idea, you know.

A fourth guerrilla, an office manager who baked chocolate chip cookies and sold them at flea markets on weekends (earning more doing that than through her office-manager salary), engaged in sampling. She baked two sizes of cookies. The tiny ones were free samples. The large ones were $1 each. She gave away the tiny ones — one per customer. More than half the customers were then tempted by the enchanting flavor and crispy goodness of the sample to purchase one or more of the $1 variety. One more case of sampling that worked.

Thus far, I've told you about two samples of merchandise that were loaned rather than given away (waterbeds and large-screen TVs) and two samples that were given away permanently (newsletters and cookies). What you can learn from this is that it does not take a giant company to engage in sampling, and sampling can be employed even if your product is too large or too expensive to give away. Free sampling can provide instant results that are not achievable through any other marketing method.

If it is at all possible to allow your prospects to sample your offering, let them. Are you a consultant? Offer a free one-hour consultation. If George, of Let George Do It, wanted to show people how good he is at home repair, he would have no trouble giving away free samples. A project, accomplished in one hour, would do the trick. And George would, in all likelihood, benefit greatly from his sampling, not to mention his new, budding relationship with a grateful prospect. The large-screen-TV entrepreneur had to make his sampling come alive through advertising. His ads called attention to his sampling. So you can see that some sampling depends upon other methods of marketing. But some sampling can work on its own.

My fifth guerrilla sampler, a person who washed windows for commercial establishments, frequently washed the windows of his prospects for free. This demonstrated his proficiency, his speed, his method of working. It also netted him several large customers. And it didn't require any advertising to get started.

Sometimes I see ads in marketing publications for writers who offer to write for free — just to prove how good they are. If they are indeed good, this advertising-then-sampling combination nets them quite a lot of business. Hardly anyone turns down something that is offered free. It seems that I'm seeing more and more ads of that type these days. It may be that the economy is tough as nails, but it also may be that people are catching on to the effectiveness of this method of marketing.

Example six also involves a person who offered a service. He offered to come to my residence weekly and wash my car, and promised to wash my car that night for free, to show how good he was. I could see the results of his work the next day, realize how convenient his service was, and then when he came back, sign up for it. Was I ever tempted to say no to his offer? Of course not. In fact, he made it nearly impossible to say no. The next morning, my car was gleaming. The next evening, he knocked on my door and asked if I wanted the same service every week. That man had earned himself a steady customer with one free sample. It probably took him fifteen minutes to wash my car. But it demonstrated to me how good he was, how convenient he was, and what a nice fellow he was. That his price was definitely not competitive didn't even enter my mind.

By giving me a sample of his great service, the car washer caused me to think positive thoughts about his offering. So I was won over quite easily. I wonder if he could have ever obtained my business through other methods. Let's see. He could have talked me into buying from him by canvassing. And in a way, his initial contact with me was a canvass. He might also have signed me up through telephone marketing, but I'm not so sure I would have signed. It certainly wouldn't have been as easy a sale as the sampling was, since he couldn't have proven his worth over the phone. A personal letter might have impressed me, but it wouldn't have given the opportunity for give and take that the personal contact did. It also wouldn't have let him prove his point. I would have read his circular or brochure with interest. But since I had never had a car washer who paid house calls, I might not have given the matter serious thought. And a sign, a classified ad, or a listing in the Yellow Pages would certainly not have won my business.

None of the maxi-media marketing methods would have worked as well. Newspapers, magazines, radio, TV, billboards, direct mail — I doubt if any of them would have made me an instant customer. Certainly if he had put his name on an advertising specialty, I would not have signed up so quickly. But sampling did the trick for him. And it might do the trick for you — in a hurry.

Instant customers

Such sampling of services is very expensive if you place a price tag on your time, and believe that terrible lie about time being money (time is far more valuable than money; stop kidding yourself), but very inexpensive if you think of out-of-pocket expenses only. Sampling is quite different from other methods of marketing because it does not depend upon repetition. One great sample will do it all. Before you purchased this book, perhaps you looked through a few pages. Maybe you looked at the table of contents. If so, that was sampling on the part of the bookstore. And it worked. I bet sampling will work for you, too. Use it if you possibly can.

Time is not money

23

Free Seminars and Demonstrations: Show and Sell

I HAVE A CLIENT WHOSE business is computer education. His classes are unique, effective, and impressive. But standard marketing methods didn't attract many customers. So he decided to hold a free seminar on computers for people who knew nothing about them. He placed an ad and over 500 people showed up for the seminar.

Had he teamed up with a great salesperson, he might have sold his program to as many as 50 percent of the people attending. But he'd never dreamed so many people would show up, so the number of people he sold on his series of lessons was closer to 5 percent. Next time he holds a free seminar, he'll be a lot better prepared to close his sales. In fact, he might even hire a professional salesperson.

Many people who give paid seminars or courses for a living advertise free seminars with ads in the business sections of newspapers. One speed-reading school advertised its free seminars with television commercials. An income tax expert markets his free seminars by means of publicity stories coupled with radio commercials on talk-oriented stations. Many entrepreneurs earn a great deal of money with paid seminars and courses. But they cannot attract large numbers of people to paid seminars and courses merely through newspaper ads, so they attract them to free seminars, then convert them to paying customers.

As one guerrilla to another, I sincerely recommend the same tactic to you. I recommend, if it is at all feasible for your type of product or service, that you advertise in the newspaper that you are holding a free seminar on the topic most closely connected with your product or service. Then obtain as many customers for your free seminar as you can. They may purchase your products or they may sign up for your service. If you hold a decent seminar, they will.

When I say seminar, I really mean lecture. Give your audience valuable information and demonstrate your expertise or your product's efficacy for, say, the first forty-five minutes. Then spend the next fifteen minutes selling whatever it is you wish to sell. What I am talking about is a fifteen-minute, straight-from-the-heart commercial — delivered by you or by someone you hire. The entire process takes one hour. After that, you sign up the prospects. Unlike professional seminar leaders, you probably won't be signing them up for a paid seminar (unless selling information is your business). But you will be allowing them to buy your offering, And they'll want it because your message, your demonstration, your enthusiasm, and your proven expertise will have created within them a desire to purchase from you.

Give valuable information

There is no question that an in-person commercial is better than a radio or TV commercial. Certainly a fifteen-minute selling opportunity will pan out better than a thirty-second selling opportunity. For this reason, seminars and demonstrations are being utilized more and more to market products and services.

In a sense, a lecture or demonstration is very much like a sample. Your prospects get to see for themselves what you have to offer. They probably get to touch it, if it's a product, and they get to ask questions, whether it's a product or a service. They get to learn more about your offering this way than they do by standard marketing methods. And just as sampling convinces many people that they should buy a good product, so can your seminar.

A seminar is a sample

Before I write one more word, I should emphasize that a free seminar/demonstration amounts to marketing in a vacuum unless two other factors are present. First, your free imparting of information must be advertised, so that you'll have a large group of prospects. Advertise in the newspaper, on the radio, or on TV. Go for the free publicity that is readily available when you're offering a free seminar. Tell the truth in your ads as to the contents of the seminar, and try to attract honest prospects, not just warm bodies. Second, be sure that either you or an associate can sell your offering to those prospects after the seminar is over. My client was a brilliant lecturer. People listened intently to his every word. They enjoyed looking at him and listening to him. As a lecturer, he was first rate. But as a salesman, he was eighth rate. He had no inkling of how to close. He had no instinct for blood. He didn't have the kind of personality that could take advantage of the momentum his lecture had built. So he signed up only 5 percent of the audience, rather than the 50 percent that was possible.

Two key factors

If you can, demonstrate your product or service at your seminar. Keep in mind that although what you are offering is free, people are giving up their time. They are traveling to the place where you are holding your seminar. And they have expectations, based upon your ad. You must give them value in exchange. You must live up to their expectations and move beyond them. You must treat them as if they have paid to hear you. You should make sure that even if they do not buy from you, they still feel that their time was well spent. Perhaps they'll buy from you later.

Where to conduct seminars

Where should you conduct your seminar? At your place of business, if possible. Just rent the chairs you'll need. Perhaps you'll conduct it outdoors, if you are demonstrating gardening skills or the like. Perhaps you'll conduct it in a gym, if you want to show and sell exercise equipment. Eventually, you'll be able to hold it on the premises of a "partner" with whom you have a *fusion marketing arrangement* — a collaboration of marketing talent, money, and ideas. (Read more about the fascinating topic of strategic alliances in *Guerrilla Marketing Excellence*, Piatkus 1993.) Most seminars are held in motels or hotels where seminar facilities are readily available. Such facilities include a lectern, a microphone, a blackboard, chairs, and easily available coffee, water, and rest rooms. It is also advisable to offer free parking. If you have a store, a free seminar held there will work best. It will show your prospects where you are and what you sell. For instance, a seminar on decorating held in your furniture showroom is a natural.

People appreciate useful information. They appreciate it all the more when it is free. When you conduct a seminar or workshop, when you give a lecture, when you demonstrate a product or service, you prove your expertise. You establish yourself as an authority. You gain credibility. Even if people do not buy from you right then and there, they very well may buy from you later. There is a tactic, however, that some very successful (and very high-pressure) businesses employ to get the maximum number of people to buy right then and there. They establish three "sales points" on the way to the exit. Upon conclusion of the free seminar, the speaker tells the customers that they can either sign up for the paid seminar at a particular table or with specific representatives located throughout the room. Probably four reps are present to sign people up. Prospects who do not buy must then pass the three sales points before leaving the room. At each, they are given a different sales pitch, stronger each time. Some people sign up in the main room, others at the first sales point, and still others at the second sales point. Another group signs up at the third sales point. Only a tiny group — who have world-class sales resistance — leave the building without putting their hands to their wallets. Sounds a bit pressured for this guerrilla.

You're the authority

This practice is common among some consciousness-raising groups. It is the hardest of all possible sells, and it is not easy to resist. As you can see, it takes several people to accomplish. But it does work. And if you care about profits more than you care about social propriety, you might employ it.

Free seminars, even without triple-teamed closes, can be a bonanza for you, and you should try to market with them if you possibly can. It may be that your business just doesn't lend itself to seminars. If you operate a window-washing business, a carwashing business, or a mail-order publishing business, perhaps seminars are not for you. But if you run an income-tax preparation, instructional, or retail furniture business, perhaps they are.

Think about the field in which you operate. Can you give a lecture for forty-five minutes on any aspect of it? Which aspect? How will this tie in with your offering? Do you have the showmanship to lecture for forty-five minutes and hold the attention of your audience, or should you delegate that task to someone else? Do you have the salesmanship to close sales right then and there, or should that, too, be the job of an associate? What will you be selling at the seminar? Will it be products? Services? Books? Lessons? A paid seminar? Products or services of a fusion marketing partner?

As with sampling, if it is at all feasible, simply try to offer one free seminar to market your business. It can be a lot of fun. And it can be extremely profitable, with a lower cost per sale than advertising in any newspaper or on any radio station. It will give you both immediate and long-term benefits. You'll get to mention in future marketing that you have lectured in your field, led seminars in your area of expertise. Giving free seminars is a very innovative way to market.

Demonstrate   Demonstrations can be given not only at seminars, but also in homes, at parties (be sure you consider party-plan marketing for your business), in stores, at fairs and shows, in parks, at beaches, almost anywhere. People are attracted to small crowds, and a free demonstration will almost certainly attract a small crowd. At a free demonstration, which is much shorter than a seminar — no more than five minutes — be prepared to sell and take orders immediately afterward. Folks who give seminars and demonstrations often have cohorts all set to accept customers' credit cards, checks, and cash. The person giving the demo or seminar is usually too busy answering questions to take orders. So be sure you have that base covered.

A free demonstration need not be marketed in the same way as a seminar. Just showing up at a high-traffic location, or placing some well-conceived signs may do the trick. Of course, it is okay to advertise and distribute circulars. But those things may not be necessary. It will be necessary, though, to provide the showmanship and salesmanship.

Can you demonstrate your product or service effectively? Be sure you ask yourself and answer honestly. If you can say yes, by all means give it your best shot. Rarely will you be afforded so golden an opportunity.

A few moments ago, I mentioned the idea of giving your free seminar or demo in a party situation. More and more items every year are being marketed through party-plan marketing. **Throw a party** Here's how it works: A person becomes a party-plan representative for a company. Let's say it's an art gallery, since so many of them engage in this kind of marketing. No, wait — let's say it's your business. You throw a party for all of your friends and close acquaintances, just as Tupperware party-planners have been doing for decades, and very successfully as I'm sure you've heard.

At the party, you serve coffee and pastries, maybe even little sandwiches. You also give a well-planned sales spiel about whatever you are selling. You show examples, conduct a brief seminar, distribute samples, or give a demonstration to the assembled throng. The lighting is optimum. Music especially selected for the occasion may be playing in the background. Your enthusiasm is bubbly and contagious. You're obviously proud of your offerings. It shows. Your friends start to like them, too. And the prices! They sound so low. A buying frenzy starts. Fifteen of your offerings are sold. They sell for an average of $100 apiece. But you purchased them for $25 each, including everything, from your supplier.

Each $100 sale results in $75 for you. You have a right to feel proud of yourself. You earned $1125 for the night and spent only $50 for refreshments — a $1075 profit. And that's just the start. Now you tell your friends that they can do the same. And some do. The word spreads. The parties spread. Soon they're being held in several towns. Naturally, you get the lion's share of sales from the parties thrown by the people you've signed up. You're raking in the bucks. Your buddies, along with strangers who are enthused about what you sell, are raking in the bucks. Your suppliers are doing very well, thank you. You are very, very, happy that you engaged in party-plan marketing.

Can you? Here are the types of companies that do already: exercise-machine companies, art galleries, kitchen-equipment companies (such as Tupperware), women's clothing manufacturers, vitamin manufacturers, X-rated product companies (the burgeoning "pleasure" industry), cosmetics manufacturers, computer companies, and lingerie manufacturers. The list is not shrinking.

Such parties are ideal places for demonstrations. And the people attending *are already conditioned to buy*. You can't beat that kind of situation if you're a practicing guerrilla. Of all the places at which free seminars or demonstrations can be held, parties certainly rank up there near the top.

Have seminar, will travel About the only disadvantage of free seminars and demonstrations (except for parties) is that you must do quite a bit of traveling. Either you or a person you delegate. You can't keep holding free demos and seminars in the same area over and over again. You've got to go on the road and talk to fresh prospects. But you can make these free sessions part of your marketing plan and give one or two per year. A guerrilla would find some way to utilize them. Will you?

24
Trade Shows, Exhibits, Fairs: Making a Public Spectacle

SOME WILDLY SUCCESSFUL ENTREPRENEURS employ only one major method of marketing: they display and sell their wares at trade shows, exhibits, and fairs. They realize that many serious prospects will attend these gatherings, so they put all their efforts into exhibiting and selling their merchandise (they usually sell products rather than services). This is not to say that their show booths are their only marketing vehicles. But they are their primary ones. And in a few instances, this is the only way a person needs to market. I don't like telling this to you for fear it might encourage a lax attitude, but it is the truth.

The marketing plan of many a guerrilla consists of appearances at four major shows or fairs, plus circulars or brochures to be distributed at the shows. Nothing else. And to be sure, nothing else is needed.

I once attended a large national furniture show with a client who owned a chain of furniture stores. He very much wanted to be one of the first people through the doors at the three-day event. When I asked him why, he told me that he would first breeze through the show, making notes and looking at all the exhibits. Then he would quickly return to the displays that had caught his attention and order a full year's worth of items, making certain to get agreements that he would be the exclusive outlet for each item.

Sure enough, it took him, with me hot on his heels, a mere thirty minutes to walk the miles of aisles. Then he spent the next two hours dickering with the manufacturers or distributors that tickled his fancy. At the end of two and one-half hours, he was delighted, having signed up for a year's worth of purchases, all with exclusive arrangements. And just as happy as he, maybe even happier, were the handful of entrepreneurs who had attracted his attention with their merchandise, displays, salesmanship, and readiness to grant concessions. I well recall the look on one man's face when he realized that in only ten minutes he had sold half a million dollars' worth of goods. Fifty thou per minute is a pretty luscious sales rate.

The $50,000 minute

Two ways to display

There are a couple of ways to display what you sell at such shows. One way, the standard way, is to rent a booth, set up a display, and give it your best. Another way, guerrilla-like in character, and a fine method of testing the efficacy of trade shows as a non-media marketing medium for you, is to visit a show, find a display booth that offers merchandise compatible with yours, and strike up a deal with the exhibitor whereby you share a portion of the next booth the exhibitor rents. That means you pay part of the rental fee, assume part of the sales responsibility, and allow your items to be displayed and sold along with those of your new compatriot.

Be a visitor

Visiting such shows is a revelation to the astute guerrilla. When you visit one or two, you will learn of products that compete with or complement yours. You will also discover products that knock your socks off — products with which you would love to become associated, and possibly could, as a fusion marketing partner. You'll learn the right way to display goods, and the wrong way. You'll pick up some dandy ideas for brochures, signs, and demonstrations. You'll learn a heck of a lot from the mistakes of others — people who have great merchandise but don't know how to market it. And you'll meet people who may be able to help you distribute what you sell.

Let's look at a case in point. A man-and-wife team who marketed greeting cards all by themselves by calling on stationery stores were soon alerted to the existence of stationery shows at which greeting cards are displayed. There, they were told, they could display their own cards and make sales, they could team up with other card manufacturers, and better yet they could meet distributors who could distribute their cards throughout the country. The two budding entrepreneurs went to the show, checked out the cards and displays of others, and met several representatives who offered to distribute their cards. Because they were greenhorns at the business, they were delighted, and they signed on with several of the reps.

Business picked up for them that next year. But in talking with a few fellow card sellers, they learned that there are basically two kinds of reps one meets at shows. Some are ordinary reps who conduct an ordinary amount of sales activity, and achieve ordinary distribution in ordinary stores. Those, alas, were the kind of reps the man-and-wife team had signed up. The other kind of reps are known as Rolls-Royce reps. They have the ability to move prodigious numbers of greeting cards by distributing only in high-volume stores and expending a great deal of selling energy.

The next year, the man and wife went to the stationery shows and signed up with only Rolls-Royce reps. By signing with them, the couple increased their sales fivefold over the year before, propelling themselves into a deliriously wonderful tax bracket. So if you are looking for national distribution of your goods, look for Rolls-Royce reps at major trade shows.

While displaying your products in your own booth — something you will most likely want to do after you are ready to take on large orders — you will have a great opportunity to engage in four other types of marketing at the same time:

1. You'll be able to hand out circulars. I suggest that you hire someone, preferably a gorgeous woman (or a

Market with more than your display

gorgeous man, if women are your prime prospects), to distribute your circulars while walking through the show. She or he will pass out as many as 5000 circulars — all inviting people to visit your booth. If you do that, you will instantly rise above most of the other exhibitors, since they will not be practicing such a guerrilla-like tactic. You'll also attract more prospects.

2. You'll be able to give away brochures. Because brochures are more costly than circulars, you won't want to give as many away. But by disseminating them at your booth only, you'll be able to narrow the distribution down to serious prospects only. And your brochures will do heavy-duty work for you. Many people attend shows and exhibits merely to collect brochures. Then they study the brochures and place their orders on the basis of the information they've gleaned. So this is a chance to make your brochure a powerful sales tool. Be sure to get the names and addresses of the people to whom you give brochures. Just ask for their card.

3. You'll have a great chance to demonstrate your goods to real prospects who are in a buying mood. You can demonstrate your offerings to large groups of people. And since your competitors will probably be at the show too, you'll have a good opportunity to prove the advantages of your product.

4. You'll have ample opportunity to give away free samples. Rarely will you be afforded the chance to give samples to so many potential customers. So if it's possible to let people sample your merchandise, a show or exhibit is the place to do it.

Perhaps now you can see how entrepreneurs avail themselves of the opportunities at shows with 100 percent effort, and why they concentrate their marketing energies and dollars on shows.

Pay close attention to this next guerrilla secret. It frequently spells the difference between astonishing success and depressing failure. It is quite obvious, or so I thought until I saw exhibitors who didn't understand the concept at all. So let me make it even more obvious right here and now. Your main purpose in having a booth at a trade show, fair, or exhibit is *to sell your product*. If it is not that, then it's to *get quality names for your mailing list*. Sure, you want to display, to demonstrate, to educate. But you really want to sell. So you've got to have the means to take orders right there at your booth. You've got to have a person there who is dedicated to selling. You should aim for a large volume of sales at the show itself, in spite of the fancy brochures you will be passing out. Don't forget the furniture store entrepreneur I wrote about at the start of this chapter. He visited the shows to look and then to buy. He didn't care about brochures. He wanted to place his orders at the show. **The main thrust**

If you do not sell a lot of what you want to sell at a show, you may have failed in this marketing effort. Don't feel great because you have given away cartons of brochures, made lots of friends, obtained loads of contacts. That's fine, but if you have not sold a large volume of what you are selling, you have not taken advantage of the glorious opportunity afforded you by such shows. I recall two competitors at a national show. Both had attractive displays. Both gave imaginative demonstrations. Both handed out compelling brochures. But the first company figured that the show was a place to display — so it made zero sales. The second company, a new, small, young partnership, figured that the show was a place to sell — so it made $4.5 million in sales during a three-day period. I believe I've made my point.

Before wandering off to the fair, there are two guerrilla tactics for you to know about trade shows. The first involves the recognition that there are prospects and there are large, hot prospects. If you've done your crucial pre-trade show homework, closely perusing the trade magazines and talking with **All prospects aren't created equal** industry insiders, you'll know exactly who the big fish are. These large hot prospects deserve to be invited to your hospitality suite at a hotel near the trade show. In it, intensify your personal bond with these people. Don't sell. Make your friendship closer.

The second tactic is mandatory for companies that didn't **Follow up** sell a lot at the show. It is to *follow up within ten days on the* **within ten** *prospects you met.* Write them, call them, and keep the **days** memory of your offerings fresh in their minds. Without follow-up, you're probably just wasting your time at a trade show. And you know how important your time is — far more important than money. If you run out of money, any guerrilla can find ways to generate more. But if you run out of time, no guerrilla tactic can alter that reality.

Many craftspeople sell all the crafts they make at one or two yearly shows. They spend most of the year making their items, then spend a few weeks selling them. Often, no other marketing is necessary for them. But generally, to succeed at marketing in a show, exhibit, or fair, you need a combination of marketing tools: a professional-looking and beckoning display; a supply of informative brochures; a larger supply of enticing circulars to be passed out at the show; a method of demonstrating, sampling, or showing off your goods; and at least two high-energy salespeople. If you have all of those, you are a guerrilla and you have primed yourself to succeed.

Your exhibit at the trade show should be as professional as you can afford. New technology in audio-visual presentations makes it possible for you to stage a continuous multimedia extravaganza — including slides, film, videotape, and music. Lighting can be combined with this multimedia display to literally spotlight your products as they are being featured in **Dancing** your multimedia show. As the visual images dance before the **visual** eyes of your prospects, and as music soothes their conscious **images** minds and gains access to their unconscious, the tape-recorded voice of a master motivator tells your audience that they should buy from you, that they should trust you, that they should give their money to you. And there you can be, order pad at the ready, all set to sign, seal, and deliver.

That's the best possible scenario for a trade-show exhibit. If you can't afford it, work down, step by step, including as much as you can.

In most big-city Yellow Page directories are several columns of "Display Designers and Producers." These businesses offer such lovelies as modular exhibit systems. They will construct or they will rent, and they will even store your exhibit while you're not using it. They'll make a miniature model of your exhibit before you give them an okay to build the real thing — or ten real things. They craft handsome exhibit displays of wood, plastic, cardboard, or metal. They make displays of any size, wired and ready to go.

I'm always impressed and educated when I walk through a display warehouse. I discover great ideas for future displays. I get a good fix on current prices, both for renting and for purchasing. Because the technology is moving so rapidly, it's a good idea to make a yearly visit to one of your area's largest display companies. Ask to see the best they have. And remember — you may be able to afford it if you go in with a few other compatible companies. Case in point: at a recent waterbed trade show, the best exhibit was a multimedia display using holograms and laser technology. It was paid for by a mattress maker, a heater manufacturer, and a bed-frame company. Each of these three compatible companies got a first-class reputation for 33 percent of the first-class price.

The display warehouse

Of course, you can always build your own display. If you have the time, talent, and equipment, give it consideration. But do me a favor. Before you do it yourself, look at what is available to you now. That's what your competitors will probably use. Can you do better? Can you keep abreast of new developments?

Just as important as an award-winning display are the people who man — or woman — your booth at the trade show. They should be talented in several areas. Here are a few tips:

1. Staff your booth with *enough* people. Not doing so can be fatal. I recall a show booth that was manned by two marvelous company reps. They were backed by a beautiful display. At one point, one of the reps was having lunch and the other was visiting another booth. The only person left was a lackadalsical fellow who didn't really understand the company's business and was really hired to be a gofer. Naturally, that was when two of the biggest customers in the industry visited the booth. They couldn't get answers to their questions, couldn't get an explanation of a new product being introduced, so they moved on and gave their business to someone else. Don't blow your opportunities. Be sure that a top-rate person is always at the booth. To do that may require at least two, and if you can arrange it, even three, top rate people to attend the show and attend to the exhibit. One of those people must always be on hand to answer questions and take orders.

2. Be sure the people staffing your booth are *personable, extroverted, and friendly.* You don't want an introverted genius up there on your stage. Some people serve best from within the inner sanctum of the company. Others are made for the road.

3. Do what is necessary to staff your booth with *knowledgeable salespeople.* Knowledgeable alone isn't enough. Salesminded alone isn't enough. At a tradeshow exhibit, your staff must be both.

4. Ascertain that the people staffing your booth have a *high energy level* and won't burn out too soon. Trade shows are exhausting. It's hard to stand up and be bright and charming all day, three days in a row.

5. Carefully select people with the *proper social graces* to represent you at trade shows. Trade shows invariably mean parties. I've seen enough people get embarrassingly drunk at such parties to realize that their energies

on the exhibit floor were wiped out by their antics on the sixteenth floor.

At trade shows, glorious things can happen for your company. It is possible — and I know of at least three instances in which this happened — to make one contact who will place an order so large that it will put you on easy street for at least a year. A woman who invented a paper-towel dispenser printed her circulars on paper towels, then gave them away at her booth — dispensed from the dispenser she had invented. One buyer placed an order with her for 250,000 units. Was this due to her unique way of supplying information? Maybe yes, maybe no. But she sure wouldn't have made a sale that size had she not been at the show. And she may not have attracted attention had she not developed such a unique way of sampling, demonstrating, and providing information.

Gigantic orders

There are more trade shows today than ever before. That means you've got to know which to attend, which to exhibit at. Except for the big national trade shows, most people attending a trade show come from a 100-mile radius. They come to buy, to see what's new, to investigate the competition, to spot trends, and to find new tools and services that can help their companies profit. If you're attending a trade show, these are the things you must know:

How to attend a trade show

- Know just what you want to accomplish.
- See the entire show; profits hide in esoteric places; small companies with exciting products are often in inexpensive locations on the fringes of a show.
- Prioritize by visiting the important exhibits first.
- Bring a sturdy, lightweight case to hold show materials.
- Wear comfortable shoes and take breaks to lighten your load. A trade show is not as exhausting as a full-court basketball game, but many attendees will tell you that it comes very close.

If you're an exhibitor, recognize that the show begins long before the show. Pre-show promotion sets your show marketing in motion. Remember that your job is to get your prospect's attention and time, then show how you can help the prospect profit. This will occur if you realize certain truisms about shows:

- Select the right shows, guiding your selection with past experience, quality of the sponsor's past shows, who the audience is, and who the other exhibitors are.
- Guerrilla rule of thumb on show selection: the more valuable the show is to your prospects, the more valuable it will be to you.
- Important criteria to consider include location, timing, convention center, on-site services, and your display.
- Guerrillas are definitely party animals and know they will ring up the most sales with a party for sizzling prospects in their hotel hospitality suite.
- Know for certain whether you want to penetrate your existing market or expand into a new market, know if you're going for sales or leads.
- Don't send any trade-show reps who will long for home so they can get down to real work. The real work is at the show.
- Be absolutely certain that your booth blends with your marketing identity and your current marketing theme.
- Because people don't like to walk into a booth where they might feel trapped, be sure your booth has an open feel.
- If you can, include a hands-on demonstration or something that people can handle. Studies show that folks love to touch things.
- Research reveals that location has very little to do with the amount of traffic at your booth; believe it.
- Keep things very easy to understand; a few large pictures are better than many small ones. Be sure your

company name is highly visible. This is all-too-often overlooked.

- Know all your costs. These include rent, displays, electricity, carpeting, furniture, transportation, lodging, food, entertaining — hey, that's a lot! Keep track or you may end up kidding yourself
- Experts say the profitability of a show is determined primarily by the quality of your people and how they work a booth. Be sure they take breaks every four hours and see the entire show as early as possible to gain a feel for the competition.
- Quickly separate the serious prospects from the browsers. Don't spend too much time even with the serious prospects; there are many others to meet.
- Have no chairs in the booth unless you *plan to close sales there — and I hope you do*. Visitors won't disturb seated staffers. If you must have a chair and table setup, put it in a quiet corner.
- Don't give away too much literature. People get overloaded. Save your best for major prospects during follow-up. With qualified leads and notes made at the show, follow-up will be effective. Start with a thank-you note within one week, or otherwise you'll probably be completely forgotten. What a waste of time, energy, and money! Don't let it happen.

A few guerrilla tactics that have worked for others before the show will also work for you:

Guerrilla tactics

- Send prospects a small packet of Epsom salts and an offer of free footpads at your booth.
- Send an invitation to pick up a free product from your booth.
- Send a photo or drawing of your booth so that your visitors can easily spot you.
- Send a map of the exhibit hall marked to show your

booth, the rest rooms, the food stands, pay phones, and all the exits.

- Send an entry form for a contest to be entered at your booth.
- Send a show schedule with a time to visit your display.

Perhaps your business simply cannot make sales at such public gatherings. But if there is any way you can utilize this marketing tool, do it. At such events, making a public spectacle of yourself is more of a virtue than a vice.

25

Miscellaneous Marketing Tools: Services, Searchlights, Contests, T-Shirts, Newsletters, and Guerrilla Media

EVERY FEW MONTHS, NEW MARKETING weapons are developed. Some are ingenious. Some are ridiculous. All are worth examining. just because a marketing device is new doesn't mean it is bad. Probably the most amazing moment I spent during my career in big-time advertising agencies occurred while I was working in England. We had persuaded a large manufacturer of anti-acne products, the largest in the country, to experiment with television advertising. This was in 1968, hardly the Dark Ages.

After a three-month test, during which sales went right through the roof, we prepared a plan calling for the year-round use of television. When we presented it to the client, he told us he did not plan to include television in his marketing program.

We wanted to know why, since our test had been enormously successful. "Because frankly, gentlemen," the client countered, "I am not convinced that television is here to stay."

Beware of fads

I suppose you can take the same attitude when examining new methods of marketing. But even if a method is hot for only one year, a guerrilla should avail himself or herself of it during that year. It doesn't have to be "here to stay" in order to help your business. Any help you can get should be gratefully accepted.

Moped marketing   Perhaps you've heard of moped advertising. That's a type of marketing in which you pay a company and provide them with a sign advertising your product or service. Then they have one of their employees, drive a moped into high-traffic areas where your sign can be seen by large numbers of people. If you are marketing sunglasses, tanning oil, or soft drinks, it makes a lot of sense to employ this medium at beaches. Mopeds can go where buses and cars cannot. They can go to parks and ballgames and parades — wherever lots of people congregate. This is a new marketing medium. It may or may not be here to stay, but it can be of help to you. It's certainly here to stay if "here" is Southern California beaches.

There are other, less obvious marketing tools that you probably have heard of. Matchbooks, for one. Package inserts, too, though they are really part of direct marketing. Searchlights are successfully used by many a retailer. But if you live in a community that frowns upon their use, better steer clear of them. Bench advertising is another medium that is available in certain towns, but not many. Might it be right for you? What about T-shirt advertising? If your business might benefit from this method of marketing, give it consideration: some businesses (and many are small businesses) get impressive results from commercials run in cinemas. The cost is very low. Can this medium influence your prospects? If they are moviegoers, maybe so.

Bumper stickers, blimps and buttons   In addition to these marketing tools, you can use bumper stickers to broadcast your message. Baseball hats with the name of an advertiser are ubiquitous. Maybe you'll market with badges like many political candidates do (though half of them lose). And then there are decals. And imprinted sun visors. There's skywriting. And you can use banners that are towed by airplanes. Let's not forget blimps, once a mainstay for Goodyear, now flying high for many other marketers. Less popular these days is the device of sandwich boards. These are worn by people parading in front of large groups of other people, and they tell of the benefits of buying from you or announce special offers. As a guerilla, you have an obligation to give serious consideration to many of these off-the-wall marketing devices.

I recall being approached by people from a company called Johnny-Ads. They told me that they placed signs on the inside of doors in rest-room toilet cubicles, renting the space from building managers. That explained their name. It also seemed to me to be an invasion of privacy. I mean, if you can't be free from advertising while on the john, where can you be? Although I did not sign up for a three-month trial of ads in latrines, I did hear some glowing stories of success achieved by others using the medium. Since that time, however, I have heard nothing about the company.

There are now several companies that offer to market your services with picket advertising. One of these is called Rent-a-Picket. Another is called Positive Picketing. You pay them a set amount and they have their employees parade in front of your place of business carrying picket-type signs that say wonderful things about you. It's unique, all right, and it may even be here to stay. It is certainly marketing. And for you, it might be worthwhile. As a practicing guerrilla, you can stage this marketing event by yourself, working only with your own employees. If you use any picket marketing, be sure to contact the media. Because the medium is such a hoot, I'll bet you can get free media coverage — in the newspapers and possibly on television. **Rent a picketer**

Such advertising methods — searchlights, skywriting, pickets, rest-room ads, computer diskettes, and the rest — should be perceived the same way you perceive billboards. They are reminder advertising. They help keep your name in the public eye, and they call attention to your prime attributes. But they probably can't do the job all by themselves. Still, one or more of them might be made part of a smart marketing plan. And computer diskettes can do a whale of a selling job for you, as they have for others. **Floppy disks as media**

Computers themselves have come onto the marketing

scene and made themselves a boon to guerrillas in six areas:

**Ways
computers
help guerrillas**

1. More fresh and up-to-the-moment customer mailing lists
2. Burgeoning-with-important-information databases
3. Motivation to publish a newsletter or catalogue
4. Ease, accuracy, and automation in direct mailings
5. Computer graphics — for print and video
6. Ability to tap into on-line information services

You can expect the computer to influence guerrilla marketing even more as we move into a new high-tech century. You'll see how by the end of this chapter.

If you have a place of business where you occasionally run promotions, a searchlight to call attention to a late-night sale may work as an attention-getter for you. I know of a waterbed retailer who once filled a waterbed mattress with helium and tied it to a rope. Then he let it float over his store, where it could be seen for miles. The cars that drove by didn't all stop, but many slowed down and noticed the store. The owner of the store says that the stunt enabled him to sell his average monthly volume in one day and to double it within one week. Crazy, but it worked.

And so it is with many unusual marketing methods. As a small entrepreneur, you can take chances that many well-established large companies wouldn't try. Take advantage of your smallness. Experiment. Try making up your own advertising implements. If you make up ten signs, you can hire ten students to affix the signs to their bikes, then ride the bikes wherever your prospects might be. Would this work for you? Or perhaps you could arrange to have a truck with bells drive through neighborhoods alerting the community to your offerings. Ice cream companies do. Political candidates do. It's worth looking into if you think it might work and won't offend the neighbors.

Just because certain marketing methods are rarely used, or

because you've never heard of them, doesn't mean they won't be effective for you. During the next year and every year thereafter, two or three fascinating ad vehicles will be invented. TV cable interconnects for low-cost prime time come to mind. Shopping trolley video monitors, too. And classified advertising TV channels, not to mention the ubiquitous home shopping networks. Marketing while people are on telephone hold was new at one time, but it's now standard for many a guerrilla company. Keep your eyes peeled for more. If you honestly feel that they can help you — not just as gimmicks, but as sales tools — give them a try. For example, if you are marketing a rock concert and you know of a beach where lots of potential concert-goers hang out, it might make a lot of sense to market your concert on a banner pulled by an airplane. And it shouldn't be too tough to find a plane owner who offers such a service.

Keep your eyes peeled for new media

Publish an annual report, especially if you're not a public company. It's a unique and rather wonderful way of communicating with your customers and prospects. It will get inordinately high readership because no small companies publish annual reports — everybody knows that. Or at least they didn't until guerrilla marketing became so necessary.

Annual reports aren't only for biggies

Market by providing extra services such as child care and baby-sitting services. Several exercise centers, for example, have increased their clientele by offering such services free of charge — and well supervised.

Remember that a videotape brochure cuts way, way down on the cost of a sales call. The 7 percent response rate to video marketing is quite attractive compared with the 2.5 percent expected of most direct mailings.

You might plan to regularly publish a newsletter, as many companies do — but some do poorly. To do yours right, you've got to know the do's and don'ts:

Newsletter do's and don'ts

● Do remember that newsletters should motivate prospects to buy while helping them in general.

- Do provide valuable, timely, brief information.
- Do make your newsletter easy to read and easy to look at.
- Do give a host of fabulous ideas; be known as an important source.
- Do let a professional designer create a great-looking format for your newsletter.
- Don't let your designer create a costly, elaborate format.
- Don't publish on a random basis; become habit-forming.
- Don't send to people who never respond to any of your offers.
- Don't give outdated, untimely, hard-to-use information.
- Don't make your newsletter too long; they're popular because they are not time-consuming to read.
- Don't forget what people buy: solutions to their problems. Newsletters, thanks to desktop publishing and a realization of the importance of time, are now easier and more sensible to add to your arsenal than ever before.

You win with contests   Also consider contests and sweepstakes. These definitely do attract people, even though they may not be attracted to your primary offering. Those who enter do become involved with you, and involvement can lead to sales. Just remember that the purposes of contests and sweepstakes are (1) to get names for your mailing list, (2) to separate you from the ranks of strangers, and (3) to entice people to enter your store in order to enter the contest. Be sure you place the entry boxes in the rear of the store so that entrants can scope out your other offerings while they try to win that free trip to Hawaii.

Certainly you have seen ads or received mail that screams "You have been selected", or "Fabulous Sweepstakes", or "You may have already won $1,000,000", or "Be a winner".

Some sweepstakes experts believe that although people may not have money for food, they do have money for sweepstakes. In fact, the experts say, "When times get bad, sweepstakes get good."

In 1990, sponsors spent an estimated $250 million on prizes, plus far more than that advertising the sweepstakes. Between 1989 and 1992, according to the Promotion Marketing Association of America, the number of contests and sweepstakes grew by more than 34 percent. Contests and sweepstakes used to be shunned as legally and morally dubious. But they have now become a mainstay of marketing. For that reason, they are worth considering. If you do get involved, be sure you do everything on the up-and-up. Check with your lawyer to be sure you are not conducting an illegal lottery when you are asking folks to guess the number of coins in a bottle.

If you want to attract a lot of foot traffic to a particular location, give thought to running a contest that requires people to come to your place of business to enter, and to return to see if they have won. These days, smart marketers are learning that everyone should win something. Whatever that is, it should be enough so that they do not resent you and associate your offering with their loss. The best prize of all, better than cruises and convertibles and round-the-world trips, is cash. No surprise there.

People seem to want to gamble; even charities are jumping onto the contest bandwagon. So let your imagination run rampant. I know a retailer who filled a gigantic container with goldfish. Then he advertised his contest: "Guess the number of goldfish in the container and win $1000!" His traffic count (and his sales) rose so dramatically that the $1000 prize didn't even put a minor dent in his budget. Because he was a guerrilla, he gave 25-cent plants to everyone who entered — after the prize winner was announced. Again, people came in to collect their prizes, and while they were there, well, they purchased something else. Are you surprised?

The gambling instinct

Different countries have different laws regarding contests. I'm sure you've seen the disclaimer "Void where prohibited by law" appended to many a sweepstakes entry form. So don't leap into this type of marketing without first consulting the local authorities.

Contests always attract attention. What you want to do is attract the attention of *prospects*, and not just people. Because people want not only to make money but also to save money, try marketing with price-off coupons. If you're a retailer, use creative tags on your merchandise. Perhaps each tag can offer a different percentage discount. Then you can advertise a "Mystery Tag Sale". It's not a completely new idea, merely a variation on an old one. But it can, and does, work.

Giving "spiffs", or special commissions, to salespeople who surpass a certain goal or sell a specific item is also an effective method of marketing. Can you put it to work to increase your own sales?

How much is that doggie in the window? Exciting, ever-changing window displays can also be effective. You're in luck if you can use them. And even if you don't have your own display window, you may be able to strike up a deal with someone who does, another person for your growing list of fusion marketing partners. Just imagine the difference between a store that has a window display and one that doesn't. Enormous!

I know of a fancy hairstyling salon that kept a poster in its window advertising a nearby clothing boutique. The boutique displayed a poster for the salon. Both gained extra sales as a result. The cost? Nil. The only price was the few seconds it took for someone to come up with the idea. As you know, guerrillas are all too happy to invest time instead of money when it comes to marketing.

Cellular phones save time, make money Maybe you can market and save time. Who does that? Users of cellular telephones, that's who. Does that mean all guerrillas need one? Here's a test to answer that for you:

- Including commuting, do you spend two or more hours

per day in your car for work?

- Do you conduct at least 20 percent of your business by phone?
- Do you often have unproductive time on the road? Are you often in locations where you are unable to be reached on the phone by others?
- Do you make frequent stops at pay phones to make calls during the day — and sometimes have to search for a pay phone?
- Have you ever lost business because you failed to get phone messages in time or didn't return a call promptly enough?
- Does your business require that customers be able to get information to you whenever necessary?
- Do you frequently need to reschedule appointments or inform people if you're running late?
- Are you often driving alone, and could it benefit your firm if you had an in-car meeting with someone?
- Do you ever get ideas while driving that you would like to put into effect right away?

If you answered yes to only two of those questions, you should look into a car phone. If you answered yes to four or more of the questions, experts say your car phone might pay for itself. I resisted having a car phone for years. Now I wonder what the dickens I ever did without it.

All of the miscellaneous marketing methods are valuable to one entrepreneur or another. They very often make the difference between a profit and a loss. But they rarely can serve as the foundation for a marketing program. They should be used as adjuncts to a solid mass-media program. You've got to prevent your public from becoming callous to your marketing, and these miscellaneous marketing tools do the trick.

Although many miscellaneous marketing tools remain forever miscellaneous — that is, never enter the marketing mainstream — they are not to be ignored. Guerrillas look under every rock, peer around every corner, examine every opportunity. You never can tell when you might make a flurry of sales from a moped sign displayed before thousands of prospects in a park on a sunny day.

Postcard decks   A decade ago, nobody heard of postcard decks — those decks of twenty or thirty postcards encased in clear plastic, addressing the same topic — business, psychology, kids, whatever — and mailed to a specific target audience. I receive postcard decks centered on business offerings. My wife receives them focused upon psychology products — books, tapes, seminars, and directories. Each postcard has a different advertiser's name on one side and room for a stamp (no need to make these postpaid). The other side has a time-limited offer: discount, freebie, two-for-one deal, something tempting. Today postcard decks are the fastest growing area of marketing. The cost is very low and the response rate is in the 20 percent range. Proof of their effectiveness is that in 1990, a full 89 percent of advertisers using postcard decks repeated the tactic. You can be sure they wouldn't have tried it a second time if it hadn't worked the first. These postcard decks are glorious ways to start the selling momentum.

So keep your eyes — and your mind — open to new media by studying the marketing publications.

Hot items for the nineties   Keep your eyes open to the hot new products of the times. Perhaps you can turn them into a marketing tool or offer them as an incentive or gift. For the nineties, the hot items and markets will be:

Rain-forest goods	Rollerblades
Portable phones	Airbags in cars
Doggie day-care	Slow food
Beach umbrellas	Liquid diets
Sports drinks	Living wills
Goddess worshippers	Birkenstocks
Vegetarians	Nannies
Depressed people	Men's hats

Environmentally friendly items	Army families
Early retirees	Oversized TVs
White appliances	Mountain bikes
Beach volleyball	Balding people
Supersized bookstores	Latchkey kids
Condoms	Step-families
Catalogue buyers	Micro-TVs
Mini-vans	Sports utility vehicles

For guerrillas with deep computer expertise but not deep **Guerrilla** pockets, digital media technology offers cost-effective op- **media** tions. These exciting new marketing tools let you support your basic message wherever you want, focus more sharply on your niche markets, open doors to new markets, and reach higher percentages of your existing customer base. With these media, you can create world-class marketing materials with the finest production values.

Lou CasaBianca, president of New Media and a leader in the field of new guerrilla media, encourages entrepreneurs to use their computers to design and print business cards, station-ery, packages, brochures, circulars, direct mailings, newslet-ters, and media ads. Off-the-shelf software can put all these tools at your disposal. And database software can help you monitor and respond to trends and to changes in your cus-tomer base.

Computer-driven voice-mail devices can help you get the most out of telemarketing media such as Freephone services. They can also prove ultra-valuable to you combined with product demos, seminars, trade-show exhibits, and the more advanced media of videodiscs, cable TV, desktop publishing, multimedia presentations, and infomercials. The proliferation of audiocassette players and VCRs makes the new media available to virtually every potential customer, and the grow-ing use of computers widens your audience even more. **When to get**

I encourage guerrillas to get their feet wet in the area of **your feet wet** computer-based production, although I warn them to tread carefully in this area. Guerrilla media production can be complex and technically demanding. So you've got to choose between doing it in-house, hiring a consultant, or retaining a company to handle the task for you. Just beware of companies that are using outmoded equipment and technology. The real truth, though, is that with the right equipment and expertise you can produce nearly every form of guerrilla marketing material in-house more cost-efficiently than by paying an outside vendor.

How do you start with these new technologies? By talking with a good consultant who will demystify the new media options for you and advise you on the *appropriate* combination of guerrilla media for your company. Note that underlined word. *Overkill is not necessary.* You don't need complicated or overly hightech media components, merely the ones that can do the right job for you for the least money with the fastest turnaround.

Even the newest and smallest companies can exploit guerrilla media techniques to the maximum. Just keep in mind that **The means** these tools are the means to an end — not an end in themselves. **to an end** Your goal is more profitable marketing communications.

Guerrillas will take advantage of the technological options that are either already at our disposal or fast approaching. These include personal computers, modems, fax machines, electronic bulletin boards, and interactive compact discs. Entrepreneurs who have technophobia will be left in the dust of the computer-literate guerrillas. Yesterday people asked if you have a fax machine. Today they assume you do. The costs of these guerrilla media devices are tiny compared to the potential return. In very little time, you will realize they have added to your personal productivity, not to mention your company's profitability.

The reasoning behind fax marketing is based upon the ideas that "less is more". People are inundated with information and have time only to glance at most of it — and the sooner it arrives the better. Speed is omnipotent. Fax marketing also helps guerrillas combat rising postal rates by aligning marketers with declining phone rates. I don't, however, recommend unsolicited faxes, or "junk faxes", as a nonadoring public has christened them.

Now that you have opened your mind to marketing with fax machines, open it more to consider voice-mail as a weapon of guerrilla marketing. To gain specific information about voice-mail in your part of the world, contact your telephone company.

Mine offers a voice-mail package that includes call forwarding, a message waiting indicator, and a special dial tone that tells you when you have a message, along with the expected message receiving capability twenty-four hours a day, seven days a week. Callers are transferred automatically to voice-mail whenever your phone is busy or unanswered, and they receive a personal greeting with your own voice (or anyone's voice, for that matter). They can leave a detailed message for you to review any time and retrieve from virtually any touchtone phone. You can use the system to send a message to one person or a whole group with a single phone call. You can even add paging notification and call transferring to an attendant.

The phone company will manage your voice-mail system and take care of all additions, deletions, and mailbox options: length of message, number of messages, messages to save, length of greeting, and paging notification. You can have a single mailbox — personal message center — or many mailboxes, one for each person in your employ if you want.

Costs for this guerrilla medium are lower than you might imagine, and the phone company owns the equipment. You don't have to purchase anything; simply pay a monthly fee.

Your prospects and customers are getting used to voice-mail and appreciating its ability to get through to you even when you're not around. As with many new technologies, people seemed to resent voice-mail when it was first introduced, but they don't mind it nearly as much these days. And owners of small businesses wonder how the heck they got around without it.

The good Mr. CasaBianca tells us that the personal compu-
At the heart ter is at the heart of the new guerrilla media. The Apple Macintosh and DOS or Windows-based IBM-compatible PCs are examples of the types of systems that can deliver the power you want. Guerrillas of the nineties are converting their computers from passive tools into pro-active assistants. The selections of your computer, software, and media peripherals will be among the most important decisions you'll make in building your guerrilla media capability. The technology of all these components will improve with time. But if you don't act now, you'll lose out on the income they can provide for you starting right now. *Waiting is not a good idea.* I purchased my own computer gadgetry ten years ago. Had I waited until prices dropped and technology improved, I would have made my purchase yesterday, losing out on the bundle of money my computer enabled me to make during that decade. Buy now and upgrade later; that's what the pros tell you to do.

The emerging guerrilla media mentioned here can give you the clout of a *Fortune 500* company, can target your message in a broad spectrum of media, and can reach a diversity of markets. Right at this moment, these are referred to as new media. But I remember when stereo music, microwave ovens, cordless phones, and quartz watches were considered new. Guerrillas have a knack for spotting the necessities from
Overcome among the passing novelties. They know that their company's
that future depends upon their overcoming any insidious signs of
technophobia! technophobia.

26
Public Relations: Instant Credibility

PUBLIC RELATIONS MEANS exactly what it says. But it's also accurate to say that it means publicity — free stories and news about you and/or your company in newspapers, magazines, newsletters, and house organs, on radio and TV, and in any other type of media.

Here's what is good about publicity: it is free. It is very believable. It gives you and your company a lot of credibility and stature. It helps establish the identity of your business. It gives you authority. It is read by a large number of people. It is remembered.

What's good about PR

Many entrepreneurs feel that there is no such thing as bad publicity; that as long as you get your name out there before the public, that's a fine thing. But guerrillas know that bad publicity leads to bad word-of-mouth marketing, known to spread faster than wildfire. Bad publicity is bad. Good publicity is great.

There are even some bad things about good publicity, though I only mean bad in a relative sense. You have no control over publicity. You have no say-so as to when it runs. You have no control over how it is presented. It is rarely repeated. You cannot buy it. You cannot ensure its accuracy.

What's bad about PR

On balance, however, publicity is an excellent weapon in any well-stocked marketing arsenal. And any marketing plan that fails to include some effort at public relations is a marketing plan that isn't going all out.

Public relations offers, as an unstated but ultra-valuable benefit, decades of staying power. Reprints of positive publicity can be framed, made parts of brochures, included in ads, put onto flipcharts, and leaned upon for precious credibility. The day the story appears is a heartwarming one, but the years afterward are when the marketing power abounds. When you can do it, use reprints of the story to empower your marketing. But you can't always do it.

PR power When I was advertising my self-published book *Earning Money Without a Job* (since revised for the nineties and published in 1991 by Henry Holt and Company, New York) in various magazines and national newspapers, I was spending about $1000 per ad. Each ad was bringing in about $3000 in sales. The book was not available in bookstores and could be purchased only through my mail-order ad. Then a local newspaper reporter purchased a copy of my book. Because I lived in the vicinity, and because he took a liking to the book, he called to see if he could come to my home and interview me, and asked if he could bring along a photographer. It didn't take me long to extend a warm welcome to him and his camera-bearing associate.

The interview lasted about an hour and included a brief photo session. A few days later, an article about me and my book appeared in the main news section of the newspaper. Accompanying it was a photo of me. Well into the article was the address to which the $10 purchase price (now it's less) could be sent. Within a week, I received over $10,000 worth of orders! The article had not solicited orders, did not really try to sell the book, and mentioned the address and selling price in a place where only serious readers of the article would find them. More than $10,000 in sales, and the marketing didn't cost me one penny.

As wonderful as I felt about the results, I felt just as frustrated at not being able to repeat the process. I sent the article to other newspapers, letting them know I was available for interviews. I continued to advertise the book, still achieving a fair degree of success. But never again have I been able to earn so much money with so little effort. Because my mama didn't raise a moron, I have made reprints of the article and used them as parts of mailings and press kits. So I have received a bit more mileage from the publicity. Although I know of similar stories, and indeed have arranged and taken part in them, never has the value of PR hit home as sweetly as in that instance.

The reporter felt that my book was newsy, since it promised honest information on how people could earn a good living without having to hold down a job. And that is probably the single most important factor in obtaining free publicity: providing news worth publicizing.

A fascinating P.S. to that PR tale is what happened to the reporter, Mel Ziegler, who interviewed me. He took the concepts of my book to heart, quit his job, and opened a store, the first of an empire, called Banana Republic. That chain hit it monstrously big with its line of safari clothes, then a harbinger, it seemed, of fashion to come. It hired professional writers to describe its offerings in its catalogue, which was beautifully written and designed. But alas, what appeared to be a trend turned out to be a fad, and Banana Republic began discontinuing its safari-oriented travel merchandise, added more mainstream clothing lines, and was since purchased by the mainstream clothing giant, The Gap. The Gap is very tuned in to the times with regard to styles, prices, marketing, and selection. Because of its demonstrated genius at merchandising exactly what its target audience wants, I predict bigger and better, although less exotic, things for Banana Republic. I don't think Mel Ziegler minds one bit.

Let me clarify here that if you want to, you can pay for public relations. You can hire a PR person, pay him or her a monthly or project fee and let that person do what is necessary to secure free publicity. PR people are experts at it. They have the contacts, the experience, the insights. They have made all

Banana Republic is born

the errors, they have learned from them, and they are usually well worth their fees.

But because you are a guerrilla, I want to let you know in this chapter of ways you can do what PR people do. That way, you'll be able to get the publicity and you won't have to pay anyone a dime.

Where it's at: publicity contacts
Moment of truth time: the way to succeed at public relations is to have *publicity contacts* — people at the media who you know on a first-name basis. It's one thing to mail a proper press kit to the proper managing editor at a publication. It's another thing to call Nancy at the paper and say, "Nancy, let's have lunch tomorrow. I have some information that will definitely interest your readers and I want you to have it first. I'll pay for the lunch."

Nancy, because she enjoys free lunches, but primarily because she knows and trusts you, has lunch with you. Never forget that *the news media need you more than you need them*. If you have news, they'll listen. So Nancy listens and the next day, there's a story about your product or service or company in her newspaper. When you pay a PR pro a steep fee, you're paying for a gob of Nancys, and those publicity contacts are usually well worth the price.

Make no mistake: a public relations pro works very hard and intelligently. So you'll have to put in the same kind of effort and intelligence. To succeed at gaining free publicity, you must have three things: the imagination to generate real news that is worth publicizing; the influential contacts to whom you can offer your news for publication or broadcast; and the persistence to follow through and see that you get the coverage you want.

Believe me, I was very lucky when I received the free publicity for my book. I had done nary a thing to get it. Didn't use much imagination. Had no contacts. Wasn't persistent. But I reaped rich rewards. Unfortunately, life does not usually work that way. You've got to knock yourself out to get the "free" publicity that helps so many companies. Instead of paying for the publicity with money, you pay with work: phone calls, writing, time, and determination. But all that effort will be worth your time. People who expend it say that PR really stands for *pro*fit.

If you do something good, you should get credit for it publicly. If you contribute money to charity, that's good — and it is a basis for PR. If you donate merchandise, that too can result in a publicity story. Just be sure you let the local media know of your altruism. And find newsy ways of being altruistic.

One of the most important public relations tools is the annual report. As a rule, entrepreneurs don't publish one. But why not? It need not conform to the usual annual report sent to shareholders. It need not talk money. It can be a report that contains information valuable to your customers. When you do publish such an annual report, send some copies to the media. Let them enjoy your creativity. Nudge them to give that creativity some "ink". And by all means, send your annual report to your prospects.

The guerrilla annual report

When you give a speech on a topic related to your business — and I recommend that you give them when you can — see to it that there is press coverage. After all, you are speaking because you are an authority on your topic. If the public learns that, they'll possibly reward your expertise with their patronage.

Recently, I went to a restaurant that was jammed. I hadn't seen any advertising for the restaurant, so I asked some friends there how they had heard of it. They told me they had been invited to an opening-week party — all the food they could eat. The restaurateur must have lost his shirt that week. But he gained it back — with a matching wardrobe and more — in the following weeks. Most likely, he wrote all that free food off as a marketing expense. That's what it was.

Members of the press are frequently invited to "press parties". At these parties, cocktails or beverages and a meal or hors d'oeuvres are served, and frequently a presentation is made. It's a short one, but attractive and hard-selling. The purpose is to woo the press with wining and dining, then win their hearts with a dramatic presentation of the facts. Naturally, the facts are about a new business or a new direction for an old business. It's no surprise that the press coverage following these parties is tremendous. Guerrillas hold their press parties at unique places such as ferryboats, railroad cars traveling to interesting destinations, penthouses, haunted houses, parks, baseball diamonds, and art galleries.

Have a press conference
If you have a relatively momentous announcement to make, consider holding a press conference. Attract the press by letting them know you will tell them something newsworthy. Be sure, however, that you live up to that promise. And be sure you can answer hard questions.

When a crisis develops in your community, do what you can to alleviate the problem and gain free publicity at the same time. When a flood hit the area in which I live, an enterprising businessman furnished free hamburgers to the volunteer relief workers. He must have given away 600 burgers. But his business was written up in five newspapers, mentioned on three radio stations, and shown on television. Well worth the 600 burgers. This is not taking advantage of an unpleasant situation as much as it is being "publicity aware". A guerrilla smells opportunities like that every time. An accident in a snowstorm closed Vail Pass in Colorado. Traffic was backed up for many blizzardy miles. Snowbound motorists were astounded when a person from the local Domino's delivered hot pizzas to their cars. Did that result in new customers and free publicity? You guess.

A major-league PR pro once told me that nearly 80 percent of the news is "planted" — sent to the media by publicity firms and lobbying groups. Sometimes planted news deals with political topics; sometimes it deals with industrial topics; and sometimes it deals with products or people. That PR pro repeated what insiders know — newspapers are hungry for real news. If you can furnish it, they'll gladly publish it. But telling a newspaper that you are having a sale is not news. Informing a radio station that you have started a business is not news. News needs a slant to it, a hook that will interest people. If I wrote a publicity release saying that I had written a new book called *Earning Money Without a Job*, that would not really be news. But if my release stated that now there is a new way to combat unemployment, It would be news. And that might be a reason for a newspaper to write about my book. **The hook**

You communicate your news by writing a publicity release. Address your release to as specific a department as you can — Sports, Entertainment, Business, Food, whatever — and use the name of the editor of that department. Get it by phoning the newspaper and asking. If your news is really hot, send it to the news or city editor. If your news item is homier than hard news, send it to the feature editor. Tailor your publicity release to the personality of the medium for which it's intended. A release for a newspaper might be longer and more detailed than a release for a radio or TV station. The latter media probably require more brevity and spice.

When writing a publicity release for any medium, you should use the format that is generally followed and that is appreciated by most media. Put the date in the upper right-hand corner. Type in the name of the person to contact for more information, probably yourself. Be sure you include your phone number. Write the release date next. The item may be for immediate release, in which case you say that — using those exact words: *For Immediate Release*. Or it may be for release after September 19th, 1994, in which case you say that. Next, you have the option of providing a headline. I always do, and I recommend that you do the same. But if you don't want to, the newspaper will do it for you. And even if you supply a headline, the newspaper will probably change it. **Writing a publicity release**

Then type your release. Double-space it. Use A4 paper and leave wide margins. Begin one-third of the page from the top. When you move on to a second page, identify your story at the top of that page, in the left-hand corner. Write in short, clear sentences. Do not use long words or adjectives. Do not give opinions. State facts. To indicate the end of your release, type either a ## or a * * * centered, below the last line.

What do you say in your release? Say who it is about, what it is, where it is, when it is, why it is, and how it came about. Say all that in your first paragraph if you possibly can. Read your local newspaper and notice how deftly most reporters can work that who, what, where, when, why, how data into the very beginning of most articles.

It also helps immensely if your release is accompanied by a very short note. It's okay if that note is handwritten. On the note, explain in as few words as possible why you are sending the release. When you can, and when it is appropriate, enclose an 8 x 10 black and white glossy photo. Make it an interesting photo because newspapers want to be as interesting as they can.

Even if you are armed with a perfect release and send it to the right person, there's a good chance it will be ignored. If you hand it to the right person, there is less chance of it being ignored. If you give it to the right person over lunch, that's even better. And if you give it to the right person over lunch and that person is an old friend of yours, that's best of all, though no guarantee of publication.

That's why I say that publicity contacts are so very important. If you lack those contacts and the time to have lunch with all the editors and news selectors at the various media, you'll have to keep phoning the person to whom you mailed your release until it gets published. That's where persistence comes in. Don't forget, there are many people trying to get their stories in. Squeaky wheels receive the grease . . . or ink.

Send out your release about ten days in advance of the date you wish it to appear. This gives you time to phone the editor and suggest that the newspaper or other medium cover your story, and allows you to make suggestions for other picture possibilities. It gives the paper — or the station — time to fit the story in, thereby increasing its chances of being used. And it lets you be absolutely certain that the release gets delivered in time.

Suppose you are George of Let George Do It. You want free publicity. You decide it would be newsworthy to build a unique barbecue pit in the local park. You secure permission, then write your release. Accompanying it is an 8 x 10 black and white glossy photo of you working on a project of which you are very proud. **How George got free PR**

You include a cutline or caption pasted (not clipped) to the bottom of the photo and folded back. It says, "Award-winning patio being built by patio designer George Richards, owner of Let George Do It, Hessel Avenue." The accompanying release says:

February 1, 1994

Contact: George Richards (707) 555-3463
LET GEORGE DO IT, sponsor
115 Hessel Avenue
Sebastapol, CA 91554

FOR IMMEDIATE RELEASE

DESIGNER TO BUILD BBQ PIT AS GIFT TO CITY

George Richards, of Let George Do It, a local contracting firm, will construct a barbecue pit of his own design in Marvin Park on Friday, April 28, as a gift to the city.

Richards, whose patios, sun decks, and barbecue pits have won awards for design excellence, said, "I've drawn up a design that will fit right in with the city's personality. I don't think there's a barbecue pit in America quite like it."

The gift to the city, to be constructed on the third anniversary of Let George Do It, has been approved by the town planning commission. "The people in this town have been very receptive to my designs," said Richards. "I feel it is high time I express my gratitude."

Richards will cook and serve hamburgers on the newly designed barbecue pit when it is completed Friday evening. The public is invited to view the new addition to Marvin Park and to enjoy the hamburgers — while they last.

* * *

The best thing that could possibly happen would be for the newspapers to publish the release as sent, then do a follow-up story on the celebration following the completion of the barbecue pit, complete with a photo of George and his creation. Perhaps you can't build a barbecue pit for your city, but you can still gain free publicity if you do things such as teach classes in your area of expertise, publish a newsletter on it (a nifty marketing tool in itself), pen a column, or write articles. All of these things help establish you as an authority. Because of the free media coverage you'll get for your work, word of your expertise will get around, you and it will sink into the minds of your prospects.

The best marketing plans usually call for a combination of advertising and public relations. The two go hand in hand. One is highly credible but gives you no control. The other has less credibility but gives you complete control. Together, they supply most of the pieces of the marketing puzzle.

Be newsy
Even if you have the best of contacts and the most dogged of attitudes, the bottom line is still that you have to provide news to get a free publicity story or interview. If a Martian lands on the roof of your store, you'll have made that news without even trying. But usually you've got to generate the news, as George did when he built a barbecue pit for the city.

There are ten ways guerrillas can create news all by themselves. Most likely, you can garner free publicity by employing at least one of them.

1. You can tie in with the news of the day. If you're a computer tutor, a person who teaches people how to operate computers, you can issue statements that pertain to the news stories about computers, positioning yourself as the expert.

2. You can stage an event — a computer fair or a free computer seminar — during which you show the public how computers work.

3. You can release useful information. In your copious reading, maybe you'll come across an item in which your community will be interested. Include it in your press release.

4. You can form a committee to study how computers can help the community — by lowering taxes, for instance. It need not be that, but find some slant.

5. You can give an award or a scholarship each year. People love awards, and perhaps you can invent one that ties in with computer education.

6. You can make a prediction using your computer. If it is startling enough, and pretty likely to be true, it will be news and will enhance your reputation as an expert.

7. You can celebrate your own business anniversary by providing free computer lessons for a week. This is the same principle as George's donation of a barbecue pit.

8. You can do something incredible. Maybe you could keep a talking parrot at the place where you give computer lessons. The parrot, naturally, would talk computerese ("Polly wants a printout"). Maybe you could get married in your computer classroom. Maybe you could paint a mural of a computer on the outside of your building. Keep it in good taste, but make it amazing.

9. You can surprise your prospects — and media — by giving something away for free such as a computer course scholarship, an award for kids using computers, an appearance by a local celebrity, a public

Ten ways to create news

demonstration of computer technology.

10. You can locate a memorable spokesperson who will serve as a living, breathing marketing weapon. It might be a local entrepreneurial success, a local sports star who uses a computer, an inexpensive, recognizable person who will appear at your demos and trade shows, maybe even in your other marketing weapons.

So as not to leave you only halfway home in your quest to be your own PR pro, and to give you a shortcut to succeeding **Guidelines** at do-it-yourself public relations, here are ten guidelines that **to obtaining** will help you get the coverage you want:
PR coverage

1. Determine exactly what sets your product or service apart from your competitors'. The media is not looking for humdrum news.
2. Practice communicating your message. Actually rehearse what you'll say to the media. Put it in writing. Say it aloud. Keep it clear, crisp, and concise.
3. Become a familiar name at local clubs, organizations, and associations likely to support your effort. Good research will pay off here.
4. Introduce yourself to newspaper, magazine, TV, and radio pros. You know all about the importance of contacts.
5. Find media biggies at social meetings, local conventions, and events likely to attract them, such as fundraisers. Join their clubs and hangouts. This includes their bars and restaurants.
6. Study all your options — magazines, newspapers, radio, TV, supermarket circulars, trade journals, free event listings, new publications, public service announcements on local radio stations, even public radio and television.
7. Watch and listen to talk shows. If you have a talk show topic, call the host. If you don't have one, develop a hot

topic. Good guests are hard to find.
8. Call radio stations and request a free media kit. This will show you what they want while giving you a handle on how to prepare your own kit.
9. Realize that the media always need *hard news* of interest to their readers. If you have any, tell them of it.
10. Consider staging your own special events to attract prospects, sell to customers, and to generate media attention. This is often an easily obtainable ticket to PR.

Join in

Another part of public relations is to join civic clubs and community organizations. That may be your most important marketing tool. Although you will be doing your duty as a member of the community, you will also make lots of contacts with people who can give you business and with people who will refer business to you. I hope you don't join just to obtain business. In fact, if you do, your true motivation may be discovered, causing you to lose business. But if you join to aid your fellow man, you'll most likely end up with important contacts. If you work hard and diligently for the community, folks will assume that you run your business the same way, and they'll want to do business with you.

Despite all the other marketing you do, possibly the most effective will be joining organizations. The only marketing many successful entrepreneurs do is to join as many clubs as possible. I'm sure you've heard that a lot of business is conducted on golf courses. Just as much is conducted in meetings, at lunches, in steam rooms, at dinners, and over cocktails with fellow members of a club.

Sponsor something

A true guerrilla puts as much effort into public relations as possible. To a guerrilla, everything that one does publicly is really public relations. That includes the sponsoring of events, teams, floats, tournaments, and more. You'll obtain sales much more slowly from sponsoring a football team, bowling team, or carnival float than you will from some other marketing methods. But some entrepreneurs report that although the sponsorship of events does not result in quick sales, it does help their other methods of marketing take effect more quickly. There's no question that you will make sales. You will gain credibility, too, and you will become known as part of the community. You'll cause folks to feel good about you. Don't underestimate the power of favorable association. Some major advertisers who spend millions on TV commercials test those commercials to find out only if they have resulted in the company's product having a more favorable association in the minds of viewers. So it is true that sponsoring events will cause more favorable public association in a hurry. But sales in a hurry? No way.

Still, if you want to establish yourself as part of the community, consider sponsorship. Sponsor a toys-for-the-homeless collection at Christmas, cricket teams during the summer, and football teams during the winter. This will do everything good for you — except win instant sales. Because you are a guerrilla, however, you will be gaining those sales from other marketing methods. And since that's the case, perhaps you should spring for a sponsorship. It doesn't cost all that much — just a few hundred bucks, in most cases. And what it does not buy in quick profits it does buy in good will.

Who should consider sponsorship? Among those who should consider sponsorship are new businesses that need to establish their identity, companies that sell items intended for the audiences of the events sponsored — for example, sporting goods stores sponsoring any type of athletic team — and companies that feel they must become more involved with the community. Sometimes community involvement is beneficial for political reasons.

Consider your own business. If there is not a good reason for you to sponsor teams or events, you probably should not do it. Don't do it just for your ego, and don't do it merely because your kid asked you to. But do it if you can, for a true guerrilla utilizes as many marketing tools as can be properly employed. And it doesn't take much cash to employ this particular tool properly. But it means you should show up for games — even if your team has one win and ten losses. Such dedication to a community team will translate, and rightly so, as dedicated treatment of your customers.

Actually, doing it for your kid isn't always bad marketing. If your company has been earning money for many years within the community, there is absolutely nothing wrong with giving some of those profits back. By putting a football team on the field, outfitted in snazzy uniforms heralding your company name, you will be making a charitable contribution and marketing at the same time. Nothing wrong with that.

Frankly, many teams and events are sponsored for the benefit of the sponsor's ego. If you want to massage yourself the same way, just be sure you know why you are doing it.

It may be that you can take advantage of the timing of certain events. For instance, if a carnival parade, featuring floats and queens and brass bands, ties in with a specific promotion you are having, Join right in. Sometimes you can collaborate with a fellow entrepreneur and co-sponsor a float.

Many astute people believe that you should not become involved in community relations for the profit motive alone. They believe that if you sponsor teams or events for the sake of the community you will prosper, but that if the sole purpose of your sponsorship is to earn extra dollars you will fail to prosper. Give that some thought. I believe it to be true. Deep down, I feel that you do owe something to your community if you are succeeding.

What sponsorship really does is lubricate the marketing wheels that are already turning for you. People aren't going to buy from you because they saw your name on a uniform. But they may buy from you if they saw your ad in the newspaper *and* your name on a uniform.

Lubricating the wheels

There is still another reason why some companies sponsor events: they may be resented if they do not. If you are operating in a small town where most of the businesses sponsor teams, you'll just have to pay those civic dues — or run the risk of offending the members of the community.

It is also true that the success of your business may depend upon the health and stability of your community. And your sponsoring of an event or a team will contribute to that health. That helps you in two ways. It helps your region and it helps your business. Without doubt, sponsoring events or teams or causes or floats gets you recognized as a solid citizen, as a kind, generous, helpful, friendly human being — a pillar of the community. And that helps your business, regardless of your intent. Guerrillas can be philanthropists, too. No law against it.

The cost of sponsorship is going to be time as well as money. Not too much of each, but some of both. You can't sponsor a team and fail to show up for its games. You can't back an event and then divorce yourself from it entirely. Word will get out that you are in it for the money alone, and that will cause you to lose more sales than you'll gain.

In some cities there are no events or teams to sponsor. Although you may want to, you may be unable to add this weapon to your marketing arsenal. If that's the case, perhaps you can create an event. Think about doing that if you have the opportunity. If yours is a growing community, your initiative, which costs very little now, will be worth a lot later. You will have positioned yourself in the right way, in the right place, at the right time. Perhaps you'll never again have that chance. Perhaps one of your competitors will start a cause, a league, or an event and assume a leadership position. Don't let that happen. As a guerrilla, you should take the leadership position.

A client of mine sponsored a 10-kilometer run with the proceeds going to the town's favorite charity. Each of the entrants received a free T-shirt with the name of the event on one side, the name of the sponsor on the other. The race is held once a year. The T-shirts are worn throughout the year.

The payoff   The payoff from sponsorships will differ from that connected with other marketing tools. Don't shortchange that payoff, however. It might be a feeling of warmth toward your business by the community at large. It might also be a new contact, a new customer, a new source of profits for your business. Perhaps at a league meeting you'll meet someone who can direct fifty new customers your way. Maybe you'll be awarded a gigantic sale seven years after you've sponsored the event. This is not at all uncommon.

By sponsoring events, you create the opportunity to meet new people, make new friends. And because your business, rather than you, is doing the sponsoring, it will probably be the benefactor of the gratitude. Little political favors may fall your way, such as better positioning in the local newspaper for your ads, better timing on the local radio station for your commercials, new contracts coming your way. None of this will be measurable, in the classic sense, but little of it will be accidental. Your sponsorship will be the cause. Increased profits will be the effect. Will it always work that way? Not always, but sometimes. Now that you know the value of sponsorship, look into it.

27

Producing Professional Marketing

IT IS POSSIBLE TO HAVE a first-rate product or service, a well-conceived marketing plan, brilliant positioning, a dynamite creative strategy, a topflight business location, a gorgeous package, an ideal name, and a memorable theme line, and still have your business fall flat on its face. It is not only possible but commonplace.

The reason? Your marketing materials look just awful. Your words sound horrible. Your advertising is a real turn-off. You have sunk all your money into media, and you have skimped on production. That is a mistake no guerrilla would ever make. A diehard practitioner of guerrilla marketing knows that marketing has an intangible quality that defies number, defies logic. It is the way marketing "feels." And that "feel" is determined by the look and sound of the marketing. If it is bad, you can't hide it. You can't hide it if it is good, either, but you won't want to.

Beyond CPM

Non-guerrillas measure advertising strictly by CPM. That stands for "cost per thousand", and it refers to the cost in media dollars to reach one thousand people. If a radio commercial costs $100 and it reaches ten thousand people, your cost per thousand — your CPM — is $10. That is considered a relatively high CPM. Some CPMs get down to $3, as is the case with widely viewed TV shows. And $3 is not a high price to pay to reach one thousand people.

But true guerrillas look far past the CPM. First, guerrillas realize that the *cost per prospect* is more important than the cost per thousand. Second, guerrillas are highly sensitive to the metamessage of their marketing. The metamessage is the unspoken part of the marketing process. It is the true emotional impact of the advertising, which really cannot be measured at all. As you might sense, it is the "feel" of your marketing. **Your metamessage**

The metamessage of your marketing reaches not merely the conscious mind of your prospects but also the unconscious. That is why it is so difficult to measure. I suppose it can be gauged only by sales results over a long period of time. One thing is certain: *You have complete control over it.* That's the good part. Here's the not-so-good part: it costs to send out a positive metamessage. Producing professional marketing materials costs quite a bit of money. On the other hand, it costs very little to produce unprofessional marketing materials. In fact, it costs so little that many would-be guerrillas are wooed away from success by the temptation to save a buck on production.

Reflecting on my own experience with clients over the years, I realize that 40 percent of them, usually the big ones, spent too much on production. This did wonders for their egos, but not their sales. They confused their prospective customers with too much style and not enough substance. Their electronic marketing — radio and TV — reeked with so much fluff and unnecessary window dressing that the message became cloudy. Another 40 percent of my clients, usually the smaller ones, spent too little on production. They invested in media advertising but not in artwork. They bought a lot of time and space but not a lot of talent. They decided that they could write the copy themselves, that their friends could do the artwork. They allowed radio stations to write their radio spots. They allowed newspapers to lay out their newspaper ads. The result was usually cheap-looking marketing that had an amateurish feel. They produced marketing like cheapskates, and it showed. That means that *only 20 percent of my clients spent the right amount on production.*

Keep in mind that it is very easy to overspend, and even easier to underspend. You will be advised to spend far more than you ought to, possibly by a friend or associate, frequently by a production facility, maybe by an advertising agency. You will probably also be advised to spend more than you ought to, by a media rep who wants those extra dollars for a commission and for more ads or commercials for you. Bad advice, all of it. Don't let it ruin an otherwise good marketing effort. Advice on spending less money may also come from your accountant and a few fellow employees. You might want to listen to them, but I'd suggest taking that advice with a grain of salt.

Ten percent should do it Here's some good advice: reserve *about 10 percent of your marketing budget for the production of marketing materials.* That means you should set aside quite a few dollars for creating professional ads and commercials, handsome signs and brochures, and motivating messages. Most likely, you'll spend a lot of that production budget up front. That's how it usually works out. You can amortize those funds over a long period of time.

If you are a new company, or if you are an old company just coming to your senses, you may want to invest in a logotype, or logo. That is your symbol — a visual representation of your company such as McDonald's golden arches or Shell's shell. It should include your name, though Shell's doesn't and really doesn't have to after nearly a century of exposure. Your logo will appear on your signs, in your ads, on your business cards, stationery, and brochures, in every single place you can think **A professional logo** of to put it. It will become associated with you. Because you'll be using it for so long and in so many different applications, invest in a first-class logo.

Three ways to produce There are three ways that you as a guerrilla marketer can produce advertisements or commercials. One way is to *do it all yourself.* You handle the graphics, the writing, and the ad production. If you are a creative genius and have experience producing ads, that will save you a lot of money. It may eat into the time you spend running your business, but if you're the best person to write your copy and create your layout, a rare bird in my experience, go to it.

A second way to have your advertising production done is to *turn the work over to an advertising agency*. For many entrepreneurs, that's a good idea. Advertising agencies earn 15 percent of your media dollars. In effect, though, you get their services free. If you buy $10,000 worth of radio spots, it will cost you $10,000. If you use an ad agency, it will still cost you $10,000, but it will cost the ad agency only $8500, since as an accredited advertising agency it gets a 15 percent discount from the media. So you get the ad agency's expertise, its planning ability, the time it invests placing the advertising for you, and even its writing talents — and you don't pay anything for services rendered. You pay only for type, illustrations, and a camera-ready mechanical.

As a guerrilla, you may want to set up your own house ad agency so that *you* can earn the 15 percent discount, but perform your own services. In this case, most standard advertising agencies charge on a fee basis these days, the fee depending upon the amount of work and time required to service your account.

If you have a too-tiny budget, most ad agencies will turn up their noses at you. But if your budget is hefty, advertising agencies can save you a lot of time and trouble. And they provide a great deal of much-needed expertise. Word-of-warning: if your budget is small, your advertising account, while pitched by senior management, will probably be assigned to green-behind-the-ears employees. That's not always bad, but it's a gentle hint that if you're going to use an ad agency, use a small one that will treat your small company like an important client.

Most entrepreneurs, however, produce their marketing materials a third way. They *use independent contractors to fill in the gaps* in their marketing ability. A success-oriented entrepreneur will hire a smart marketing consultant to help draft a marketing plan and a creative strategy. The consultant is paid a fee — one time — and that's it. The fee covers either several projects or anywhere from one to three months. If he or she is needed down the road, then another fee is charged. Maybe you'll want to keep a consultant by paying a monthly retainer fee for continuing counsel.

A smart entrepreneur might also have an ongoing relationship with an art director. That person designs the logo, the ads, the brochures, the circulars, the Yellow Pages ads, the mailing pieces, the signs — everything that needs designing. The art director is paid by the hour, by the ad, or by the project. Usually, it is by the hour.

You might also hire a copywriter who charges by the hour or by the ad. And you might employ a media-buying service to place all your ads for you, at a charge of from 3 percent to 10 percent of the cost of running the ads. Since a media-buying service can save you 15 percent, the 10 percent it may charge actually amounts to a saving of 5 percent for you. At times, you might also wish to hire a professional research firm that charges by the project. And you might need the services of a photographer or an illustrator. Be sure they all follow your marketing plan and pull in the same direction.

As I have counseled a number of times, and will continue to harp on because it is so important, you should utilize as **Use properly** many methods of marketing as you can *properly* utilize. The **or not at all** same holds true for marketing production. Do as much of it yourself as you can do properly. Farm out the rest to talented professionals. In all likelihood, you are a pro at your business. And you should use people who are pros at the business of advertising production. That combination of pro and pro is a tough combination to beat.

An effective printed piece, be it ad, brochure, circular, or **Seven areas** point-of-purchase sign, requires expertise in seven different **of expertise** areas.

The first area is the idea. *Don't forget that all great*

marketing starts with a great idea. It is not important that you be the person who gets the idea. It is very important that you be able to judge the idea. If you can't distinguish a good idea from a bad idea, find someone who can. That's the most important part of marketing.

The second area is *copywriting*. To begin with, somebody has to come up with a winning headline. To be successful, the headline should either state the idea succinctly or interest people so much that they'll want to read the copy. The copywriter must have the ability to write flowing, motivating copy. No particular style is right or wrong. But in general, copywriting should be clear, easy to follow, crisp, and believable. Many people believe that because they can write, they can write copy. If that were the case, there wouldn't be such a large number of copywriters earning large salaries for their golden prose. There is a huge difference between writing in the English language and writing advertising copy designed to create a desire to buy.

The third area is *graphics*. The most important aspect of graphics is the design and layout. An art director must take the words and pictures and arrange them in such a way that the reader's eye will flow from one element to the next, free and easy. There must be no hint of confusion. The ad should look appealing, should invite readership by its look. It is not easy to create such ads. That's why some art directors are paid fancy salaries to lay out advertisements. They possess a graphic sense that combines aesthetics with motivation, art with psychology. You need an ad maker to design ads, not merely a designer. An ad that merely looks good is a bad ad. The ad must look good and also communicate exactly what you wish to communicate.

The fourth area is *pictures*. The pictures may be illustrations or photos, black and white or color, small or large, one or many. The art director makes that decision. The illustrator or photographer then takes over and draws or shoots the picture that helps bring the marketing plan to life. I have had clients pay $12,500 for a single photo session and feel that the shots were worth every cent. I've had clients spend $150 for a photo session, too. They weren't as captivated as the big spenders, but the $150 did the job of helping them grow to become a company that could afford the higher figure. If you are superb with a camera or if you can illustrate with pizzazz, perhaps you can handle the picture portion of your advertising. But chances are, you'll be better off hiring a pro. Fortunately, most people recognize their lack of talent at art. Unfortunately, most people fall to recognize their lack of talent at writing.

The fifth area is *typography*. There are books and books of typefaces you can select. With such a wide selection, which is the right kind of type for your advertising? Should it be a serif typeface — one with letters that have little tails and curlicues? Or should it be a sans serif typeface — one with clean, streamlined letters? Should you use italics? Boldface type? All capitals? What is the right size of type for the headline? The subhead? The body copy? The theme line? A type expert or art director must be able to answer all of those questions and answer them correctly. Otherwise, a lot of money may go down the drain. I've seen many ads that had everything right except that the type was unreadable — either unclear or too small. Any ad with unreadable type is a sad waste of money, space, time, and energy. Daily, you see typefaces that can and do give people headaches.

The sixth area is *paste-up*. That means pasting on a board or sheet of paper the type that has been set, the headline, the illustration or photograph, the logo, the border, and any other element that goes into the ad. The paste-up person, when preparing the mechanical — a term used to describe the pasted-up ad — must place and paste with precision. He or she follows the design formulated by the art director and pastes all the pieces together to make a camera-ready ad.

The seventh area is *photostating*. Once an ad has been thought up, written, laid out, illustrated, set in type, and pasted up, it must be photographed and a photostat of the ad must be made. That's what you send to the newspaper. That ensures that the ad will appear as you want it to appear. The art director should already have contacted the publication to find out its printing idiosyncrasies, so that the ad will print well. Once that is done, your ad quality is assured if you send a perfect stat to the paper.

It is the rare guerrilla who possesses expertise in all seven areas. Even the most proficient ad makers are expert in but a few. Generally, one person thinks up and writes the ad, a second person serves as art director, paste-up person, typographer, and stat maker, and a third person handles the photos or illustrations. That, as I said, is generally the case — meaning more than 50 percent of the time. In many cases, however, the art director thinks up the ad. In some cases, one person does the writing, a second person handles all graphics and production responsibilities, and either of the two people gets the idea for the ad. It doesn't matter where a good idea comes from.

Your job, as a guerrilla, is to exercise the right judgment in all of these areas. You need not be able to do any one of these tasks, but you must be able to distinguish good from bad in all seven areas.

Judgement is all

One of the most successful entrepreneurs I have ever known, Mike Lavin — a true guerrilla in every sense of the word, inventor of the BioFirm Mattress, the best-selling mattress in Berkeley, California, and proprietor of the Berkeley Design Shop, which became a local landmark because of his marketing — had zero talent in all seven areas but had exceptional judgment and resourcefulness. His judgment helped him recognize his own limitations, helped him distinguish a good ad from a bad ad, a good commercial from a bad one, good copy from bad copy. His resourcefulness led him to the people who could supply the talent he needed to run prime-quality ads. Although he didn't contribute one word to his copy, he never ran a bad ad. His success, both financial and personal, was astonishing. He built a company that used all of the media — and I mean all. First, he sold waterbeds, then added other beds, then futons, then invented a breakthrough mattress design, then added space-saving furniture, then added children's furniture — changing with the times and the needs of his market. There was not a single major marketing tool that he failed to use. And yet he had no innate marketing talent, merely brilliant marketing judgment and instincts. That's all you need to be a guerrilla. That plus patience and aggressiveness.

Needless to say, it will cost you money to secure talent in the seven areas required. And remember, I'm just talking about printed marketing materials. You'll require even more talents for television marketing. And radio advertising calls for professionalism in six areas: the idea, the writing, the voicing, the music, the sound effects, and the mixing. As with print advertising, you yourself don't have to have talent in these areas, merely good judgment. And you must know how to locate expert production studios.

As with cognac, when it comes to marketing production, you usually, but not always, get what you pay for. Learn what you'll be paying for by checking the portfolios of the pros you **Results over** plan to select. Be wary of those who talk of awards. Be **awards** attracted to those who speak of results.

In most parts of the country, seminars are often presented for entrepreneurs. Some seminars are geared to teaching you how to produce your own marketing materials. If such seminars come to your area (check with a local community college, a chamber of commerce, or the extension division of a local university), sign up for one. Sign up for more than one if production turns you on. If it does, ask yourself, "Is this the best use of my time for the business?"

Now that you are taking the marketing process seriously, start developing a radar for good marketing and bad marketing. Both kinds are all around you. The more you observe, the more you learn, and the more you learn, the better you'll be able to market.

With all of my recommendations that you handle much of the marketing yourself, I encourage you to hire a pro to create your marketing materials. Unless it is something at which you really excel, you are usually far better off giving it to a pro — or to several pros. To find them, merely set aside a few days to visit graphic-art firms and view the work they have done for others. Visit writers and art directors and look at ads they have created. Listen to radio spots they have written and produced. View TV commercials for which they have been responsible. Only if you do it that way will you get a feel for the marketplace. When looking at the work of these people, ask two questions: (1) How much did it cost to produce? (2) What were the sales results? Concern yourself more with the answer to question two than question one.

Guerrillas use pros

You can save sacks of money and get to use beautifully produced ads, commercials, brochures, and signs if you make use of co-op advertising. If you are a manufacturer, you can gain a lot in local sales by joining a good co-op program. If you are a retailer or distributor, you can gain welcome funds for your marketing budget by obtaining co-op money. Co-op funds and materials are made available to entrepreneurs by large companies. If you deal with one, ask about their co-op advertising program. If they don't have one, ask them to create one for you. Never hurts to ask. To obtain first-class marketing help in the way of money, ads, and more, co-op advertising is an area worth exploring.

Co-op advertising

Only after you have assembled the proper marketing aids will you be able to combine the best stated message with the best metamessage. It is the combination of the two that will result in success. One without the other just won't do it.

When thinking about marketing — an activity in which you should engage more and more — try to think long-term while you are thinking short-term. Don't just look at the week ahead. Look also at the months and years. Your marketing efforts will add up. Your identity will not come easily or quickly but will be built over time. And everything you do in the way of marketing will contribute to that identity. If you see that you may have to spend $1000 to produce an advertising piece, think of other ways the piece can be used. Maybe you can turn it into a sign. Perhaps it can also serve as a customer handout. Possibly it can be the basis for a brochure. Maybe it can be used with interchangeable headlines and become two ads. Perhaps it can be the major part of a mailing. And you may be able to use it for five years or longer. By getting the most mileage out of your marketing materials, you will save a lot of money. Suddenly, that $1000 figure looks a lot more reasonable. Why, with enough deep thought on your part, it might even seem inexpensive.

Become a brand name

In addition to getting as much mileage as possible from your marketing, do everything you can to create brand names for your products. People trust brand names. They have confidence that a brand-name item will perform better than a non-brand-name item. Don't make the mistake of thinking that brand names belong only in the province of the big guys. Brand names can be used by anyone who wants to create them. Smart marketing people, big and small, want to create them.

Mike Lavin, of Berkeley Design Shop fame, has only one retail store but he created a brand name for the mattress he invented. He calls it the BioFirm Mattress. He has marketed and advertised and promoted it so long and so enthusiastically that local people now ask all over town for the BioFirm Mattress. The mattress is available only at his store, of course. He has created a brand name that, in his community of 125,000 people, outsells Serta, Sealy, Simmons, Sears — all the big guys. And he's just a little guy with limited resources and a single showroom, but a stunning profit and loss statement, along with a permanent grin. Ask him about the Herculean power of brand names.

According to the *Harvard Business Review*, entrepreneurs are going to have to start developing their own brand names. There is a new selling environment. People want uniqueness, want names they can trust. Creating a brand name gives the people what they want and gives you what you want: consumer confidence. A good approach to take is to give your customers *more than their money's worth*. If you sincerely try to do that, to go the extra distance, provide the extra service, give the extra quality, you'll be able to convey that attitude in your marketing. You'll be a better marketer if you think that way. And word will spread, too.

The department store, Nordstrom, is famed for its customer service. Its name is synonymous with superlative service. One day, the store received a call. Something a customer purchased had broken and the customer wanted it fixed — pronto. That day, Nordstrom had a salesperson stop by the person's house to make the repair. The broken item hadn't come from Nordstrom, after all, but from Sears. The Nordstrom person fixed it anyhow, charged nothing, and contributed yet another tale to the treasure trove of service stories that has made Nordstrom a name that people know they can trust. Do that for your company, too.

There is no mystique to marketing, as you have seen. It is nuts and bolts and is fairly easy to dissect. But marketing is difficult to do properly. Never forget that no matter what your business really is, *people will think of it as your marketing portrays it*. If you run cheap-looking ads, that's what people will think of your product or service. Don't believe those people who tell you that you'll never go broke underestimating the intelligence of the American public. Instead, figure that the American public is about as intelligent as your mother. And you know that she is no dodo. In reality, she is a good representative of the public. She won't be won over by gimmicks and special effects.

If you have employees, make sure they are completely aware of your marketing program. They must reflect all that is conveyed in your marketing. After all, people will come to you because of that marketing, and they will expect certain things from you. Your salespeople or representatives must have attitudes that are consistent with the messages you have

Involve your employees

been putting forth. Guerrillas not only have all employees and associates read their marketing plans but also insist that all employees read every ad and hear every commercial. If they do, they'll be able to relate that much better to customers and will know what the customers are looking for. They will know what is being communicated in advertising and will be able to help the business live up to its marketing.

One of the most important attributes a guerrilla can have is patience. Wait for that marketing plan to take hold. Stick with it. If you have thought it through, it will pay rich dividends. If you expect instant results, your plan will never have a chance to shine, to motivate, to sell. Lean on your marketing materials as much as you can. Post your ads on your door, in your window, on your walls. Be proud of them. Create each ad with the care you would use if it were your only ad.

You are probably reading this book because you own your own business or because you are considering owning your own business. I doubt that many people would invest money and time in a marketing book unless they were involved in the marketing process. It may be that you are in the marketing department of a company. But it is more likely that you have your own company. Merely by purchasing or taking the time to read this book, you have proven that you already know the crucial importance of marketing. In our competitive society it is more important now than ever. Because you purchased a book dealing with guerrilla marketing, you are a person who wants to market more effectively than your competitors. You are now equipped to put better marketing to work for you.

Entrepreneur magazine, a worthy publication for any person who considers himself or herself an entrepreneur, publishes an entrepreneur's credo in each issue. Because I suspect that you are a small businessperson who wishes to become a **Words to** big businessperson, and because I believe you are an entrepre- **live by** neur, I will repeat the credo by which you may already live:

I do not choose to be a common man. It is my right to be uncommon — if I can. I seek opportunity — not security. I do not wish to be a kept citizen, humbled and dulled by having the state look after me.

I want to take the calculated risk, to dream and to build, to fail and to succeed.

I refuse to barter incentive for a dole; I prefer the challenges of life to the guaranteed existence; the thrill of fulfillment to the stale calm of Utopia.

I will not trade freedom for beneficence nor my dignity for a handout. I will never cower before any master nor bend to any threat.

It is my heritage to stand erect, proud and unafraid, to think and act for myself, to enjoy the benefit of my creations and to face the world boldly and say: This . . . I have done. All this is what it means to be an entrepreneur.

Now you have risen above the level of entrepreneur. Just as the entrepreneur has advanced beyond the wage slave, being freer, more responsible, and a greater taker of risks, the guerrilla has advanced beyond the entrepreneur, being a mite harder working, a bit sharper, slightly more of an explorer, often more successful. As the age of the entrepreneur and individual enterprise comes more and more into the forefront, the need to be a guerrilla is more and more acute. And to be a guerrilla requires an attack.

Section V

Launching Your Guerrilla Marketing Attack

A WELL-EQUIPPED ARMY led by a top-rate general in possession of a well-conceived battle plan will win no battles — unless those battles are launched. In real life, that army can assure a blessed peace merely by its presence. But marketing isn't as simple as real life.

You are constantly under attack by your competitors — all vying for that limited disposable income to be spent by your prospects. Your presence, plan, and general don't amount to a hill of Rice Krispies if they just sit there, snapping, crackling, and popping. You're going to have to launch your own attack. To some people, this is a sorry situation. They don't have the smarts, the stomach, or the imagination to launch, much less succeed at, an attack.

But you do. You've got it all — the data, the motivation, the insights, and the arsenal of weapons to stake out a territory and get your fair share, even more. You'll be able to achieve your goals because you know what those goals are. They are clearly spelled out in your marketing plan.

You also must now realize that if you don't attack, you'll lose the battle. Others are coming down the pike by the hundreds of thousands, and they're all bent on victory. You are dead meat unless you act. So you've got to do something. You've got to do it with the acumen of a guerrilla, and although you must act with patience, you must also act now — right after you complete this book. No shilly-shallying around.

One of the hallmarks of the guerrilla is a penchant for *action*. When they hear there's a battle coming up, they plan, anticipate, visualize, and understand victory. They take the actions that victors take, and they keep up the attack permanently, always aware of what the heck is going on — information most small-business owners lack.

These people have learned that marketing is not an event, but a process. It begins in a room where they map their battle plan. Then they take it to the streets in the form of mini-media, maxi-media, and non-media — utilizing the weapons that they can use with skill. Understanding how and why marketing works, they are armed with their ten-word guerrilla credo: commitment, investment, consistent, confident, patient, assortment, subsequent convenient, amazement, and measurement. They are now ready to take the actual steps to launch an attack.

Do they launch all of their weapons at once? Of course not. That would be time-consuming, confusing, intimidating, and expensive. Guerrilla marketing attacks are precise, easy to control, inexpensive, and intimidating only to the competition. Success requires knowledge of specific aspects of the science of psychology, plus an unstoppable inner will to win. The knowledge and the will aren't usually to be found between the covers of a book. But they're in this manual for guerrillas, and they're coming in just a moment.

But first, step back and take a look at marketing in the context of business, in the context of *you*. Use this perspective for honest self-evaluation. I'm asking you to do this because in a study to determine why so many products fail, the answer turned out to be painfully obvious: *the boss*.

A 1992 Innovation Survey from Group EFO Limited, the eighth annual survey of its kind, showed the number-one reason for product failure isn't the competition, the trade, the recession, a failure of creativity, or a shortage of ideas. It's the chief, the honcho, the top banana. A starting 63 percent of new-product managers say *top management at their companies do not have a clear strategic vision of the role of new products.* "Lack of strategic direction" is the leading factor in new-product failure. Absence of management commitment tied for second with such factors as price-value relationship, product delivery, and point of difference. Guerrilla marketing can't save companies that have low marks in those areas.

Fully 83 percent of new products brought to market in 1993 failed to reach their business objectives, according to the respondents' projections. Fingers were also pointed at guilty parties for failure to market aggressively: only 47 percent said their companies put their best marketing people on new products. To illustrate the pitiful lack of creativity in creating products, 87 percent of the products respondents' companies brought to market in 1992 were line extensions — new versions of old products — while only 4 percent created a new product category. These figures pertain to new products and to large companies, but all entrepreneurs can learn important lessons from them.

Management for the twenty-first century must improve on them. Guerrillas will require new skills and will have to fill new management roles in addition to running the marketing show:

- You'll have to scale economies.
- You'll have to offer speed and flexibility.
- You'll have to understand data processing.
- You'll need the knowledge to create intelligently.
- You'll have to know the exact way to position.
- You'll have to know how to maximize profits.
- You'll have to know how to create value.
- You'll have to constantly refine your operation.
- You'll have to consistently reexamine your strategy.

How will you possibly do all these things? By being a true entrepreneur and not an implementer, by developing coaching and not just controlling skills, by identifying and nurturing employees with the right attitudes, and most of all, by understanding your customers inside and out, backward and forward, upside and down.

The more you know what makes your customers tick, the better able you will be to push their hot buttons, gain repeat business from them, enjoy referrals from them — and create the kinds of products and services they want. All this takes is a knowledge of human behavior, and you'll start gaining that knowledge when you turn the page.

28

How Guerrillas Use Psychology

THE FIELD OF PSYCHOLOGY has undergone a major transformation since I was majoring in the subject at the University of Colorado. I remember how upset I felt upon hearing, as we approached graduation, that there were no fixed laws in psychology, only theories.

Here, I had spent nearly four years of my life learning theories (and skiing) instead of hard, tangible facts. No wonder so many people majored in engineering, where the numbers add up in no uncertain way, or English Literature, where the words are unarguably printed right there on the page. But psychology and theories? Didn't sound very solid, though it certainly was fascinating.

Since my college days, psychology has changed even more than I have. Many of the theories have been discarded after proving worthless or false. Other theories have emerged, and marketing guerrillas have learned how some of these aspects of human behavior can be applied in marketing.

The best example of this — and the one you've just got to
Where remember as long as you market — is that *purchase decisions*
purchase *are made in the unconscious mind.* You do not, as you may
decisions have thought, consciously select a brand to purchase. Instead,
are made your unconscious mind, that inner, deeper portion that comprises about 90 percent of your brainpower, figures out what brand you should purchase, then sends its message to your

conscious mind. There, where the words are spoken, you order or pick up a specific brand. You thought you were making a conscious decision but your conscious mind was merely a tool of your unconscious one.

All alone, that's a fairly shocking piece of information different as it is from the conventional wisdom. But marketing geniuses do not look at that law all alone. They also are entranced at the law that tells us *how to access the unconscious mind*. We didn't know how to do that while I was studying about minds in college. We figured that hypnosis was one way, but we weren't sure. *Today we are sure that you can access the unconscious mind through repetition.* Advertising leaders from Rosser Reeves to Leo Burnett have frequently made the same point.

How to access the unconscious

So you put two and two together and you see that by repetition of your message, you can gain admission to that holly place where purchase decisions are made. Empowered by that simple fact, you begin to understand why marketing works the way it does. And you make a mental note to apply this new awareness in all of your future marketing. It will manifest itself in repetition. That will be one of the "secrets" to your profitability.

When I was in college, none of the professors talked about left-brained people and right-brained people. Today, still, not many advertisers, even the biggies, act upon the enormous economy this discovery represents to enlightened entrepreneurs.

Studies show that 45 percent of people are left-brained and react to logical appeals while ignoring emotional appeals. Another 45 percent are right-brained and are stimulated by emotional appeals, disdaining logic for the most part. The final 10 percent of us are balanced-brained. Because most marketing is created without regard to this psychological reality, nearly half of mass marketing is wasted. Better still, *I know which half*: in some marketing, it's the kind aimed at the nearly half who are left-brained; in other marketing, it's the

Left-brained and right-brained

type created for the nearly half who are right-brained. Most marketing aims in the opposite direction of about half of its potential audience. As a guerrilla, you can hit 100 percent of the people to whom you market if you *aim your marketing at both left- and right-brained people.*

Left-brained people love logical, sequential reasoning. You offer them a brochure with ten reasons to buy from you and they'll read every word. Is that good? Not necessarily. Since half the population is left-brained and half is right-brained, you're missing half of your market. Those right-brained people, who are influenced by emotional, aesthetic appeals, have zero interest in your ten reasons to buy. So you create a brochure with gorgeous graphics and words that tug at their heartstrings. Is that good? Not necessarily, because such a brochure would miss out on all those left-brained people who don't care a whit for pretty pictures and mushy words.

Aim at two targets *Guerrillas, therefore, are very careful to aim their marketing materials at both left-brained and right-brained people.* They know that their target audience is probably 45 percent left-brained and 45 percent right-brained. So they put forth logical appeals to buy — blended with emotional reasons. Nobody is overlooked. Their brochures have both the ten reasons to buy plus the appeals directly to the heart. This is not a big deal, but the losses suffered by ignorance of this aspect of human behavior are a humongous deal.

There are exceptions to the left-brained, right-brained aim I advise you to take. If your audience is computer scientists, they're probably left-brained to begin with, so your marketing can be the very model of logic.

The basic appeals However, if your audience is artists, most likely they are right-brained and will buy because of emotion. And you should know that except for the most analytical of souls, almost everyone is influenced by appeals to the basic emotions. To add force to your marketing by giving your prospects motivation to buy, you can rely on one of the following emotional appeals:

- Achievement
- Pride of ownership
- Security
- Self-improvement
- Status
- Style
- Conformity and peer pressure
- Ambition
- Power
- Love

Your job is to find out which of these emotions will most set your customers and prospects into motion — or to find another that will do the job better.

As you can benefit by appealing to emotions, maybe you're in a business where you can also appeal to the senses. Do it whenever you can and consider yourself lucky to have the opportunity. Guerrillas do all they can, by conversation and observation, to learn which senses most motivate their prospects. These examples show how they put their findings into action by enlisting the senses as allies: **Sense their senses**

Sight: "That looks great on you."
Sound: "Hear the massive power in that engine?"
Touch: "Feel the richness of those fabrics."
Smell: "The clean, fresh aroma is pure delight."
Taste: "These are remarkably delicious tomatoes."

As you can surmise, guerrillas are both emotional and sensible. This sensibility manifests itself in their understanding of the need to create powerful bonds.

A great deal of repeat business never occurs because the business owner makes a strong business bond with his customer, then leaves it at that. The guerrilla is all for business

The human bond bonds, but knows the human bond that the strongest are braided with the strength of a human bond. So the guerrilla first makes the human bond, then the business bond. As the years pass, both bonds are intensified, strengthened, made permanent. This does not mean that the guerrilla spends a lot of time socializing with his or her customers. Instead, it means that in all interactions, the person is treated first like a human being — with a family, a business, hobbies, interests, opinions — and then like a customer. When the human bond is powerful the business bond is lasting. When the business bond exists without the human bond, its existence is fragile.

Psychologists have asserted that one of a human's most powerful needs is for an identity. A way to cater to this need is to form a club and make the customer a "member" of your "customer club". Membership privileges might include a membership card, framable certificate, newsletter, special discounts, advance notice of special events or sales, free gifts, car window sticker, refrigerator magnet, a greeting card or gift at holiday time, maybe even a birthday card. Sometimes it includes a gift that is personalized with the names of both the guerrilla marketer and the customer. This further strengthens the individual's sense of identity with your business.

Stay in touch with your members, offering them new products, new services, and offerings of your fusion marketing partners. Naturally, these offerings will be in the best interests of your customers, so life is working out well as your customer benefits first and you benefit as a direct result.

To add more power to your human bond while increasing your members' sense of identification with your company, **Educate your customers** educate them on how they can succeed better at their businesses. Sometimes that will mean purchasing from you; sometimes it will mean purchasing from others — or not purchasing at all. Educational marketing is effective, potent, rare, and just the ticket for a guerrilla. By helping your customer — even if there is no immediate gain for you — the eventual gain will make the wait worthwhile.

The whole concept of "eventually" takes on special meaning to guerrillas who know that most, but not all, people respond to determination — another law of human behavior.

Dennis Holt, a friend who happens to also own what may be the world's largest media-buying service, tells this story about himself. While he was about halfway through a sales presentation for his company to an advertising executive, the exec, his face only inches from Holts, snarled, "I don't like you. I don't like what you do. I don't ever want to see you again. I'm insulted that you came into my agency to pitch me. Get out." Holt got up, pulled out a pencil and paper, and said, "I'm putting you down as a firm maybe."

Holt never let up. He called the executive weekly. The first four years the agency chief refused to take his calls. The fifth year, he finally picked up the phone only to beg Holt to stop calling. Thirteen years after their first encounter, that same executive hired Holt's company, and more specifically, Dennis Holt, to handle his media buying. Holt's determination, along with the fact that *he is always a pleasure to be with* — a crucial guerrilla tactic — is why his little media-buying service purchased over $1 billion in media in 1991. Determination alone wouldn't do the job. Charm was part of the recipe.

Don't think you're limited in your canvassing and sales presentations to only the approximately 250,000 words commonly used in the English language. Guerrillas aren't limited by such paltry numbers. They've boned up on the latest findings from the psychology world, and they know there are 600,000 non-verbal gestures they can use. Even better, they've learned that *people respond more to non-verbal cues than to verbal ones.* So they learn the proper stance, the right facial expressions, when to smile, when to lift an eyebrow, what crossed arms mean, what a furrowed brow means. Non-verbal communication, ie., body language, is part of communication and, therefore, part of marketing.

Non-verbal marketing

Sophisticated sales training techniques include videotaping the top salespeople, then showing the other sales staff members the video — pointing out the non-verbal gestures that lead to sales. Dissected, a fifteen-minute sales pitch may have 500 non-verbal gestures, most subtle, many highly effective. When you learn that in most organizations, 20 percent of the people accomplish 80 percent of the sales, you've got to figure that the 20 percent do a lot of non-verbal communication — unless they're in telemarketing. In that case, their voice inflections, volume, and pitch do as much selling as the words they use. Do they understand the science of speaking effectively? They do. They do. Success hardly ever happens by accident.

Make each feel unique
Guerrillas pay close attention to another critical maxim of marketing that focuses on the psychology of human beings: *make every customer and prospect feel unique.*

This guerrilla tactic leads right to the vault, yet is the most unusual to see in practice. It describes the best possible way for your customer or prospect to *feel* after an encounter with you — either by phone or in person. It's almost like asking you to be a psychologist.

I admit it is difficult to get people to feel this way without appearing phony. It is also difficult because it requires hard work and cannot simply be finessed with a warm smile or a firm handshake.

Still, you've got to make each customer and prospect feel unique and important, not like a consumer, not like a member of a demographic group, not even like a well-treated customer. Instead, each should be made to feel like the special individual that he or she is — with feelings, beliefs, values, problems, and personality traits unlike those of any other human being on earth. If you convey knowledge of the person by your remarks, actions, and service, you will go a long way toward making that person feel unique. This is not easy to do. But if you do it, you will have a customer for life — *because hardly any other companies do it*. Even if they know the importance of making a person feel unique, they haven't got the knack, the data, or the information to accomplish it. As a guerrilla, you've got the small size to do it with every one of your customers.

Just ask yourself: when was the last time a business owner made you feel unique like an extraordinary, one-of-a-kind person? Maybe once or twice, but probably never. That's because it's too hard to collect the information and remember it when dealing with the person. But that's a piece of cake to a guerrilla because the guerrilla has made customer reverence part of his very essence. That's your job.

It is now possible to add still another reason for people to buy from you — to aid a social cause. If they patronize your business, they'll gain all the benefits you offer — *plus* they can help save the environment, or stop AIDS in its tracks, or cure multiple sclerosis, or save whales.

Remember that aligning yourself with a noble endeavor gives you an opportunity to engage in *cause-related marketing*, a method of overcoming the "purchase guilt" that many consumers feel, and another method of using psychology along with your normal competitive advantages. If you can let them feel that they've helped the world while buying your product, you're doing a favor for them, for you, and for the world. Cause-related marketing is an act of philanthropy on your part, and the world needs and appreciates it. There are many sick, homeless, displaced, and disabled people who need all the help they can get. If your business can devote even a small percentage of its profits — or better still, its sales — to a good cause, there's a good chance that many winners will emerge.

Cause-related marketing

The eighties were a "greed" decade. The nineties are a "green" decade with more awareness of environmentally safe or damaging products than at any other time in history. In 1991, a poll revealed that consumers said they'd be willing to pay a 5.5 percent premium for green products. Since 1989, recycling has been up 15 percent for glass and cans, up 21 percent for newspapers. Seventy percent of consumers are against postponing tougher emission standards for the auto-

Greed then, green now

motive industry. The world, and so the marketing directed at it, is always changing, as if you didn't know.

As you pursue the psychological edge that can make or break a sale, these days, a call to patriotism in purchasing is often heard and heeded. The appeal to buy British is strong.

The downside of this patriotic marketing is that it might appear to cater to the hate and fear instincts in people. Be sure if you embrace cause-related marketing, especially the red, white, and blue variety, that it is not at the expense of other peoples or ethnicities. Guerrillas never alienate potential prospects.

To gain the closest psychological bonding with your prospects and customers, be certain that you know the most possible about them, then marry that information to the understanding you have of your own product or service. Just what is its identity? What does it symbolize to your market? What are its inherent emotional appeals? Logical appeals? Cultural appeals? As true product differentiation is harder to come by and even tougher to sustain, perceptual associations will play a greater role in setting products and services apart from one another.

See yourself as others see you That's why it's so crucial for you to understand precisely what your business really stands for in the eyes of your target audience. Research can tell you. Ideally, it's what you want it to stand for. If not, changes are in order. Understanding what your offering means to your market is something you should always strive for. You must be aware that the public perception of your product or service will probably change over time, necessitating continuing research via questionnaires.

In 1992, a national poll by advertising agency Warwick Baker & Fiore revealed that people who shop at stores have changed their shopping habits. Nine out of ten shoppers who go to the store for frequently purchased items go armed and ready with a specific shopping strategy in mind for saving money. These shoppers have been categorized into five basic groups:

- *The Practical Loyalists*, 29 percent of shoppers, look for ways to save on the brands they will buy anyway. The confidence they have in these brands cannot be shaken by low price alone. **The psychology of shoppers**
- *The Bottom-Line Price Shoppers*, 26 percent of all shoppers, buy the lowest-priced item with little or no regard for brand. This number is up from 14 percent in the mid-1980s.
- *Opportunistic Switchers*, 24 percent of shoppers, use coupons or sales to decide among brands and products that fall within a mentally preselected group.
- *The Deal Hunters*, 13 percent of shoppers, flat out look for the best "bargain" and are not brand-loyal. Understand that "bargain" refers more to value than to price.
- *The Non-Strategists*, only 8 percent of shoppers in the nineties, do not spend the time and effort to strategize their shopping.

As you might expect, the recession is largely responsible for this fundamental change in consumer behavior, yet the behavior is expected to continue even after economic recovery is in full swing again. Although confidence will reign supreme as the unconscious motivator for selecting one brand or business over another, recessions cause consumers to clip coupons, shop in bulk, and patronize warehouses and price clubs.

Nineties consumers arc savvy shoppers, buying on pure benefit and price relationships. And although the largest group of them are loyal to their brands, increasing numbers are loyal to their dire financial straits and are forced to forsake longtime loyalties. Guerrillas do all they can to maintain their current customers while winning over the new breed of sophisticated, yet savings-minded consumers.

If you use psychology in your marketing, you'll do every single thing in your power to cater directly to your audience and capitalize not only on its universal buying habits, as I've just described, but also on its special idiosyncrasies, regardless of how would this may make your marketing appear to the outside world.

A Mad example Mad magazine, known for its irreverent humor and wacky views of American life — also for its consistent profitability — gave a free pin to all new subscribers. In keeping with its identity, it didn't treat the pin as it deserved to be treated, as an insignificant object, but instead wrote of it in terms that only its subscribers could love:

> Each and every *Mad* Pin is precision crafted by machines that are turned On and Off by hand. These Mad Pins will not be sold in any store — we know, we tried getting any store we could find to sell them and nobody would touch them. Due to the special nature of this offer, the number of Official *Mad* Pins commissioned shall never exceed the demand. Each Official *Mad* Pin is so valuable it will be personally delivered to your home by an official United States Government employee, dressed like a mailman.

You can be sure that each person who received a pin felt unique and identified just a wee bit closer with *Mad*.

Do I recommend this tactic to all guerrillas? I definitely recommend the tactic of being sensitive to your own market. The accuracy of your marketing attack will depend upon that sensitivity.

29
How Guerrillas Win Battles

THERE IS ABSOLUTELY NO MYSTERY to why guerrillas prevail
when others fall by the wayside. They know how to launch a
marketing attack and when to do it. They know which battles
to fight and which to ignore. They know where to turn for
support. They have learned how to win, beginning with one
battle, and continuing as the battles get larger and more
numerous. They have also learned how to avoid the greed and
blind instinct to grow beyond their capabilities and into a heap
of trouble.

Working backward, assuming you're going to do what it
takes to be a guerrilla, be sure you know how to deal with
success. Most people lack the skill. It is an infrequently
encountered talent, and yet without it, you're going to find
yourself in deep waters. A good rule of thumb is to *engage in
no expansion until you have eliminated all of the mistakes in
your current operation*. Otherwise, your mistakes will be
magnified and multiplied. When you begin to hit new profit
highs month after month, you'll be tempted to go for the gold
and grow. If that's what you really want, go for it — but not
until you've fine-tuned your mistake-radar to the realities of
your company. Any mistakes you find are red flags warning
you against growth. Don't ignore those flags.

To get to the point where you even seriously *consider*

**Don't expand
yet**

The four steps expansion, you're going to have to engage in the four steps necessary to launch your marketing attack, then launch it at the right time.

The four steps seem to get harder as you take them, not a bad arrangement since it always helps to have the easiest part in the beginning to build your confidence.

Step one is to plan your marketing. This entails a few crucial tasks, all of which can easily be accomplished by a good, hardworking guerrilla in one tough week, not counting the research time that must precede this endeavor:

- Select the marketing weapons you'll use.
- Create a guerrilla marketing plan.
- Create a guerrilla creative plan.
- Create a guerrilla media plan.
- Develop a guerrilla marketing calendar.
- Decide the priority order of launching your weapons.
- Decide who will be responsible for launching each.
- Decide who will be responsible for tracking each.
- Decide exactly when each weapon will be launched.

It starts out easy There. That's all there is to the first step of launching your devastating attack. I told you it would be relatively simple. I also told you that the second step would be a bit harder.

Step two is to launch your weapons. Non-guerrillas, if confronted with a list of, say, fifty-five weapons to launch, would be so overwhelmed they'd run for cover, or more likely, never launch an attack at all. But the guerrilla knows that there is no reason to launch all the weapons at the same time. A sane way to look at it is to figure on about eighteen months, maybe a year, to launch all the weapons you said you'd launch. There never has to be or should be a rush. And every weapon must be used properly. The people responsible for launching your weapons know who they are; those same people know when to launch them, so there are no surprises — except to your competition.

Step three is to maintain the attack. Sorry, this is no arena **Hang in there** for devotees of instant gratification. Little that you do will give you instant results. Feedback will be sparse or nonexistent. You won't be able to stop yourself from questioning your marketing plan. But don't ask too much of it. Remember the Marlboro man and take a horse ride into the sunset. Bide your time.

Unless you maintain your attack, there is no way it will succeed for you. The money — and the time, energy, and imagination — you have invested in marketing will be lost forever. It would be like shredding a stock certificate because the stock dropped a couple of points. Keep embedded in your mind that this is the way it's supposed to be. It is tough to continue investing your money while seeing little or no return. Some business owners might construe this state of affairs as a failure on their part.

But guerrillas know that people don't fail; they only quit trying. They cease maintaining.

This is the time to hang in there and win that all-important confidence that guerrillas are supposed to win. But, sadly, this is where most business owners get cold feet and sweaty palms. They panic, abandon their marketing plan, change their media, fire their advertising agency, and decide that newspapers, direct mail, telemarketing, television, or any combination of these doesn't work for them. Of course it doesn't! It has to be maintained over a period of time — three months to a year — to work.

Just last week, a client excitedly called to tell me that he was overloaded with business. I wasn't surprised. He was shocked! He had been actively marketing for six months, and during the first five, not much happened. During the sixth month, *everything* happened. And it all was good. Those prospects he had spoken to five months earlier decided that now was a good time to take him up on his offer. Those *other* potential customers he contacted, also five months ago, figured that this was a good time to buy from him. His telephone was ringing incessantly and the callers were all ready to undergo that magnificent transition from prospect to customer. The seeds had been planted; they had been lovingly nurtured. Now the harvest was taking place and the farmer was shocked! If you maintain, you'll harvest. If you don't, you won't. Maintenance is not glamorous work. But it does work. And don't be shocked when it does.

Don't be shocked when it works

Step four is to measure your attack. This is where you will work the hardest because it is one royal pain to measure the effectiveness of marketing, but it's your job — and if you do it, you can double the effectiveness of your marketing budget. Stated another way, if you don't do it, you can halve the effectiveness of your marketing budget.

Only by measuring can you improve your marketing calendar. Only by finding out which weapons worked and which were duds can you maximize the good ones and eliminate the bad ones. You learn about the effectiveness of your marketing by asking people where they heard of you.

Ask them in person, when completing a sales receipt, at the outset, in a questionnaire, at any opportunity — because it is so important for you not to waste one cent of your marketing money. If you don't find out where people first learned of your company, you are wasting your marketing money. That's just no way for a guerrilla to conduct business, and so the guerrilla devises methods and policies that capture this information from every customer, and in many cases, from every prospect.

Measuring becomes a mite easier when you've formalized the procedure for any employees who are in a position to track responses, such as including a blank space on your order form with room for the original source of this customer, "forcing" the employee to ask and learn it. Some businesses that do this or have their phone operators ask prospects "Where did you first hear of us?" say that they've got their measuring chore "on automatic" — that is, have devised a system where everybody is asked for this data.

But measuring is never a cup of tea. Keep it forever in mind, however, that measuring actually will double your efficacy and translate to dramatic increases in your profits — the whole purpose of guerrilla marketing in the first place.

The ideal small business of the 1990s and the decades beyond will realize that *the past is not the key to the future.* Although the sun continues to rise in the east and you are required to pay your just share of taxes by the ides of April, marketing has changed and will continue to change. Guerrillas are positioned for these changes. To adapt, they know that survival and prosperity are not so much a matter of money as a matter of time, energy, and determination.

To market with acumen and success today, you've just got to launch a guerrilla marketing attack. Stock your arsenal with these profit-producing tips for the nineties:

An arsenal of profit-producers

- Forget the past when planning the future. Changes that represent opportunity will take place in service, technology, prospect sophistication, quality expectations, available options, and competitive marketing savvy. Be ready or be lunch.
- Refocus on your marketing strategy. Anticipate response. Be sure your plan is clear and brief enough for all major employees to read it. Don't change your marketing merely for the sake of change, or a bad case of nerves.
- Expand your niche. Expand it by offering what your competitors don't do well. Expand it by targeting markets too small for big competitors. Expand it by discovering the new markets that change creates. Strategies to consider for expanding your niche are: *speed, service,* and *specialization.*
- Assess your passion. Assessing is done with your mind, a left-brained activity, as you now know. Passion you feel with your heart — a right-brained characteristic. Combine your mind and heart to see if you truly still feel passion for what you do. If the fire's gone out, move on

to your next bliss. No guerrilla attack can succeed without a burning desire to win.

- Trust your marketing. In a world with much change, marketing can stand out by changing the least. Maintain your thrust and identity, but broaden your media, add more target markets, and reexamine your pricing.
- Become your customers. The moment you are in their shoes, you'll see changes from their perspective, see your company from their viewpoint, see any changes that are needed.
- Make each customer feel unique. I repeat this because most of your competitors will be unable to do it, and you'll gain an enormous advantage if you can. Learn so much about your customers' lives and businesses that when they see or hear from you, they'll instantly remember that you recognize what makes them special.
- Hang in there. When times change, the normal tendency is to make changes in wholesale lots. This is not necessary. What is necessary is that you make some changes, even make them on a constant basis. Hang in there with your mission, but in service and quality, be a rolling stone.
- Hone your awareness of needs and problems. Guerrillas know that the path to profits is smooth when it is directed to filling needs and solving problems. Needs and problems change, but guerrillas have methods for spotting them.
- Do more fusion marketing. Many businesses, large and small, are aware of changes, yet unaware of how to act. One way to act is to team up with new collaborative marketing partners who can help you spread the marketing word and cut marketing costs — benefiting both fusion marketing partners.
- Know what your prospects and customers expect. Be assured that they expect more and better. You've got to be ready to exceed those expectations, even new ones.

- Create a new competitive advantage. Change opens many doors, and guerrillas rush through to offer exactly what new consumers want. They want speed. They want service. They want value. They want technology that works.
- Do more follow-up with existing customers — and prospects — than ever. Do more than any competitor.
- Engage in constructive discontent. Stop talking up your business with your associates, and start questioning it. Informed criticism helps you keep abreast of changes.
- Don't lower your prices just because others are doing it. Instead, consider maintaining or even raising your price, then justifying it with more service or increased convenience.
- Develop a reverence for measurement. Become an accountability freak, measuring marketing weapons, employees, staff and company performance. Every component is accountable, so change won't leave you behind.
- Recognize that your best marketing investment is yourself. Invest time and energy learning to negotiate the subtle intricacies of change in your marketing and your managing. The times, your competition, your marketing, the marketing process itself, and you — they all are a-changing.

Be sure that you realize these changes are all working for you when you launch your guerrilla marketing attack. The two best times to launch it are exactly the same as the two best times to plant a tree: twenty years ago — and today.

When to launch your attack

Regardless of your lofty achievements, regardless of your successes, regardless of the size to which you grow, it will always be possible to bring to marketing the imagination, the ingenuity, and the comprehensiveness of thought of a guerrilla. If you approach your task with the soul and the spirit of a guerrilla primed for the times, in spite of the hordes of competitors, my bet's on you. I'll see you in the trenches. And at the bank.

Index